W9-BCZ-566

Praise for Bearing Witness

"At the centenary of the worst maritime disaster in Canadian history, what better way to re-live the harrowing moment than through the vivid dispatches of journalists from all over North America who converged on Halifax to capture the traumatized responses of Haligonians to the devastation of their city. In *Bearing Witness*, Michael Dupuis introduces us to these men and women of the press and allows us to vicariously experience a time when newspapers were the only window on the world."
— Marjorie Lang, author of *Women Who Made The News:*
Female Journalists in Canada, 1885-1945

"Michael Dupuis' book appeals to me not just as a Mackey, but as a former print journalist too. To an inspiring reporter, whether formally trained or self-proclaimed, there are all kinds of lessons tucked away in the newspaper articles reprinted here."
— Frank Mackey, former *Montreal Gazette* and *Canadian Press* journalist,
grandson of *Mont-Blanc* pilot Francis Mackey

"*Bearing Witness* is an indispensable and meticulously researched book for those who seek to know every detail of the events surrounding the Halifax Explosion. A large debt of gratitude is owed to Michael Dupuis, much like the people who fill this book, for researching and compiling this essential information for posterity."
— Ben Proudfoot, Founder and CEO of Breakwater Studios

"On the eve of the centenary, Michael Dupuis in *Bearing Witness*, has published a remarkably insightful study that should forever change the way we see the Halifax Explosion event. What *Bearing Witness* does is examine the stories behind the story — the remarkable piecing together of the conflagration and aftermath by an echelon of committed journalists who responded with courage and insight."
— Paul Heyer, author *Titanic Century Media, Myth and the Making of a Cultural Icon*

"Michael Dupuis has shown tremendous resourcefulness in tracing the movements and activities of virtually all the Canadian and American journalists who covered the devastating Halifax Explosion of 1917. This account, together with extensive examples of what they wrote, provides a fascinating and richly detailed case study of how, in the face of great danger and many obstacles, journalists covered one of the biggest stories in Canadian history."
— Gene Allen, Professor, School of Journalism, Ryerson University

"Michael Dupuis has given us a definitive account of the coverage of the tremendous tragedy that struck Halifax, Nova Scotia, during World War I. The blast, which was the biggest explosion in world history before the atomic bomb, still reverberates today for both Canadians and Americans. *Bearing Witness* fills a gap in the history of the journalism with a readable tale of censorship, heroism and professionalism.

As a native Bostonian, I had heard bits and pieces of this story, but I had never been able to read the first-hand accounts of the New England journalists who raced to Halifax with the relief teams to bear witness. Their stories moved me one hundred years later. As a former Associated Press reporter, I was proud to learn of the daring work by members of the AP, the Can Press, and many newspapers in the region.

We are lucky to have this book to remind us of the suffering, heroism, and international cooperation that marked the response to the great catastrophe."
— Christopher B. Daly, Boston University

"Michael Dupuis' exhaustive chronicle of the wartime disaster that altered Halifax is masterful. Told through the typewriters of a bygone era – my grandfather's among them — the book is a compelling read for all Canadians."
— Barry O'Leary, grandson of *Ottawa Journal* reporter Grattan O'Leary

"In *Bearing Witness* Michael Dupuis has collected a wealth of first-hand narrative from reporters who were actually in Halifax at the time of the Explosion or soon afterward. The graphic and painful information they offered to the outside world, under extreme difficulty, certainly helped to stimulate the outpouring of generous assistance to the suffering city.

And now, one hundred years later, Dupuis offers timely praise to those writers as well as a wonderful resource for historians still writing about that disaster and its lessons. Not surprising, some of their reportage was inaccurate and contradicts other accounts, reflecting the confusion and anxiety of that time, but Dupuis attaches footnotes and offers more recent correct information. Changing the narrative to dispel some persistent myths is just one of the virtues of *Bearing Witness*. It is also a compelling read, and a tribute to the courage and determination of those reporters who had to confront scenes of terrible misery, at considerable risk and with compassion."
— Janet Maybee, author of *Aftershock The Halifax Explosion*
and the Persecution of Pilot Francis Mackey

"The centenary of the Halifax disaster will witness an upsurge in serious scholarship on the devastating 1917 explosion in Halifax Harbour. Apart from Jacob Remes's *Disaster Citizenship*, Michael Dupuis's uniquely original work has pride of place. Lavishly illustrated with maps and photographs, extensively annotated, and including a bibliography of both primary and secondary sources as well as two valuable appendices and an index, this documentary history will immediately establish itself as an indispensable handbook for all students of the Halifax disaster."
— Barry Cahill, biographer of the Halifax Relief Commission

Bearing Witness

Bearing Witness

Journalists, Record Keepers and the 1917 Halifax Explosion

MICHAEL DUPUIS

Foreword by Alan Ruffman

FERNWOOD PUBLISHING

HALIFAX & WINNIPEG

Copyright © 2017 Michael Dupuis

All rights reserved. No part of this book may be reproduced or transmitted in
any form by any means without permission in writing from the publisher,
except by a reviewer, who may quote brief passages in a review.

Editing and text design: Brenda Conroy
Cover design: John van der Woude
Front cover: Front page of *Halifax Herald*
7 December 1917, story by *Herald* journalist Peter Lawson.
Photo of damaged railway footbridge from the bottom of Duffus Street
to the head of Pier 7. From a portion of View From Pier 8,
a panorama by W.G. MacLaughlan (courtesy of Joel Zemel).

Printed and bound in Canada
Published by Fernwood Publishing
32 Oceanvista Lane, Black Point, Nova Scotia, B0J 1B0
and 748 Broadway Avenue, Winnipeg, Manitoba, R3G 0X3

www.fernwoodpublishing.ca

Fernwood Publishing Company Limited gratefully acknowledges the financial support of
the Government of Canada through the Canada Book Fund, the Manitoba Department
of Culture, Heritage and Tourism under the Manitoba Publishers Marketing Assistance
Program, the Province of Manitoba, through the Book Publishing Tax Credit, the
support of the Province of Nova Scotia through the Department of Communities,
Culture and Heritage and the support of the Canada Council for the Arts.

Canada   Canada Council   Conseil des arts   NOVA SCOTIA   Manitoba
          for the Arts   du Canada

Library and Archives Canada Cataloguing in Publication

Dupuis, Michel, 1948-, author
Bearing witness : journalists, record keepers and the 1917 Halifax
explosion / Michael Dupuis.

Includes bibliographical references and index.
Issued in print and electronic formats.
ISBN 978-1-55266-875-7 (softcover).--ISBN 978-1-55266-876-4 (EPUB)

1. Halifax Explosion, Halifax, N.S., 1917--Press coverage.
2. Journalists--Nova Scotia--Halifax--History--20th century.
3. Journalism--Nova Scotia--Halifax--History--20th century.
4. Halifax (N.S.)--History--20th century. I. Title.

FC2346.4.D87 2017   971.6'22503   C2016-908064-1
                           C2016-908065-X

Contents

Dedication

This book is a tribute to the Halifax–Dartmouth journalists and record keepers and the visiting Canadian and American journalists who in December 1917 wrote about the Explosion in Halifax Harbour. I have been able to identify most of these writers. To those I could not but whose work I have included, I apologize. Their names may be lost to history but their accounts still inform us.

Although he never wrote a single word about the disaster, Bearing Witness *is dedicated to twenty-three-year-old* Halifax Morning Chronicle/ Daily Echo *marine reporter John "Jack" Ronayne. Acting upon journalistic instincts, he rushed to the vicinity of Pier 6 to investigate the burning Mont–Blanc. When the munitions–laden ship unexpectedly and spectacularly exploded at 9:04:35 on 6 December 1917, he was fatally injured and died soon afterwards. As the* Chronicle *eulogized two days after the Explosion, "Mr. Ronayne was only in the first flush of young manhood, nevertheless his death is a distinct loss to the City as well as to the newspaper profession."*

Acknowledgements

Various colleagues, librarians, archivists, friends, journalists' descendants and members of the public helped in the research and writing of this book. Journalist Frank Mackey, grandson of *Mont-Blanc's* pilot Francis Mackey, and Explosion historian John Armstrong generously offered advice after early readings. Gene Allen at Ryerson University reviewed a draft of the section on James Hickey, Maxwell Backer and the role of the Halifax Canadian Press Bureau in covering the disaster.

In Halifax-Dartmouth, I thank the following: Creighton Barrett (digital archivist, Dalhousie University), Barry Cahill, Harry Chapman, Don Connolly (CBC Information News Radio), Paul Coote (branch manager, Superline Fuels), Cathy Driscoll-Cainen (Catholic Cemeteries of Halifax), Anthony Edwards, Dr. Norman Fergusson, Philip Hartling (reference archivist, Public Archives of Nova Scotia), Janet Hathaway (Archives and Special Collections, University of King's College), Rick Howe (News 95.7 Radio), Karen Kavanagh, Stephen Kimber, Janet Kitz, Chris Lambie (business editor, *Chronicle Herald*), Diane Landry (archives assistant, Dalhousie University Archives and Special Collections), Laurent Le Pierres (editorial writer/columnist, *Chronicle Herald*), Louise Le Pierres (librarian, *Chronicle Herald*), Crystal Martin (curator, Dartmouth Heritage Museum), Janet Maybee, Susan McClure (municipal archivist, Halifax Regional Municipality), Joe McSweeney, John and Paul Moore, Joan Payzant, Patricia Poll, Nancy Ring, Alan Ruffman, Garry Shutlak (senior reference archivist, Public Archives of Nova Scotia), Carolyn Simpson (Spring Garden Library Reference Department), Katie Wooler (museum and communications coordinator, Nova Scotia Sport Hall of Fame) and Lois Yorke (provincial archivist and director, Nova Scotia Archives).

In Ottawa, Library and Archives Canada senior archivist Robert Fisher and reference archivist Sophie Tellier gave valuable assistance in providing archival records related to the *Toronto Daily Star's* mystery woman reporter and *Ottawa Journal* reporter Grattan O'Leary. In Vancouver, Paulus

Vrijmoed kindly provided a translation of Explosion-related information in the 29 December 1917 Dutch newspaper *Nieuw Rotterdamsche Courant*. I am also grateful for the assistance of Kate Rutherford and Lucy Lariviere (Greater Victoria Public Library), Amber McAlpine-Mills (New Brunswick Museum), Quaestio Virtual Reference Service staff (New Brunswick Public Library Service, Provincial Archives of New Brunswick), Patti Johnson and Francesca Holyoke (University of New Brunswick, Library Archives and Special Collections), Nan Harvey (Colchester Historical Society), Esther Bye (human resources advisor, Canadian Press), Liisa Tuominen (*Ottawa Citizen)*, Jessica Blackwell (librarian, Special Collections and Archives, University of Waterloo), Toronto Public Library reference department members, Monica Ball (Reference Services, Manitoba Legislative Library), Bibliothèque et Archives nationales du Quebec (BAnQ) staff and Sarah Hull (administrative assistant, City of Beaumont, Texas).

Assistance with American journalists was kindly provided by Boston Public Library Reference Department staff, in particular Katie Devine, Michele Brann (librarian, Maine State Documents), Charles Shipman (reference librarian, New Hampshire State Library), Gerrie Denison (reference librarian, Vermont Stare Library), Ann Poulos (reference librarian, Providence Public Library), Professor Jacob Remes (SUNY Empire State College), Professor Richard Musser (Kansas University), Professor Chris Daly (Department of Journalism, Boston University) and Roy Flukinger (senior research curator, Harry Ransom Center, University of Texas).

I am profoundly thankful for help from the descendants of several Canadian and American Explosion journalists whose writing is featured in *Bearing Witness*: Patricia Brennan and Eileen Rouse, granddaughter and great granddaughter of Halifax Canadian Press Bureau superintendent James Hickey; Lucinda Boucher and Susan Lynch, granddaughters of Canadian Press journalist Andrew Merkel; Rhonda LeBlanc and Donna Sheldon, great nieces of *Daily Echo* reporter John Ronayne; Margaret Brooker and David Gowen, granddaughter and great grandson of *Daily Echo* reporter James L. Gowen; Jim O'Regan, nephew of *Morning Chronicle* columnist Mary "May" O'Regan; Barry O'Leary, grandson of *Ottawa Journal* reporter Grattan O'Leary; Diana Zimber and David Gorman, grandchildren of *Ottawa Citizen* reporter Tommy Gorman; Thomas O'Leary, son of *St. John Globe* reporter Thomas O'Leary; Carol Eagles and Heather Bagg, great granddaughters of George Yates (Prime Minister Robert Borden's private secretary); Dr. Scott Pigford, grandson of *Halifax Herald* editor Peter Lawson; and Vermont Senator Dick Sears, grandnephew of *Boston American* reporter/photographer Richard Sears.

I owe a special debt of gratitude to award-winning Halifax Explosion author, historian and musician Joel Zemel and Halifax marine geophysicist, author and Explosion/*Titanic* scholar Alan Ruffman. Joel prepared the book's photographs and maps and Alan contributed the Foreword. Both also provided generous feedback as the work progressed. Finally, *Bearing Witness* would not have been possible without the assistance of my editor Errol Sharpe at Fernwood Publishing and the support of my wife Christine Moore.

Preface

This book began with research into an earlier Maritime disaster involving journalists and an equally momentous twentieth-century news story: the sinking of RMS *Titanic*. While writing "Canadian Journalists in New York" for Paul Heyer's 2012 book *Titanic Century: Media, Myth and the Making of a Cultural Icon*, I learned that as many as twenty Canadian journalists were sent to New York to cover the arrival of *Carpathia* with *Titanic's* survivors. Among these reporters were Grattan O'Leary of the *Ottawa Journal* and Tommy Gorman of the *Ottawa Citizen*. Five years later both were assigned to the story of the Explosion in Halifax Harbour.

I reasoned that if O'Leary and Gorman were released to Halifax, there must have been other Canadian and likely American journalists sent to cover the sensational story. Also, what about Halifax-Dartmouth newspaper reporters and record keepers, who were eye-witnesses to the disaster? Eventually, I learned that more than two dozen individuals published accounts of the disaster in newspapers and magazines between 6 and 29 December 1917. Each of their stories presented in this work is distinctive yet reflective of a common event.

Journalists' stories as well as record keepers' accounts and impressions in *Bearing Witness* are reproduced as originally published. For American "or" endings instead of Canadian "our" endings — as in harbour, armoury and endeavour — I do not use (*sic*). Similarly, I do not point out the outmoded use of the feminine to refer to ships. However, other grammar and spelling errors etc. are so noted. Finally, unless specified, all currency amounts are in Canadian dollars of the day and are not converted to present-day equivalents.

Foreword

In today's world we find it hard to conceive of a modern city completely cut off from all means of communication beyond its borders when a catastrophe strikes. Yet that was Halifax and the town of Dartmouth across the harbour at shortly after 09:04 a.m. on Thursday, December 6, 1917, when the *Mont-Blanc* and its 2.9 kiloton cargo of explosive materials detonated in a microsecond. In an instant, nothing worked.

Telephones went dead, electrical wires came down, telegraph wires parted, gas service ceased, Morse code messages ended in mid-word, electric trams stopped running, streetlights did not come on at night and debris blocked train tracks and roads. About 10 square kilometres of Halifax's northern suburbs in Richmond were laid flat and had begun to burn. Well over a thousand residents, tradespeople, military and vessel crew members were killed in the same split second. Whole families had vanished; 9,000 more were injured. Nothing worked!

Initially, getting news on the Explosion to senior military officers in Ottawa involved despatches via a motorcycle courier to the Camperdown Marconi facility near Portuguese Cove, 12 kilometres south of Halifax, which were sent to the Marconi station in Sydney and relayed on to Ottawa.

Canon Charles W. Vernon, writing in *Church Work* of February 14, 1918, noted: "One of the most helpful things in connection with the disaster, and one which probably has not been fully recognised was the splendid zeal and efficiency shown by the press representatives in getting stories of the disaster off to the Associated Press and the leading newspapers at the earliest possible opportunity. This speeding up of press reports, written in graphic style, and full of human interest was probably the greatest factor in starting the magnificent wave of sympathy and of practical assistance which swept over the American Continent and indeed over the world."

The role of the press in reporting the Explosion has never been compiled — a deficiency that has persisted for a century. In *Bearing Witness* Michael Dupuis addresses that gap. So read on.

Michael Dupuis devotes one chapter to the role of Canada's Chief Press Censor, Lieutenant-Colonel Ernest Chambers. On the morning of December 6, Chambers was oblivious to any aspect of the Explosion that had beset Halifax Harbour. At 11:38 a.m. EST a telegram arrived in Chambers' Ottawa office with a quite unexpected request from the editor of the *Sydney Record* on Cape Breton Island: "In reference to Halifax explosion without mention of cause permissible *Record* is afternoon paper, so please rush answer." Chambers did not flinch, and in twelve minutes the editor had his permission: "No objection publication all facts you can get regarding Halifax explosion. Thanks for query."

Michael Dupuis quotes Philip Graham of the *Washington Post* in saying, "Journalism is the first rough draft of history." We might paraphrase Graham by noting that the historical writing of Michael Dupuis is the second draft.

— Alan Ruffman, co-editor *Ground Zero:*
A Reassessment of the 1917 Explosion in Halifax Harbour

Introduction

The complete story of the disaster will never — can never — be told. There will be a chapter here and there lacking continuity but each with a theme filled with vital interest.
— front-page editorial, *Halifax Herald*, 11 December 1917

The first in a series of events causing Canada's greatest Maritime disaster began in the early hours of 6 December 1917. Painted a sombre wartime gray and flying the French tricolour, the munitions-laden freighter *Mont-Blanc*, with a crew of forty-one, raised anchor near McNabs Island at 7:30 a.m. and proceeded north from Halifax's outer harbour to the lake-like expanse of Bedford Basin.[1] To reach this sheltered inner anchorage and await convoy, the French steamer needed to navigate the "Narrows," a 1600 metre long 440 metre wide strait separating the city of Halifax and the town of Dartmouth. On *Mont-Blanc's* bridge were Captain Aimé Le Médec, age thirty-eight, and Pilot Francis Mackey, age forty-five. Both were mindful of the ship's potentially dangerous cargo below and on deck.[2]

Meanwhile, in the southwest corner of Bedford Basin the Norwegian owned Belgian Relief vessel *Imo*, eighteen hours behind schedule for New York and empty except for ballast,[3] weighed anchor at approximately 8:00 a.m., and after making its way through a maze of ships, reached the entrance to the Narrows at 8:30 a.m.[4] The two main figures on *Imo's* bridge were Captain Haakon From, age forty-seven, and Pilot William Hayes, age forty. To protect the neutral freighter and crew of thirty-nine from German submarine (U-boat) attacks, "Belgian Relief" was emblazoned in large red block letters against a white background on both sides of the ship.[5] Soon after *Imo* entered the Narrows, the vessels sighted each other for the first time. They were between 500 and 600 metres apart.

And so the prelude to the Explosion in Halifax Harbour began.

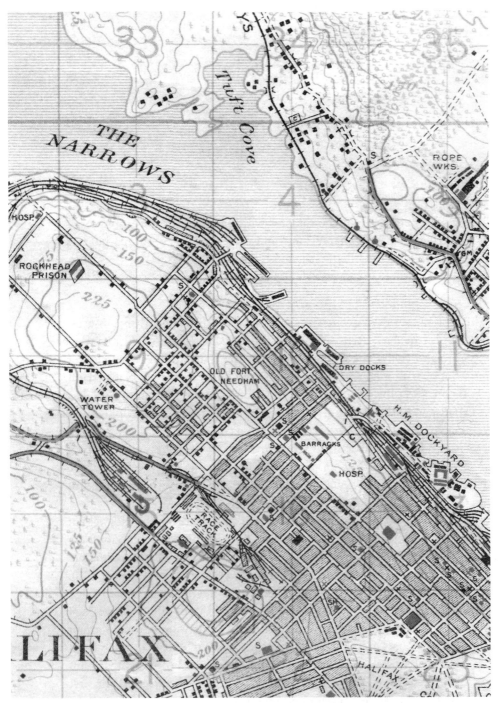

Halifax–Dartmouth inner harbour before Explosion. Courtesy "Halifax, N.W.", Canada, Department of Militia and Defence, Survey Division, 1918; NSA Map Collection: V5 1:31,680 no.133a

Although it is not my intention to furnish a detailed account of the disaster, the reader might benefit from a summary of what happened next and when.

It was a crisp, early winter morning with frost in outlying areas of the city. There was a light northwest wind, little tide, no precipitation and a slight mist on the Narrows.[6] Due to a series of steam-whistle miscommunications and navigational decisions by both vessels, at approximately 8:45 a.m. *Imo* struck *Mont-Blanc* slicing the ship's starboard bow and cutting a three metre gash in its forward hold.[7] The contact punctured several of *Mont-Blanc's* treated benzol (high octane gasoline) drums, and when *Imo* pulled out, sparks were created. Almost immediately, thick, black smoke followed by flames erupted on *Mont-Blanc*. Shortly after the fire broke out, Pilot Mackey, Captain Le Médec and the vessel's entire crew abandoned ship and rowed in two lifeboats towards the Dartmouth shore. Seeing the blazing vessel drift toward Halifax's Pier 6 and the community of Richmond, *Imo* unsuccessfully attempted to steer back to Bedford Basin.

After the collision, onlookers on the Dartmouth side of the Narrows watched *Mont-Blanc* drift almost directly towards Pier 6. On board the ferry *Halifax*, which had departed Dartmouth at 9:00 a.m., passengers gathered on deck and in the cabins below to watch the fire.[8] On the Halifax side sailors on nearby ships assembled on decks, housewives peered out windows, children on their way to school stopped to look down the slope overlooking the Narrows, and shop clerks came outside to view the blazing vessel and rising column of smoke.[9] All were unaware of its deadly cargo.

As the wood pilings of Pier 6 began to burn and exploding barrels of benzol periodically rocketed skyward from *Mont-Blanc's* forecastle deck, both depot ship HMCS *Niobe* and light cruiser HMS *Highflyer* sent boat parties to investigate the situation on board the French steamer. Following a call from Richmond grocer Constant Upham, on fire call box 83, located at the corner of Roome and Barrington Streets, the city's new pumper fire truck "Patricia" raced to the waterfront from Fire Station 2 on West Street.[10]

Unaware that *Mont-Blanc* was a floating time bomb, longshoremen, stevedores, freight handlers, railway, foundry and factory workers in the nearby industrial area temporarily halted work to view the burning ship. Soldiers at Wellington Barracks came outside for a better view of the spectacle, and a score of employees from the fifteen-storey Acadian Sugar Refinery watched from the building's rooftop. Others watched from the crest of Fort Needham and perhaps as many as 150 bystanders viewed developments from the railway footbridge overlooking Piers 6 to 9.[11] Sensing a story, *Daily Echo* marine reporter John Ronayne left his North Street residence near the King Edward Hotel and accompanied by a friend hurried northward along Barrington Street where he met Upham, whose store was less than

Halifax Herald *owner/publisher Senator William Dennis.*
Courtesy William Dennis, Clara Dennis, photographer;
NSA, Clara Dennis fonds, 1981-541 no.1085

300 metres from Pier 6. Ronayne then continued futher north to the bottom of Duffus Street and crossed the footbridge leading to the head of Pier 7.

At 9:04:35 a.m. *Mont-Blanc* suddenly and unexpectedly self-destructed.[12] Survivors claimed they first saw a blinding flash of light and giant fireball, then heard a horrendous, ear-splitting roar and crash. The 2.9 kiloton blast was so powerful that *Mont-Blanc* virtually disintegrated and Pier 6 vanished entirely both above and below the waterline. In the process a shrapnel-like barrage of razor-sharp steel, wood and iron fragments rained down onto the streets of Halifax and Dartmouth. A tsunami was created in the harbour, and a massive pressure wave levelled buildings, snapped and toppled trees and utility poles and bent metal rails for a radius of approximately two kilometres. Soon a kilometre-high pillar of dense, greyish smoke rose over the Explosion's epicentre and a greasy black mixture of oil, soot and water rained down on Halifax-Dartmouth.

Some measure of the Explosion's cataclysmic force can be calculated by the ejection of a 450 kilogram piece of *Mont-Blanc* through a classroom roof of the nearby Naval College, a 136 kilogram twisted stern post onto *Imo's* deck, a 564 kilogram anchor shank hurled over three kilometres across Halifax's Northwest Arm onto Edmonds grounds and *Mont-Blanc's* stern cannon, its barrel partially twisted and misshapen by the blast, launched nearly four kilometres to the vicinity of Little Albro Lake on the Dartmouth side.[13] *Imo*, its superstructure twisted and destroyed, was jettisoned sideways onto a shoal off the Dartmouth shore by the tsunami.[14] Captain From, Pilot

Hayes and First Officer Ingvald Iverson died on *Imo's* bridge.[15] Near Pier 6, *Echo* reporter John Ronayne lay fatally injured.[16]

While the Explosion rattled and broke windows 100 kilometres away in Truro and was heard as far as Sydney to the north and Yarmouth to the south, the magnitude and scale of the destruction at and near ground zero were catastrophic.[17] In a 10 square kilometre area of Halifax-Dartmouth populated by approximately 65,000 people, 2,000 died, most immediately, 9,000 were injured, including 6,000 seriously, and more than 200 were partially blinded and some lost all sight.[18] Over 1,600 houses were destroyed and 12,000 damaged, more than 6,000 people were made homeless, and an additional 12,000 were left without adequate shelter. In the city's North End Richmond district, gas mains and water pipes were ruptured, telegraph and telephone lines disabled, railway and streetcar tracks wrecked, tree trunks splintered, and roads littered with debris and human remains. The severing of the telephone cable link between Halifax and Dartmouth compounded communications difficulties.

Among the businesses in the city's core affected by the Explosion were the five daily newspapers and the Halifax Canadian Press (CP) Bureau — all

Damaged Halifax Herald building, 7 December 1917, from Views of the Halifax Catastrophe *by Harold T. Roe*

Granville Street, directly opposite Province House, Halifax, showing Fisher House #86, the Acadian Hotel and the Acadian Recorder Building. Courtesy Notman Studio, photographer, 1900; NSA Notman Studio Collection, 1983–310 no. 7300

located approximately three kilometres south of ground zero. The Chronicle Publishing Company, owned by Halifax lawyer G. Fred Pearson, published the *Morning Chronicle* and afternoon *Daily Echo*. Senator William Dennis owned the rival Herald Publishing Company, which published the morning *Halifax Herald* and afternoon *Evening Mail*.[19] The evening *Acadian Recorder* was owned and published by Charles Coleman Blackadar.[20] Due to damage from the blast the city rooms of these dailies were silenced and the presses stopped; none would publish an evening edition on 6 December, a rare news blackout for the city.[21] The following day all five daily papers reappeared, albeit with smaller editions.[22] In Dartmouth, the Saturday weekly *Patriot* was unable to republish until 15 December.[23]

Meanwhile, the country's commercial press — the major mass-media news source available at the time — bumped front-page news of the war, conscription and the impending federal election with bulletins on the Explosion story.[24] In Ottawa, Canada's Chief Press Censor (CPC) Lieutenant-Colonel Ernest Chambers became increasingly concerned about the credibility and impact of headline-grabbing and confusing newspaper accounts rippling across Canada and the United States. Deciding that significant facts and not unconfirmed and fragmentary details of the disaster were of national importance, he used his considerable influence with Canada's two telegraph companies to facilitate timely transmission of accurate press reports by the Canadian Press. As a result of his intervention, on the afternoon of the Explosion, Halifax CP bureau superintendent James Hickey was able to wire 3,000 words of on-the-scene reporting to the news agency's Montreal bureau, and from there to member newspapers in Canada and the United States.[25] Equally important, through Chambers' efforts over the next few days, visiting Canadian and American journalists, who began arriving in Halifax on 7 December, were able to wire despatches about the blast's aftermath. Although their independent accounts were at times hyperbole-laced and graphic, for the most part they emphasized facts and not opinions.[26]

Immediately after the disaster, local officials, federal authorities, citizens and the Halifax press began asking questions. Why was a ship with such a potentially dangerous cargo allowed into Halifax Harbour? Did one or both of the vessels fail to follow the rules of passage? Was the unthinkable calamity, as many people initially believed, the work of German armed forces, spies or saboteurs? Where were the safeguards for the lives and property of the citizens of Halifax? And ultimately, who was to blame?

As a result, an official inquiry into the Explosion headed by sixty-year-old Justice Arthur Drysdale and assisted by nautical assessors Captain Walter Hose, Royal Canadian Navy (RCN) and Captain L.A. Demers (Dominion

LOCATIONS OF JOURNALISTS AND RECORD KEEPERS AT TIME OF EXPLOSION

1. John Ronayne - Near Pier 6; **2. Nieuw Amsterdam Editor** – Bedford Basin near Fairview Cove; **3. Joseph Sheldon** – 48 Commercial Street (near Dartmouth ferry terminal); **4. James Hickey** – 85-93 Granville Street, Chronicle Building; **5. Maxwell Backer** – 85-93 Granville Street, Chronicle Building; **6. Leo Hinch** – 85-93 Granville Street, Chronicle Building; **7. William Barton** – 97-103 Granville Street, Halifax Hotel; **8. Peter Lawson** – 30 Buckingham Street (now Scotia Square); **9. Hervey W. Jones** – 88 Cedar Street; **10. Archibald MacMechan** - 72 Victoria Road; **11. Arthur Lismer** - 8 Cliff St., at the end of Bedford Basin, overlooking the Sackville River.

Map created by Joel Zemel

Wreck Commissioner) commenced in Halifax on 13 December.[27] After sitting nineteen days, examining sixty-one witnesses and taking 2,143 pages of testimony/summation, Drysdale concluded that the Explosion occurred because of "violation of the rules of navigation." Despite contradictory testimony and conflicting evidence, he placed complete responsibility for the collision of *Imo* and *Mont-Blanc* on Captain Le Médec and Pilot Mackey. Acting Commander, RCN Frederick E. Wyatt was found guilty of neglect in performing his duties as Halifax's Chief Examining Officer.

Although the three men were quickly arrested for manslaughter, charges against Mackey and Le Médec were dropped on 15 March due to insufficient evidence to prove criminal culpability, and a jury acquitted Wyatt on 18 April. Mackey was fully exonerated and eventually restored to work as a pilot, Le Médec continued his career without censure from the French government, and Wyatt was suspended from duty on 26 January and then discharged from the Royal Canadian Navy on 3 May.[28] Soon after Drydale's decision, the owners of *Mont-Blanc* and *Imo* sued each other for $2 million. On 19 May 1919 the Supreme Court of Canada reversed Justice Drysdale's earlier findings and ruled that both vessels were equally to blame. This ruling was later upheld on 22 March 1920 by the Judicial Committee of the Privy Council in London, England.

Over the past ten decades much has been published about the Explosion.[29] To date however there has been no systematic collection and presentation of accounts attributed to Halifax-Dartmouth journalists and record keepers who experienced the event firsthand, and visiting Canadian and American journalists who reported the disaster's aftermath.[30] *Bearing Witness* is an attempt to fill this gap and recognize the work of editors, reporters, correspondents, photo-journalists and record keepers. Chapter 1 explores the role of Canada's Chief Press Censor in facilitating transmission of Explosion news by the press. Chapter 2 features the accounts of journalists and record keepers in Halifax and Dartmouth who experienced the Explosion firsthand. Chapters 3 and 4 are devoted respectively to visiting Canadian and American journalists and record keepers who reported the blast's aftermath. Appendix A provides the reader with a timeline of the activities for each journalist and record keeper between 6 and 16 December.

For almost a hundred years, researchers, novelists, filmmakers and historians have utilized journalists' Explosion press matter and record keepers' accounts to provide context, details and images about the disaster and its aftermath. Now the collected and unscripted "personal experiences," "graphic pen pictures," "exclusive descriptive stories" and "living pictures" of notepad-toting reporters and correspondents, as well as impressions and "quick-fire sketches" by local record keepers, reveal a unique perspective of the disaster, offer new details about the tragedy and provide insight into those who struggled to articulate the scale and magnitude of an event that was spectacular, shocking and surreal. In the final analysis, most of the accomplishments by these Explosion chroniclers were the result of perseverance and resourcefulness, others of ingenuity and audacity, and a few came from intuition and luck.

Chapter 1

The Role of Canada's
Chief Press Censor

In view of contradictory reports abroad regarding Halifax explosion
I hope everything possible is being done to facilitate a transmission
of all press reports.
— Canada's Chief Press Censor Ernest Chambers to George D. Perry,
general manager of the Great North West Telegraph Company,
and to J.J. McMillan, manager of Canadian Pacific Railway
Telegraph Company, 6 December 1917

Lieutenant-Colonel Ernest J. Chambers

Born 16 April 1862 in Penkridge, Staffordshire, England, Ernest Chambers had extensive journalistic experience. In 1885 he covered action during the 1885 North-West Rebellion as a field reporter for the *Montreal Star*, in 1888–89 was managing editor and publisher of the *Calgary Herald* and from 1893 to 1896 was joint editor of the *Canadian Military Gazette*. He well understood that a news report obtained credibility from the reputation of the journalist who wrote it.

Involvement with the federal government began on 1 March 1904 when he was appointed Gentleman Usher of the Black Rod, the Senate's head of security. In 1908 Chambers became editor of the *Canadian Parliamentary Guide*, a position he maintained until death on 11 May 1921. In 1912 he was appointed Secretary of the Canadian branch of the Empire Parliamentary Association. On 10 June 1915 the Canadian government created the office of Press Censor through an Order-in-Council under the War Measures Act. Chambers was immediately appointed Chief Press Censor (CPC) and held the position until 1 January 1920.[1]

Although his Ottawa staff consisted of only two press censors, an office manager and messenger and by late 1916 a German translator/assistant censor,

Chambers held sweeping powers to block any source, including newspapers, which would hinder the war's successful promotion.[2] As Canada's official news manager, he conscientiously and successfully used a combination of regulations under the War Measures Act and voluntary regulation by newspaper proprietors, publishers and editors to ensure press censorship. In an address before the September 1915 annual meeting of the Canadian Daily Newspaper Publishers Association, Chambers assured his audience that "the extreme penalties provided were not intended to apply to well-meaning, careful, decent papers that had any sense of responsibility or loyalty about them."[3] Nevertheless, as the war persisted he tightened the rules making it illegal for reporters and editors to discuss the origins of the war or to advocate a negotiated peace.[4]

In facilitating transmission of information about the Explosion by the media, Chambers called upon his experience as a journalist as well as his influence and credibility with newspaper publishers, editors, telegraph company general managers and Canadian Press management. On the morning of the blast, he received an unexpected and urgent request from the *Sydney Record*. Reflecting a looming deadline, the paper's editor wired: "In reference to Halifax explosion without mention of cause permissible Record is afternoon paper, so please rush answer."[5] The *Record's* extraordinary telegram arrived in Ottawa at 11:38 a.m. Eastern Standard Time (EST), approximately three and a half hours after the blast. At 11:50 a.m. Chambers tactfully replied: "No objection publication all facts you can get regarding Halifax explosion. Thanks for query."[6] In stating *all facts* were permissible, Chambers established the criteria for press coverage of a disaster in one of the war's most crucial military installations: only substantiated details should be published. In doing so he decided that the nation would be better served by disclosure rather than suppression of information.

As the Explosion story quickly gained momentum in newspapers across Canada and the United States, Chambers became increasingly concerned about the reliability, completeness and value of press reports. As a result he influenced the country's two main telegraph companies to facilitate accurate news dissemination by Canadian Press (CP), Canada's fledgling national wire service. At 3:45 p.m. (EST) on 6 December Chambers telegraphed identical messages to George Perry, general manager of the Great North West Telegraph Company and J.J. McMillan, manager of Canadian Pacific Railway Telegraph Company: "In view of contradictory reports abroad regarding Halifax explosion I hope everything possible is being done to facilitate a transmission of all press reports. This most desirable from a national point of view."[7]

An hour later Chambers telegraphed Charles Knowles, a fellow press censor and the newly appointed general manager of CP in Toronto.[8] Adopting a congenial tone, Chambers offered to assist Knowles to disseminate news: "Considering the gruesome and exaggerated character of reports in circulation about Halifax explosion I have requested from both telegraph companies to give every facility for transmission of press matter. Can I do anything to help your service and have you found any interference other than due to injuries sustained by telegraph plants?"[9]

While CPC files do not contain a reply from Knowles, the heads of both telegraph companies soon complied. McMillan responded: "Canadian press ass'n now have (*sic*) direct wire to Halifax and other press matter will receive every consideration,"[10] and Perry answered: "I shall be glad to do everything possible in the direction requested in your message just received."[11] By day's end Chambers summarized the importance of CP's despatches: "Up to midnight [6 December] no communication had been received by the Naval Department [from Halifax] and at their request I telephoned to them a synopsis of the press service reports."[12]

Chief Press Censor Lieutenant-Colonel Ernest J. Chambers c. 1925. Library and Archives Canada/ Department of the Interior

In Halifax, thanks to the organizational efforts of Eastern Superintendent A.C. Fraser, by the evening of the Explosion the CPR Telegraph Company had six direct multiplex wires to Montreal, three to Saint John and one each to Boston and New York.[13] Moreover, in addition to messages by private individuals, during the next few days the company's telegraph operators handled press matter for Montreal, Saint John, Ottawa, Toronto, Boston and New York consisting of 45,000 words daily. To accomplish this feat, local staff was supplemented by men from Nova Scotia, New Brunswick and Quebec, with operators averaging twelve to twenty hours on duty.[14]

Over the next three days Chambers continued to facilitate daily transmission of press material from Halifax to a news-hungry world and issued no directives to Canadian newspaper editors to spike stories.[15] However on 7 December he did caution CP's Knowles about compliance with local censorship regulations in Halifax: "In connection with reports of Halifax disaster it is important that nothing be published revealing information as to defences, strength and disposition of garrison etc. Neither should details be given as to naval and transport activities at the port during the war. No photographs of Halifax or vicinity taken since commencement of war should be published. Desirable that special correspondents despatched to Halifax inform themselves as to local censorship requirements."[16]

On the same day Chambers was contacted by representatives of "the local [Ottawa] newspapers" questioning the "delay in transmission of their reports by [Halifax] landlines."[17] After noting the papers' grievance in a memorandum, he telegraphed Colonel A.E. Curren, the federal government's Halifax censor: "Newspapers are complaining of delay in transmission of their reports by land lines. Most desirable that no obstacle be placed in the way of promptest possible despatch of press matter. Anxiety throughout the country extremely keen and I have issued instructions to telegraph companies to extend every facility to correspondents."[18]

Since the United States had already entered the war, Chambers' efforts to help reporters disseminate accounts of the disaster extended to American correspondents. On 7 December he sent a telegram to George Creel, head of the influential Washington-based Committee on Public Information: "If any of your editors find trouble in securing transmission of their stories I hope they will let me know."[19]

On 8 December *Ottawa Journal* editor John Crate complained to Chambers that on the CPC's instructions CPR Telegraph officials in Halifax had delayed transmission of press despatches on 7 December. Chambers immediately contacted J.J. McMillan for an explanation of this apparent news suppression: "As you know my instructions were that every facility was to be offered to transmission of press despatches. Early reply will greatly oblige."[20] The next day the *Journal's* reporter in Halifax, Grattan O'Leary, was able to wire his stories.[21]

Due in large part to Chambers' behind-the-scenes involvement to preserve as much freedom of the press as possible, by 9 December visiting journalists in Halifax were able to send full-length despatches to their papers, supplying readers not only with graphic details of the Explosion and its aftermath but also identifying many of the dead, injured and missing. On the same day Chambers telegraphed George Perry thanking him for help in "facilitating news dissemination." After mentioning his own "experience as a telegraph editor" Chambers observed: "You will thoroughly appreciate the anxiety caused to newspapermen by the disorganization of the telegraphic services."[22]

On 14 December, the second day of the inquiry into the disaster headed by Justice Arthur Drysdale, Chambers arrived in Halifax at the request of Major-General Willoughby Gwatkin, chief of the general staff of the Canadian Militia. Significantly and symbolically, Chambers arrived in uniform reflecting his status as a lieutenant-colonel in the militia and a representative of the chief of general staff. The purpose of his visit ws to discuss security and censorship problems caused by the disaster.[23] The next day Chambers convened a closed-door meeting at the Halifax Hotel with representatives of the *Mail, Herald, Chronicle, Echo, Recorder* and Halifax CP Bureau.

Following the "little conference," as Chambers described the press briefing, he sent a letter to James Hickey, superintendent of Halifax's CP Bureau. After requesting Hickey to transmit to local reporters in attendance "suggestions offered for the guidance of the press in the treatment of matter relating to the recent catastrophe," Chambers added, "it has given me peculiar satisfaction to hear through those best able to judge, such very general approval of the admirable manner in which the local members of the press, and visiting correspondents have co-operated with authorities during the past terrible week."[24] Furthermore, in separate communication to Gwatkin, Chambers reported that Major-General Benson "expressed himself as much pleased with the general attitude of the press."[25]

Additional praise for the professionalism, diligence and assistance of the press would follow. Prior to his departure from Halifax, Abraham Ratshesky, Commissioner-in-Charge, Halifax Relief Expedition, from 8 to 12 December, stated: "The newspapers and their staffs have our sincere thanks for their kindness and attention."[26] Also, visiting journalist Stanley Smith of the *St. John Daily Telegraph*, who reported the disaster from Halifax between 7 and 9 December, would later write that the men on relief and recovery "were ably seconded by the Halifax press which, recovering quickly from the disaster, gave invaluable assistance not only as a medium for dissemination of necessary information but editorially inspiring the people."[27]

Chapter 2

Journalists and Record Keepers Who Experienced the Explosion Firsthand

Among those who escaped with their lives in the Halifax catastrophe and sharers in the widespread destruction and injury from the explosion were two members of the Canadian Press staff. J.L. Hickey, the superintendent at that point, was himself injured, his house partly wrecked, and two of his children injured. M.L. Backer, day operator, on the leased wire, has to face the destruction of his house, with serious injuries to his wife.
— *Manitoba Free Press*, 8 December 1917

Lawyer and *Halifax Chronicle/Daily Echo* owner/publisher G. Fred Pearson founded the Eastern Associated Press (EAP) in 1909. The following year EAP became part of Canadian Press Ltd., which delivered Associated Press news from New York to Canadian newspapers as well as a small domestic Canadian news service. On 1 September 1917, Pearson, who would play a role in the Explosion's recovery efforts, brought EAP into the newly established national wire service agency Canadian Press.[1] The Halifax CP Bureau was established in the three-storey Granville Street building housing Blackadar Brothers Printing Company and the *Recorder* daily newspaper, approximately three kilometres from where the Explosion would occur three months later.[2]

In normal circumstances Halifax CP Bureau staff did very little independent news gathering and reporting. Instead, each day the wire service received "dupes" (carbon copies) of stories forwarded by news or city editors of Halifax's newspapers, after which an agency editor revised such local items as were "judged of interest outside the newspapers' own immediate territory."[3] The revised material was then sent over a leased wire to the Montreal CP Bureau, and from there disseminated nationally through a network of regional bureaus. Given the co-operative news sharing agreement between CP and Associated Press (AP), the same material was also distributed to CP's New York Bureau and AP in New York, which in turn made the copy available to hundreds of American wire service's member newspapers in the United States.[4]

James Hickey and Maxwell Backer, Halifax Canadian Press Bureau

The Halifax CP Bureau consisted of forty-eight year-old Superintendent James Hickey,[1] thirty year-old American-born telegraph operator Maxwell Backer[2] and sixteen-year-old messenger boy Leo Hinch.[3] Born 7 July 1869 in Halifax, Hickey joined the *Chronicle* in 1883 serving as an office boy, reporter and by 1903 the paper's news editor. During his career he met many notables including King George V, Prince of Wales, Prince Louis of Battenberg and Sir Wilfrid Laurier. Hickey also interviewed William Howard Taft who was later to become successively president and chief justice of the United States. After Hickey stepped down as the *Chronicle's* night editor in the late 1920s, he remained active in the newspaper field as a member of the *Halifax-Mail Star*.[4] He became the last surviving member of a once large group known as the "Spring Gardens Group" a fraternity of youths whose homes were located in the area bounded by the Halifax Common, Tower Road, South Street and the North West Arm.[5] Described as the "dean of Maritime newspaper men," Hickey died in Halifax on 28 November 1954.[6]

In April 1912 Hickey played a central role in the paper's coverage of the *Titanic* disaster. He arranged to have Cathedral Church of All Saints Reverend Canon Kenneth Hinds, who was the chaplain on board the recovery vessel *Mackay-Bennett*, provide a summary of the number of bodies recovered and the names of the most prominent persons.[7] Before the *Mackay-Bennett* docked in Halifax the ship was daringly intercepted by a tug carrying two *Chronicle* reporters, who obtained a written record from Hinds and rushed the highly sought after "manuscript" to Hickey. He immediately wired the information to New York via the Western Union Telegraph Company, thus scooping all other Halifax reporters, three correspondents from Upper Canada and representatives from American press associations and newspapers.[8]

Prior to December 1917 Hickey was appointed superintendent of the Halifax CP Bureau, although his official title remains uncertain. In one contemporary press report he was identified as "Superintendent of

*James Hickey and family, c. 1917; back row (l-r) Jim, May, J.
Howard; middle row (l-r) Abigail, James Hickey; front row (l-r)
Parker, Hilda. Courtesy Pat Brennan*

the Eastern Division of the Canadian Press."[9] However, Ernest Chambers addressed Hickey shortly after the Explosion as "Superintendent, Maritime Section."[10] At the time of his CP appointment, Hickey was also Halifax correspondent for the *New York Times*[11] and news editor of the *Halifax Chronicle.*[12]

Maxwell Backer was born in New York in 1887 and married Sadie Oxner of Lunenberg on 21 February 1914. While in Nova Scotia they had two children, Lawrence Louis and Muriel. The Backer family left Nova Scotia for Bridgeport, Connecticut, in 1919, and according to the 1930 American Census they were still married.[13]

Leo W. Hinch was born in Canada [likely Ontario] on 12 December 1901. He attended school in Halifax and joined CP as a messenger boy in 1917. Leo left Nova Scotia after the disaster and settled in Welland, Ontario, where he married Nora Vernon on 28 March 1921. They soon moved to Schenectady, New York, where Leo worked as a welder for more than twenty-five years for the American Locomotive Company. He died in Schenectady on 9 October 1979.[14]

The involvement by Halifax CP bureau staff, particularly James Hickey, in news gathering and reporting on the day of the Explosion can be determined from five sources: a 14 March 1918 story in the *Royal Gazette* (Bermuda, Hamilton), Hickey's recollections in a 1949 newspaper interview,

From a panorama by Walter G. MacLaughlan. James Hickey first went to the CPR Telegraph office in the Dennis Building to telegraph news of the Explosion but the wire was dead.

Hickey's 6 December 1917 Halifax CP despatch, mention in Halifax and Canadian and American newspapers between 7 and 10 December 1917 and information from CP historians Mark Nichols and Peter Buckley.

Royal Gazette News Story

On 14 March 1918 a story was published in the *Royal Gazette* (Hamilton, Bermuda) describing how James Hickey overcame injury as well as shock, terror and struggle of the Explosion's immediate aftermath to break news of the disaster to the outside world.

How The News Was Sent From Halifax

The explosion on the French munition ship Mont Blanc in the harbour at Halifax December 6, 1917, that laid waste a large part of the city and brought death or permanent injury to thousands of its citizens, threw James Hickey, for many years correspondent of The Associated Press, through a shattered glass door in the office of the Halifax Chronicle.[15]

When he picked himself up, Hickey was bleeding from cuts on his left arm and hand, but, without realizing that he was injured, he rushed into the street with but one thought in his mind — there had been a disaster and it depended upon him to sound the alarm to the outside world before telegraphic communication collapsed, as he felt it inevitably would.

At the shock the Canadian Press lease wire snapped. Struggling through a street choked with panic stricken men and women, Hickey reached the Western Union office only to find it dismantled and deserted. At the Canadian Pacific Railways Telegraph office a broker's operator still stood by his wire, but the wire went dead a moment later.

Near the building occupied by the Postal and Halifax & Bermuda Cable Company, Hickey stumbled upon Superintendent Hagan (*sic*) of the Cable Company and asked him if he could get off a bulletin to the Associated Press by way of Havana.[16] Mr. Hagan with considerable peril to himself crawled over the debris in what had been his office and touched a wire.

"It's alive," he said. Then as Hickey dictated, the Superintendent transmitted the only news message that went out of Halifax that day, finishing it only seconds before the isolation of the stricken city, so far as wire communication was concerned, was complete.[17]

Hickey's Recollections in a 1949 Interview

In a special issue on 20 June 1949 honouring Halifax's bicentennial, *Chronicle* reporter Graham Allen interviewed Hickey related to his more than sixty years as a Halifax journalist. Among Hickey's recollections was a description of how he scooped all reporters and correspondents in providing first news bulletin of the Explosion to the outside world.

Veteran Newsman Had Ringside Seat For City's History

Mr. Hickey believes, and with good reason, that he was instrumental in giving the world its first news of the Halifax Explosion in December 1917 half an hour after the disaster occurred.[18]

Like thousands of others he rushed from his office amid the welter of broken glass but unlike many he had a definite plan as a trained newsman his first idea was to get a taxi to go to the scene of the explosion. But there were none in sight. The street cars stood immobilized on the tracks.

Then he began to walk towards the North End. He met thousands on the streets, for all had rushed out when the blast came and as he went farther north he met hundreds of women and children crying and bleeding from their wounds, fleeing the devastated area and seeking doctors.

Soon naval and military men were on the streets warning all to make for open spaces as it was feared the Dockyard magazine might blow up. The military men were difficult to pass, Mr. Hickey recalls, but the bluejackets after he explained his errand permitted him to go ahead.

"I went up Cornwallis street to Gottingen street and found conditions worse," he recalls. "The sight was appalling. Masses of humanity were flocking to the Commons. Citadel Hill was crowded, most of the people huddling on the south and western slopes. I talked to many of them."

Then he rushed down the slope to the telegraph offices but found them deserted as were stores and offices throughout the downtown section.

However, John Hagen, manager of the Halifax and Bermuda Cable Company came along the street and Mr. Hickey asked him if there was any chance of getting a message to New York. "We'll try," said Mr. Hagen, and, after clambering over some of the debris in the office he touched the Morse key pad and said "Yes."

Then Mr. Hickey stood by Mr. Hagen and dictated the following message:

"Associated Press."

"New York."

"Hundreds killed, thousands injured, and millions of dollars property damage as result of collision between two steamers in Halifax Harbour this morning and terrific explosion which followed one of the ships said to have been loaded with ammunition. Then fire broke out in ruins and flames raging fiercely with no means to check them. Half of extreme North End of city now levelled."[19]

Hickey's 6 December 1917 Halifax CP Despatch

Through further news gathering after his bulletin to AP in New York, Hickey was able to provide a follow-up story with numerous details of the Explosion to outside world news centres during the afternoon of 6 December.[20] However, in conforming to agency practice, he was not permitted a byline. His on-the-spot reporting, which appeared on 7 December in several Canadian newspapers, demonstrated the work of an experienced legman. The *Montreal Gazette* ran his unattributed account of the chaotic scene under the following lengthy spreader headline.[21]

Belgian Relief Ship Gored Hull Of Explosive-Laden French Craft Damaged Vessel Caught Fire — 25 Minutes Later Terrific Convulsion Spread Death, Injury And Destruction Over Wide Area — Property Loss Will Reach Millions, Every Structure In The City Being Shaken — One In Each Two Surviving Residents Injured — Temporary Morgues And Hospitals Improvised — Relief Directed To Stricken City From Many Points In Canada And United States.

By Canadian Press Halifax, N.S., December 6 — As the result of a terrific explosion aboard a munition ship in Halifax harbour this morning a large part of the north end of the city and along the waterfront is in ruins and the loss of life appalling. Estimates places (*sic*) the number of dead at more than one thousand. On one ship alone forty were killed. Thousands have been injured. The property damage is enormous, and there is scarcely a window left in a building in the city.

Chief of Police Hanrahan tonight estimates that the dead may reach 2,000. Twenty-five wagons loaded with bodies have arrived at one of the morgues.

Among the dead are the fire chief and his deputy, being hurled to death when a fire engine exploded. Fire followed the explosion, and this added to the greatest catastrophe in the history of the city.

All business has been suspended and armed guards of soldiers and sailors are patrolling the city. Not a street car is moving, and part of the city is in darkness. All the hospitals and many private houses are filled with injured.

The offices of the railway station, the Arena rink, military gymnasium, sugar refinery and elevator collapsed, and injured scores of people.

The munition ship was bound from New York for Bedford Basin, when she collided with a Belgian ship bound for sea.

Following the collision the explosion occurred, and in an instant the whole city was shaken to its foundations. Thousands rushed for the open, and some of the children in the schools became panic-stricken. On every street could be seen adults and children, with blood streaming from their wounds, rushing to the nearest doctors' offices. The work of rescue was greatly impeded by the piles of debris in the devastated area.

A part of the town of Dartmouth is also in ruins.

Nearly all the buildings in the dock yard are in ruins.

Practically all the north end of the city has been laid to waste. The destruction extends from the North Street Railway Station north as far as Africville to Bedford Basin, and covers about two square miles.[22]

The buildings which were not destroyed by the explosion were laid waste by the fire that followed.

Thousands Are Homeless

Thousands of people have been rendered homeless.

The Academy of Music and many other public buildings have been thrown open to house the homeless.

Five hundred tents have been erected on the Commons, and these will be occupied by the troops, who have given up their barracks to house the homeless women and children.

Temporary hospitals and morgues have been opened in the school houses in the western section of the city. The doctors and nurses worked heroically in rendering aid to the injured.

The collision between the two steamers occurred near the point of the harbour known as Pier 8, and was between a French munition ship, the Mont Blanc and a Belgian relief ship, the Imo.

The Mont Blanc lies in the Narrows, a battered, torn wreck, while the Belgian relief boat is beached on the Dartmouth side of the harbour near what is known as Tuft's Cove.[23]

At nine o'clock this morning the city was enjoying its usual period of calm, the streets were crowded with the usual number of people who were wending their way to work. Then came an explosion. From one end of the city to the other glass fell and people were lifted from the sidewalks and thrown to the pavements. In the down-town offices, just beginning to hum with the usual day's activity, clerks and heads alike cowered under the showers of falling glass and plaster which fell about them.

25 Minutes After Collision

The collision was a terrific one, the munition boat being pierced on the port side practically to the engine room. The relief vessel, which was practically uninjured, kept going ahead, shoving the damaged craft ahead. When the fire was seen to break aboard the Mont Blanc, the other ship backed away and the crew started to abandon her.[24]

The Mont Blanc drifted off, a burning wreck, while the relief boat was beached near Tuft's Cove on the Dartmouth side of the harbour.[25] Twenty-five minutes after the collision the explosion occurred. Under the force of the explosion, houses crumpled, while the unfortunate residents met death in the debris.

In the main portion of the city, where the buildings are more or less of stone or concrete, the damage was confined to the blowing in of windows, and the injuries sustained by the citizens were in the main due to the cuts from flying glass. Proceeding south to the extreme end of the city, the same thing was observed.

In the west and northwest end, the damage was more extensive, and the walls of houses were in places blown to atoms, and the plaster and laths strewn on the streets, making them more like a shelled section of Flanders than a Canadian town.

The main damage, however, was done in the north end, known as Richmond, which was opposite the point of the vessels' collision.

Here the damage is so extensive as to be totally beyond description. Street after street is in ruins and flames swept over the district.

In this section many of the larger buildings are smouldering heaps of ruins, and ordinary frame houses are mere piles of shattered flattened ruins.

Automobiles scurrying here and there in this section of the city, each bearing a blanket-clad burden, told of serious injuries or, in many cases, death.

The hospitals with admirable order were rendering aid, and in the military hospitals the soldiers injured while on guard duty were being hurried to the wards for relief.

A few minutes after the explosion occurred, the streets were filled with terror-stricken people trying to make their way as best they might to the outskirts, in order to get out of the range of what they thought to be a German raid.

Women rushed terror-stricken through the streets, many of them with children clasped to their breasts. In their eyes was a look of terror as they struggled on with blood-stained, horror-stricken faces, endeavoring to get anywhere from the falling masonry and crumbling walls.

By the littered roadsides as they passed, there could be seen the remains of what had once been human beings, now torn and mangled beyond realization of what had occurred.

Here and there lay the cloth-wrapped bodies of children, scarred and twisted by the force of the horrible explosion.

By the side of many of the burning ruins were women who watched the flames as they consumed the houses which in many cases held the bodies of loved ones. With dry eyes they watched their homes devoured by the flames, and as others passed with inquiries as to whether they could render any aid, they shook their heads in a dazed manner, and turned their gaze once more to the funeral pyres.

One particularly sad case was that of a Canadian Government employee named MacDonald, who on rushing to his home after the explosion, found that all his family, consisting of his wife and four children had perished. Before him on the roadway was the mangled remains of his little two-year-old child, who had met death while playing on the roadside.

Many of the men composing the crews of ships in the harbour were killed and injured. The damage along the waterfront is very serious.

On one steamer, the Picton, it is reported that 38 of the crew of 42 have been killed. Many bodies of seamen have been picked up in the harbour and rescue parties are working among the ruins of buildings, removing bodies of the dead.[26]

Mention in Canadian and American Newspapers between 7 and 10 December 1917

Between 7 and 10 December 1917 several Canadian and American newspapers reported the presence of Canadian Press staff in Halifax on the day of the Explosion.

Press Men Escape (*Manitoba Free Press*)

Toronto, Dec. 7 — Among those who escaped with their lives in the Halifax catastrophe and sharers in the widespread destruction and injury from the explosion were two members of the Canadian Press staff. J.L. Hickey, the superintendent at that point, was himself injured, his house partly wrecked, and two of his children injured. M.L. Backer, day operator, on the leased wire, has to face the destruction of his house, with serious injuries to his wife.[27] These cases help to illustrate the handicaps under which the citizens of Halifax are labouring to effect reorganization (*sic*).[28]

Halifax Appeals For $25,000,000 To Aid Victims
(*New York Times*)

Halifax N.S., Dec. 9 — An Associated Press dispatch from Pittsburgh telling of a munition plant explosion there, was coming over the leased wire of the Canadian Press at five minutes after 9 o'clock Thursday morning [6 December] and the operator here had just copied the word "explosion" when the building rocked with the concussion from the explosion of the munitions ship. Reading faster than he wrote, M.L. Backer, the operator, was getting "the cause of the explosion has not been determined." The wire broke on "explosion" but while the typewriter was trying to jump away from him Backer finished the sentence. That was the last word that came for six hours.

Less than an hour later Backer entered his home to find his baby in a cradle safe under a blanket which was covered with a shower of glass.[29] His wife was severely injured. Part of a shell weighing eighteen pounds had plowed through the wall of his home two feet above the place where the baby slept.

James Hickey, Superintendent of the Eastern Division of the Canadian Press, working at his desk in the same building with Backer, was hurled through a door, but not seriously hurt. Every big plate glass window in the three-storey structure was shattered.[30]

Operator Leaves To Succor Wife And Press Story Of Disaster Has To Wait Till Substitute Found (*New York Times*)

At ten o'clock last night [6 December] there was a sudden break in the story of the Halifax disaster coming into the New York offices of the Associate Press over the wire of the Canadian Press, the only one in operation into that city since the explosion.

Efforts to raise Halifax were ineffectual. An hour later it was learned that the operator who had been sending from the stricken city had left his key when a messenger brought him news that his wife had been dangerously injured. While sending the story he had expressed the fear that something must have happened to her because she had sent him no message since he went on duty.

The regular Canadian press operator at Halifax has been missing since the explosion and his place was taken by a substitute. Sending further details of the disaster was perforce suspended until a second substitute was found.

Halifax was cut off for a time from all communication with the rest of the world by wire or cable according to officials of the Western Union Cable Company in the city. All land lines were down and the plant of the United States Direct Cable Company at Halifax was so damaged by the explosion that the line could not be operated.[31]

Cause Of Collision (*Montreal Gazette*)

In conversation with one of the nurses, a *Canadian Press correspondent* [my italics] was informed that the suffering of the badly-wounded victims was intense.[32]

Terrible Sadness Of The Great Disaster
(*St. John Daily Telegraph*)

Dr. Almon, C.M.O., said to *Canadian Press* [my italics] last night [6 December] that nobody was seriously injured in that [military] hospital at Rockhead.[33]

CP Historians Mark Nichols and Peter Buckley

Mark Nichols and Peter Buckley both provide information about day one coverage of the Explosion by the Halifax CP Bureau.[1]

Excerpt from (CP) The Story of the Canadian Press by Mark Nichols, 1948

Strangely enough, news of the Halifax disaster that claimed 2,000 lives came first to the outside world at 9:25 a.m. from Amherst, NS 140 miles west (*sic*) of Halifax, in the form of a bulletin:

American (incorrect) ammunition boat collided with another boat at Rockingham, three miles from Halifax. A section of the city is on fire.

This was followed half an hour later by an AP bulletin from Boston:

A great disaster has occurred in the vicinity of Halifax. Number of people killed.[2]

Succeeding bulletins at few-minute intervals reported destruction of many buildings, scores of lives lost, sections of Halifax in flames and all crews of the boats in collision killed.

Canadian Press leased wires were put out of business upon the instant of the explosion. Canadian Pacific Telegraphs was unable to give The Canadian Press use of its Halifax wire, which intermittently "went down," but enough news was picked up to produce a dispatch that was filed for distribution at 4 p.m.[3] It contained the first really accurate estimate of the dead — 2,000 — and also reported that it was a French ship, not an American, that was in collision.

The dispatch was used in the late editions, not only in Canada, but in United States papers served by The AP. A review of American papers of December 6 revealed that The Canadian Press supplied more than ninety per cent of the Halifax story used by AP newspapers.

The nearest Canadian Press member was *The News*, published in Truro, sixty-one miles west (*sic*) of Halifax. A telephone call via Amherst asking assistance of A.B. Coffin, the Truro publisher, had immediate response.

We received a long distance message from Amherst asking us if we could get a story out of Halifax where wires were dead. Within an hour the writer was on the road for Halifax with the best taxi in town, the chauffeur carrying a machinist with him. Roads were in worst possible condition, having been guttered badly before freezing and in places covered with ice and snow.

In spite of the roads we made the trip in three hours. You would know that in the lightly-loaded car we didn't spend much time on the seat. At Bedford (10 miles from Halifax) we made all arrangements for telegraph and telephone at any time during the night on our return.[4]

Coffin's dash to Halifax proved to be unnecessary. Shortly after his arrival, wires were restored and at nine o'clock 3,000 words were sent to Montreal. *We left Halifax at eleven o'clock,* Coffin's letter continues, *carrying back as many people as could be crowded into the car, all of them anxious to get away.*[5]

Excerpt from *The National (CP) Link* by Peter Buckley, 1997

Barely three months after starting operations, *The Canadian Press* faced the challenge of covering the most devastating tragedy in Canadian history.

At 9:04 a.m. on Dec. 6, 1917, the French ship Mont Blanc — crammed with explosives for the Allied forces in Europe — blew up in Halifax harbour. The blast flattened much of the city and left some 2,000 people dead and dying.

A telegraph operator in his dockside office saw the Mont Blanc being struck amidship by a Belgian relief ship. Flames shot up from the benzene stored on her deck. Realizing the danger, he tapped out: "Ammunition ship on fire and making for Pier Eight. Goodbye."[6] In the explosion that followed, all the telegraph and phone lines went dead.

The shockwave from the blast was felt a hundred kilometres away. In Montreal, CP got a first vague report from Amherst, 225 kilometres to the west of the ruined city. The Associated Press in Boston also began sending out bulletins, fed by tattered Western Union lines from the Halifax area. Truro and other Maritime points relayed whatever information they could get from refugees and other sources.

There were only confused details in that day's afternoon papers across Canada, but by the time the morning papers came out the next day — not only in Canada, but around the world — CP's increasingly descriptive reports dominated the news coverage.

CP's Halifax office was silenced by the first blast (there may have been only a single person, a telegrapher, stationed there in any case).[7] So were the Halifax papers, the agency's normal source of news. Desperate for information, CP sent out a call for help to A.R. Coffin, publisher of the Truro News.

Coffin's news instincts were fired up. He and a taxi-driver skidded for three hours over icy roads to the outskirts of Halifax to gather information. But by the time Coffin arrived, the first outside relief efforts were in place and at least some telegraph contact was being restored.

CP's new board of directors had been bitter from the start about the failure of many papers to provide their local news to the co-operative. They decided Coffin's eagerness to help CP was an example of how things should be done and voted the Truro publisher a warm recommendation.[8]

William Barton, Former Telegraph Editor at the *Montreal Gazette*

> In ten seconds it was all over.
> — William Barton, former *Montreal Gazette*
> telegraph editor, *New York Times*, 8 December 19

William Barton was a former telegraph editor of the *Montreal Gazette*.[1] After World War I began he became a travelling auditor for the Canadian Imperial Munitions Board, and on 6 December 1917 was in Halifax representing the organization. When the Explosion occurred Barton was having breakfast with approximately thirty other guests in the Halifax Hotel on Hollis Street.[2] His eye-witness account of the blast and its immediate aftermath was first published in the *New York Times* on 8 December 1917 and two days later in the *Manitoba Free Press*.[3]

Blizzard Stops Rescue Work (*New York Times*)

Associated Press Dec. 8 – William Barton, former telegraph operator of the Montreal Gazette, and now a traveling auditor for the Canadian Imperial Munitions Board at Ottawa said he was at breakfast at the Halifax Hotel.[4]

"In ten seconds it was all over," Mr. Barton said. "A low rumbling, an earthquake shock, with everything vibrating, then an indescribable noise, followed by the fall of plaster and the smashing of glass. In such moments the human mind does not hesitate: a cry went up 'A German bomb!' A rush for the door, heading down the hallway amid falling pictures, glass and plaster, to the swing doors of a few seconds before, now ripped from their hinges, through great projecting triangular pieces of glass to the street.[5] Here I found myself with a burden. How she had come into my arms I do not know, yet here she was hysterically shrieking: 'Oh my poor sister. My poor sister!'

My aid, for I was unscathed, was probably needed for more there. I made my way upstairs to the rooms of two friends. The rooms were vacant but normal, even the glass unbroken — and few panes of glass remain unbroken in this area. Once more I was in the street, meeting my companions on the threshold. They, too, were unscathed.

Our plans were quickly made. We were off to the immediate vicinity of the disaster, for among many theories, we accepted as most plausible the blowing up of a munition. Toward Citadel Hill we wended our way, and the further we went the more horrid the aftermath. The improvised stretcher met us on all sides, converging into the main thoroughfares from the highways and byways. The wounded were everywhere, but most of these unfortunates could hobble or walk; we kept onwards.

Our hurry-scurry had led to the armory.[6] Here the khaki-clad men were already on parade. Many of the soldiers showed wounds bound with handkerchiefs, conjuring to the mind base hospitals of overseas.

As we passed they were already on the march toward the more devastated area. The order had gone forth. 'Commandeer all vehicles, auto or horse.' A cordon was drawn across the streets and passengers were forced to alight and resume their journey afoot.[7] There was grim work ahead."[8]

Joseph Sheldon, *Dartmouth N.S.Patriot*, Arthur Pettipas, *Halifax Herald*, and Mary "May" O'Regan, *Morning Chronicle*

> My God, what is happening; is this the end for me?
> — Joseph Sheldon, *Dartmouth Patriot* editor, 9 December 1917

One of three Dartmouth journalists known to have survived the Explosion was thirty-five-year-old Joseph Sheldon. He resided on Victoria Road, several blocks northeast of the town's waterfront, and was editor of the eight-page Saturday weekly *Dartmouth N.S. Patriot* and manager of the Dartmouth Printing and Publishing Company Limited.[1] When the blast

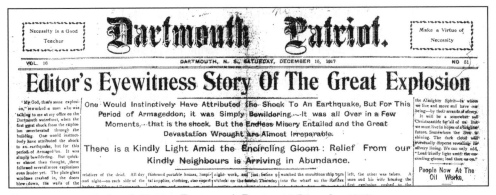

Front-page story by Joseph Sheldon, Dartmouth Patriot *15 December 1917*

occurred Sheldon was in a meeting in the *Patriot's* office at 48 Commercial Street, one block east of the Dartmouth ferry terminal and approximately 1,600 metres from the blast.[2] His eye-witness description of the Explosion and its aftermath was first published in the *Toronto Daily Star* on 14 December 1917. When the weekly republished on 15 December, the same story (with slight revisions) appeared on the *Patriot's* front page under the headline "Editor's Eyewitness Story Of The Great Explosion."[3]

In 1918 Sheldon wrote two further Explosion-related accounts: *A Bolt from the Blue*, subtitled *A Vivid Story of the Halifax Explosion by an Eye Witness,* published by Cox Brothers in Halifax, contains thirty-two unnumbered pages, twenty-three of which are illustrations, and little text, and "Death Calls too Soon: Scenes at Chebucto Morgue," an article based on his experience of the Explosion and a subsequent visit to the Chebucto Morgue.[4]

Two other Dartmouth journalists who survived the blast were twenty-seven-year-old Arthur Pettipas and twenty-six-year-old May O'Regan. Pettipas was born in Dartmouth in 1889 and received his education at public schools. After completing school he first worked for a Dartmouth plumbing company and then was employed as a clerk in the office of the Chronicle Publishing Company. Between 1908 and 1912 he was on the editorial staff of the *Chronicle* and then went west to work as a reporter for the *Saskatoon Daily Star*. After two years he returned to Dartmouth and was employed as a reporter for the *Halifax Herald* and *Mail*. In 1916 he became temporary assistant secretary of the Halifax Board of Health and was appointed permanently in 1919.[5]

In 1917 Pettipas lived at the corner of Windmill Road and Dawson Street but was not home when the Explosion occurred. His wife Gertrude survived because minutes before the blast she opened the house's east facing window to call to women on the street below. This act likely saved her life and her eyes because she was standing in front of the open window when the concussion hit and left the house in ruins.[6] Following the disaster Arthur supervised Dartmouth's #2 relief food depot, which began operations on 9 December, and was also a member of Dartmouth's Fuel Relief Committee.[7]

Mary "May" O'Regan was born in Dartmouth on 30 April 1891.[8] She had a forty-year career in journalism with the *Chronicle*, *Echo* and *Star* and after 1949 the *Mail-Star*. Although unable to walk after 1945 due to severe arthritis, she supplied the *Mail-Star* with a Dartmouth social column and general news of women's activities. She continued as the paper's Dartmouth correspondent until her death on 29 March 1957. *Chronicle-Herald* reporter Berton Robinson said that, in the mid-1920s May "was the first women's lib character I ever met. Anything a man could do around a newspaper, she often asserted, she could do better."[9]

In 1917 May lived with her mother and younger sister Teresa at 67 Ochterloney Street and was on staff at the *Chronicle* and *Echo*. She wrote the children's feature "Sunshine Club Mailbag" under the pseudonym Cousin Peggy.[10] Teresa worked as a secretary at the Royal Litho and Print Company on Argyle Street next to the Herald Publishing Company. On 6 December, Teresa was on the 9:00 a.m. ferry *Halifax* crossing from Dartmouth to Halifax. When the Explosion occurred, *Halifax* was about five minutes out and almost in mid-channel — approximately two kilometres south of the burning *Mont-Blanc*.[11] The ferry survived the blast and continued to the Halifax side. However, Theresa was seriously cut across the face and the bridge of her nose.[12] At the time of the Explosion May O'Regan was either home in Dartmouth or at work in the Chronicle

Arthur Pettipas, c.1905. Courtesy collection of the Dartmouth Heritage Museum

Mary "May" O'Regan, Chatelaine, *June 1954*

Building on Granville Street. There is evidence to suggest that later in the day she identified the body of fellow *Chronicle/Echo* reporter John Ronayne in one of the city's morgues.[13]

In the disaster's aftermath, May as Cousin Peggy provided two columns related to the disaster's relief work. On 21 December she wrote "A Steady Stream Of Gifts—This Is What Cousin Peggy Wants," in which she outlined the needs of the Children's Christmas Fund.[14] Then on 27 December she wrote a much longer story, "How The 'Sunshine Rays' Sent Father Christmas to the Little Children," describing how "Every Hospital and Every Shelter Yesterday [25 December] There Was a Tree, a Glittering, Gaily-Decorated Tree, Weighed Down With Toys and Other Gifts."[15] Later in her career May would write about the Explosion as part of a story on sensational local events since 1900.[16]

Joseph Sheldon's initial account of the Explosion was published by the *Toronto Daily Star* on 14 December and given a three-line deck.[17] The story's dateline, *Dartmouth, N.S. Sunday, Dec. 9*, indicates it was written within three days of the disaster.

Dartmouth Man Tells Of Halifax Explosion
Bewildered, Instinctively Rushes To Back Room,
Then Out To The Street, Only To Meet Blood-Bespattered
People Crying Out In Anguish For An Explanation.
My God! Is This The End For Me? He Asks.

The Personal Experience Of Joseph Shelden (*sic*), Editor of the
Dartmouth N.S. Patriot, in the Great Disaster.[18]

Dartmouth, N.S. Sunday, Dec. 9 – "My God, that's some explosion!" remarked a man who was speaking to me at my office on the Dartmouth waterfront, when the first great shock from the explosion reverberated through the building. One would instinctively have attributed the shock to an earthquake, but for this period of Armageddon. It was simply bewildering. But quicker almost than thought, there followed several more explosions even louder yet.[19] The plate glass windows crashed in, the doors blew down, the walls of the wooden building cracked and bent inwards. Almost without thought — just from the natural instinct of self-preservation — I backed from the window to a small stock-room as the explosions continued. As I stood there bewildered, just one conscious thought passed through my mind: My God, what is happening; is this the end for me? It was all over in a few moments — that is, the shock from the explosion. But the endless misery entailed and the great devastation wrought are almost irreparable.

I rushed to the street, there to meet scores of fear-stricken men, women, and children — blood-bespattered — crying out in anguish for some explanation of the awful catastrophe. All manner of rumors were forthcoming: Explosion at the dockyard! Munitions ship blown up! Etc. etc. But the thick spiral cloud, reaching as it were to the heavens, told its own tale of calamity. Gradually the truth leaked out: A collision in the harbour, munitions ship exploded.

Rumors Create Panic

Then came news that the magazine at Halifax Dockyard was in danger, and that another explosion was expected at any moment. This news caused somewhat of a panic. People rushed from their homes and stores in confusion — even the banks were deserted. Sick ones — including children suffering from diphtheria, mothers in a delicate state of health — the old and decrepit, many thinly clad, were brought out-of-doors into the bleak December weather. Thank God! Within a short time news came that all fear of further explosion was at an end. The people gradually regained their equilibrium and began to

return to their houses — that is where the buildings were still standing.

In the meantime, doctors, nurses, ambulances, etc., were all astir. People forgot their fear in the desire to render help to the injured and comfort the relatives of the dead. All day and night — on each side of the harbour, Halifax and Dartmouth, our people were busily engaged on errands of mercy; rescue parties to recover bodies from the ruins of houses and buildings that had been razed to the ground; fire brigades fighting the terrible flames which broke out in every part of the city of Halifax, the town of Dartmouth and vicinity.

Next day a furious blizzard swept over the scene of the disaster. The wrecked buildings and the dead beneath the ruins were mantled in snowy-white. It was a pathetic scene.

The full extent of the calamity will not be known for many months — perhaps never.

Trees Torn Up By Roots

Both sides of this section of the harbour suffered terribly. On one side a sugar refinery was razed to the ground; on the other a brewery entirely collapsed.[20] In each case, with few exceptions, all the occupants were killed. The people at the southern end of the harbour suffered chiefly from shattered glass. One woman had her throat cut by a piece of glass; she bled to death. Trees were torn up by the roots. The Indian reserve north of Dartmouth was practically wiped out. One poor Indian woman was taken from the debris with her leg hanging by a small piece of flesh. The mutilated condition of the injured, as well as that of the dead, was indescribable.[21]

There is a kindly light amid the encircling gloom. Relief from our kindly neighbour, the United States, is arriving in abundance. Massachusetts sent a specially equipped train of supplies, and another is expected from New York. A thousand portable houses, hospital supplies, clothing, also engineers and nurses, are coming to our rescue. Three cheers for the Stars and Stripes!

Bureau Falls On Him

I interviewed an eye-witness of the collision. He resided, before his house was destroyed, on the Dartmouth waterfront, in full view of the scene of the collision. He had been on night work, and just before nine o'clock Thursday morning went upstairs to sleep. He glanced out the window just as the French munitions ship, Mont Blanc, and the Belgian relief ship, Imo, were zigzagging across the narrows of the harbour. "What the deuce are they trying to do?" was his inward comment.

The young man watched the munitions steamer turn into the wharf on the Halifax side of the harbour. He watched for some time, but eventually, feeling somewhat sleepy, he retired to the back of the bedroom and lay down. No sooner had he done so than the explosion occurred. He remembers seeing the bureau jump in the air. It landed on top of him. He remembered no more until some of the family came to his rescue. He was badly injured in the face and body, and for the time was rendered unconscious. "I never heard the noise from the explosion," he remarked to me. "I simply remember seeing the bureau leap at me, and all was blank."

One Taken, The Other Left

A man and his wife, on hearing the first explosion, rushed to the doorway, the wife a little ahead of her husband. She was killed instantly by a projectile from the exploding ship; her husband was unscathed. At the Halifax dockyard

and in the immediate vicinity of the explosion men were pitched high up in the air, landing practically unscathed, while their comrades around were blown to atoms. Oil and water poured down like rain.

The ferry steamer, which was crossing the harbour at the time of the explosion, quivered as though it had struck a log or chunk of ice, shattering the glass and causing one or two serious cases of injuries to the eyes of the passengers.

Even the dumb animals are bewildered.

Manufactures Are Stopped

The Dartmouth Patriot office, which is close to the waterfront, suffered severely. The type was scattered all over the floor among broken glass and other debris.[22] It was impossible to get out the regular weekly edition last Saturday [8 December]. All hands are working hard to restore order out of the chaos. It is hoped that the regular issue of the paper will appear next Saturday [15 December].[23] All the manufacturing concerns of the town of Dartmouth and pretty nearly all in Halifax, too, are temporarily out of commission. Some of them are not likely to be running again all the winter. Windows of works, shops, and houses, are fastened up with tar paper and strips of wood.

There is no ritual in the churches to-day (Sunday) — they are restitiute (*sic*) of windows and doors.

It will be a somewhat sad Christmastide for all of us. But we must live in hopes of a brighter future. Somewhere the sun is shining. The dark cloud will eventually break, revealing its silvery lining. We can only add, "Lead kindly light, amid the encircling gloom, lead thou us on."[24]

Peter Lawson, *Halifax Herald*

It was not long before a special messenger came to me from the late Senator Dennis telling me to get busy on the story.
— Peter Lawson, *Herald* news editor,
letter to *Berwick Register* 27 January 1943

Peter Lawson was born in Hamilton, Bermuda, on 7 September 1875 and taken as a child by his parents to Halifax, Nova Scotia.[1] In 1882 the family moved to the Annapolis Valley, where Peter's father established a general store in Waterville. Lawson attended schools in Waterville and in Berwick and left home at sixteen to spend two years at sea. In 1893 he enrolled at Dalhousie University but took off time and started again in 1897.[2] Between 1898 and 1914 he worked for the *Berwick Register, Parrsboro Leader, Kentville Advertiser, Middleton Outlook* and *Western Chronicle* in varying positions and in the United States as a printer at R.R. Donnelly and Sons Company in Chicago, Illinois, and managing editor of the *Galesburg Gazette* in Galesburg, Illinois. In 1908 he married Maude Tryon.[3]

In October-November 1914 Lawson represented the Nova Scotia government on board *Tremorvah*, the first Belgian relief ship to reach Europe.[4] In 1915 he accepted a position on the editorial staff of the *Halifax Herald*. After reporting the Explosion for the *Herald*, Lawson left Halifax in early 1918 to edit the *Glace Bay Gazette* and then a labour paper in Fernie, British Columbia. However, within a few months he left Fernie for Stuttgart, Arkansas, to publish the *Stuttgart Free Press*. In December 1923 he joined the *Beaumont Journal* (Beaumont, Texas), where he worked as a reporter for several years. In the early 1930s he became public relations director for the Beaumont Chamber of Commerce (BCC). Lawson retired from the BCC in 1946 and worked for the Texas Department of Public Welfare until his death in Beaumont on 9 September 1949.

A fellow journalist once described Lawson as "a rather smallish man with a slight Scottish burr ... with a mate's ticket in his pocket, sailed at least some of the seven seas. If you sniffed, you'd still detect salt about him."[5]

According to colleague Harold B. Jefferson, on the day of the Explosion, Lawson, "news editor of the Halifax Herald, veteran of disasters in the United States and Canada, made his way out the

Peter F. Lawson, c.1915. Courtesy Dr. Scott Pigford

railroad to the nearest undamaged telegraph office and sent the first real news."[6] Jefferson also recalled that following the blast, press operators gossiped "GXP" over their leased wires, meaning "Great excitement prevailed."[7]

In a letter written to the *Berwick Register* in January 1943, Lawson reconstructed his role in news gathering and reporting on the day of the Explosion.[8]

At the time of the Great Explosion in Halifax I was living on Buckingham Street and employed on the Halifax Herald.[9] Having seen the Herald "put to bed" on explosion morning I went home about four o'clock to put myself to bed.[10] When the windows and doors smashed in I was sure a German sub had arrived in the harbour and lobbed over some shells, one in our backyard. When I was awakened by the two blasts of the explosives on the French S.S. Mont Blanc, I said I thought a German submarine was shelling the city. It was not long before a special messenger came to me from the late Senator Dennis [the *Herald*'s proprietor/publisher] telling me to get busy on the story.

There were no cabs or taxis. The street cars had all of them, been put out of commission. I crossed Sackville Street, ran across the citadel on the snow of the Old Town Clock, noting that it was still running with its old imperturbability. What was an explosion in its history! Over toward Richmond there was a dense pillar of smoke in the sky. I ran in that direction.

The story of the Great Explosion has often been told. There is not space for me to tell of my experiences that morning. The big stories were without the edge of "news" for there was no electricity or gas; the linotypes could not be run and the metal in the pots could not be melted for lack of gas.[11] The Herald and Mail had an old hand press such as The Register once had. On The Register I had learned to hand set type and in addition to writing the first story [for the 7 December edition] I had the privilege of putting a part of it in type. We got out a one-sided edition of The Herald on the old hand press. It was a small edition.[12] I think a copy of it framed still hangs in the Halifax Herald office. Getting a few copies of it over the province was a problem for the [North End] rail terminal had been badly wrecked. A special messenger carried them to the train somewhere near Bedford.[13]

According to a subsequent story in the *Mail*, "It was a woe begone (*sic*) and yet optimistic group that stood round that old hand-press at 4 o'clock on the morning of December 7th, watching the slow grinding out of the sheets, glad with each impression made that one more sheet was added to the number of those that must be made to go round among the more than 14,000 subscribers eagerly watching for the Herald with an account of the terrible disaster."[14] In the predawn hour Lawson would have been among the tired group in the composing room who had worked through the night and was now watching the "Halifax Wrecked" story come off the hand press.[15]

"Halifax Wrecked," front-page story by Peter Lawson, Halifax Herald *7 December 1917; a reproduction from a supplement in the* Mail-Star *6 December 1967*

HALIFAX WRECKED
More Than One Thousand Killed In This City, Many Thousands Are Injured And Homeless

More than one thousand dead and injured, many of them fatally, is the result of the explosion yesterday on French steamer ship Mont Blanc, loaded with nitroglycerine (*sic*) and trinitrotuol (*sic*). All of Halifax north and west of the depot is a mass of ruins and many thousands of people are homeless. The Belgian Relief steamer Imo, coming down from Bedford Basin, collided with the Mont Blanc which immediately took fire and was headed in for Pier No. 8 and exploded.[16] Buildings over a great area collapsed, burying men, women and children. Tug boats and smaller vessels were engulfed and then a great wave washed up over Campbell Road.[17] Fires broke out and became uncontrollable, stopping the work of rescue. Not a house in Halifax escaped some damage, and the region bounded on the east by the harbour, south by North street and west by Windsor street is absolutely devastated.

The wounded and homeless are in different institutions and homes over the city. The Halifax Herald is collecting information regarding the missing, and citizens who have victims of the disaster at their homes are requested to telephone to the Herald office. Hundreds of the bodies which were taken from the ruins are unrecognizable and morgues have been opened in different parts of the city. Citizens' committees are being formed for rescue work. Bulletins will be issued thruout the day giving information for the assistance of those who have lost relatives and friends. While practically every home in the city is damaged, those who are able to give any temporary accommodation are asked to notify some of the committees.

Military and naval patrols are keeping order and superintending the rescue work.

The Awful Story Of Disaster

At 9.05 o'clock yesterday morning a terrific explosion wrecked Halifax killing over a thousand, wounding at least five thousand, and laying in ruins at least one-fifth of the city.

The Belgian Relief steamer Imo coming out of the Basin in charge of Pilot William Hayes collided with the French steamship Mont Blanc in charge of Pilot Frank Mackay (*sic*). The French steamer was loaded with nitroglycerine and trinitrotoul. Fire broke out on the Mont Blanc and she was headed for Pier 8. It was eighteen minutes after the collision when the explosion occurred. The old sugar refinery, and all the buildings for a great distance collapsed. Tug boats and steamers were engulfed and then a great wave rushed over Campbell road carrying up debris and corpses of hundreds of men who were at work on the piers and steamers.

Without the loss of a moment hundreds of survivors rushed to the rescue of those buried in the ruins. Fire broke out in scores of places and soon the great mass of wreckage was in the grip of an uncontrollable fire checking the work of rescue.

The military and naval authorities almost immediately took charge of the situation. Fearing that the fire would reach local magazines of explosives military messengers were sent over the city warning the people out of the buildings and advising them to take to the citadel and open spaces. This was not by authority.

Practically every house in the city was damaged. The entire business district was windowless and to prevent pillaging patrols from warships in port were paraded thru the streets.

All along Gottingen street and throughout the northwest part of the city there was a pitiful scene as women and children lacerated with flying fragments of glass rushed from their homes. Truckmen, hackmen and taxi-cab drivers rushed victims to the hospitals for dressing. At the Naval hospital many of the sick sailors were badly cut and, fearing an explosion from the magazine at the Wellington barracks, they were taken away.

The home of The Halifax Herald and The Evening Mail is badly wrecked. Every pane of glass and window in the building is smashed. Partitions have been blown down. Our press is filled with glass. Some employees have lost their homes and families. Our power service is cut off.[18]

We are sending out a copy of this hand printed bulletin to every town in order that as many of our readers as possible may know at least some details of the disaster. We hope to be in a position to publish tomorrow. In the meantime we ask for patience.

A public meeting is called for city hall at 11[p.m.].[19]

Lawson's remarkable story would reappear over the next fifty years, the first time in the special "Reconstruction" edition of the *Evening Mail* published on 22 March 1918. Beside the story was the editorial comment: "The work of the reporters [on the Explosion story] was hardly less arduous [than the work of the hand compositors]. It was overwhelming — the prospect of trying to tell anything about the catastrophe, knowing that only a small fraction of what they would write could be printed.... They did what was possible — that was all."[20]

Damage to the *Halifax Herald* Building

In 1918 *Views of the Halifax Catastrophe* was published by the Royal Print and Litho Limited. The booklet contains forty photographs including a picture of the damaged south and east corners of the Herald building with the following description:

> The Herald building is situated more than two miles from the scene of the disaster, and so great was the explosion that every pane of glass in the building was shattered. On the north and west sides (not shown in the picture) the greatest damage was caused, frames and glass being blown in on the presses and other parts of the plant.

Although the publication of *Views of the Halifax Catastrophe* is dated 1918, author William March claims that the illustrated booklet was offered for sale on 'the eighth day after the event.' [14 December 1917] March *op. cit.* 135. In support of March's claim, on 14 December an advertisement for the publication appeared on page 9 of the *Herald*. It is almost certain that the broken windows are an early example of photo shopping.

The story's second reappearance was in 1943, when Halifax author William Borrett used the "Halifax Wrecked" story for the opening page of "The Halifax Explosion" chapter in *More Tales Told Under the Old Town Clock*. Finally, on 6 December 1967, Lawson's story was republished as the front page of the special fiftieth anniversary edition of the *Halifax Mail-Star*.[21] In this supplement, Explosion survivor Dr. J.P. McGrath accurately described the one-page 7 December 1917 *Herald* issue as "a little larger than a large letter sheet" and claimed he read a copy on 7 December at the Queen Hotel.[22]

Hervey Jones, James L. Gowen and John "Jack" Ronayne, *Daily Echo*

Was in the party first to board the "Imo" on the evening of December 6th. Went On Pickford and Black's tug, agents for the ship. Found body of [William] Hayes, pilot, crouched under the life-boat on the bridge, as if he tried to shelter himself from the effects of the explosion."

— personal narrative of Hervey Jones, 17 December 1917

Hervey Jones

Born in Halifax on 13 April 1892, Hervey Jones was educated in Halifax and received a BA from Dalhousie University in 1912. In September 1917 he became the *Echo's* editor and remained in this position until 1925, when he became the *Chronicle's* first managing editor.[1] In 1917 he also served as the acting vice-consul for Spain.[2] Jones moved to South Africa in 1934 to work in the gold mining industry, and from 1942 to 1951 was manager of New Consolidated Gold Fields Limited. He died in Johannesburg, South Africa, in May 1979.

Halifax Disaster Record Office Director Archibald MacMechan described the twenty-five-year-old journalist as a "small, slight build, neat, dark, worn out and tired gentleman."[3] At the time of the Explosion Jones lived at 88 Cedar Street with his wife, Gertrude, who was also on staff with the *Chronicle* and *Echo*.[4]

On the day of the Explosion, Jones accompanied Captain Le Médec by automobile to the

Hervey Jones, 1912. Courtesy Dalhousie University Photograph Collection, Dalhousie University Archives

Northwest Arm residence of French Consul Emile Gaboury. However, during the ride to the French Consulate, Le Médec would not talk.[5] Afterwards Jones returned to the devastated Richmond district where he witnessed several fires, observed a large crowd on the Common and saw a man's leg drop out of a truck.[6] Later that night he was among the first inspection party to board *Imo* as it lay beached on the Dartmouth side of the Narrows.[7] They found the body of Pilot William Hayes "crouched under the lifeboat on the bridge, as if he had tried to shelter himself from the effects of the explosion."[8]

The *Echo* did not appear on the day of the Explosion.[9] However, it did resume publication the next day under the banner headline "Death Toll In Great Disaster Growing."[10] The main story was almost certainly edited by Jones.

Thousands Dead And Thousands Are Homeless As A Result Of The Terrific Explosion Yesterday

Whole Families Wiped Out Of Existence, Homes Wrecked, And Intense Suffering Prevails — Relief Is On The Way But In Too Many Cases It Is Too Late

A stricken city, racked by Fire, with a thousand families homeless and twice that number dead, Halifax today is suffering as it has never suffered before. The collision that occurred on the harbour yesterday morning has made a shambles of the North End of the City, has inflicted damage that will mount in the millions of dollars and has created untold sorrow among our people.

While there is no official estimate as yet of the death toll, it is considered a surety that it will be well over two thousand. Whole families were wiped out of existence when their homes were knocked down like so much cardboard. Buildings in which where (*sic*) many employees were swept to the ground and in some cases there was not a single survivor.

The hospitals are filled to overflowing and some of the cases there have

Front–page story Daily Echo, 7 December 1917

been heart-rending. One wee tot, five years old, was taken into the Camp Hill Military Hospital sadly mutilated. Despite her wounds she was cheerful and bright, though she wanted "her Mammy." The hospital nurses could not bring themselves to tell her that her mother, father, brothers and sisters were all dead. The admissions at Camp Hill and Cogswell Street have been well over three thousand and it is estimated that the number of injured, more or less seriously, is over five thousand. Doctors from outside points have been rushed to the City and the heroism of some of the local medical men is worth more than passing notice. Some of them, with their faces badly cut or limping

from leg wounds, kept at their duties unflinchingly and save (*sic*) many a life.

A Daily Echo reporter yesterday interviewed the Captain of the French Steamer Montblanc (*sic*), the munition ship which exploded and caused the frightful loss of life and property. The Captain was not willing to talk. "C'est terrible, c'est effroyante" [It is terrible, it is frightful] was all he would say.[11] He stated that he would reserve his statement until the official inquiry was held.

Relief trains are coming in from various points in the Province and even from the United States. Yesterday trains with hundreds of wounded left Halifax for Truro and Kentville.[12]

James L. Gowen

Born in Halifax on 12 February 1864, James L. Gowen began work as a cub reporter at the *Chronicle* in 1888 and later transferred to the *Echo* until it was renamed the *Star* on 22 January 1927. After 1905 he was also Halifax correspondent for United Press Association wire service. Every Sunday between August 1914 and November 1918 he prepared and posted war news on the Prince Street windows of the *Chronicle*.[13] Gowen had a reputation as a "newspaperman of the old school who never rode to a story in a car and seldom used a telephone to obtain information."[14] He was a traditional figure in county court

proceedings who enjoyed the assignment so much he once refused an editorship to avoid relinquishing the court beat.[15] At the time of his death in Halifax on 14 April 1936 he was the *Star's* city editor.[16]

Fifty-three-year-old Gowen survived the Explosion without injury and rushed home to 179 Morris Street to check on his family. After 7:00 p.m.

James L. Gowen, 1900. Courtesy Nova Scotia Sport Hall of Fame

James E. Gowen 1923. Courtesy Nova Scotia Sport Hall of Fame

he left Morris Street in a snowstorm that turned into a blizzard to gather news for the *Echo* and did not return from the all-consuming task until 3:00 a.m. in "three feet of snow."[17] Later that morning he went back out in the bitter cold to all known shelters and hospitals to compile lists of survivors.[18] During the ensuing Wreck Commissioner's Inquiry, Gowen reported the proceedings for the *Echo*.[19] Gowen's seventeen-year-old son James E. Gowen, who would follow in his father's footsteps as a Halifax journalist, acted at the Inquiry as the *Echo's* "runner" by running his father's copy of proceedings to the nearby Chronicle building.

The results of James L. Gowen's on-the-ground news gathering in extraordinarily difficult circumstances appeared in the first post-Explosion issue of the *Echo* under the headline "Relief Work Among The Grief Stricken People Of The City."

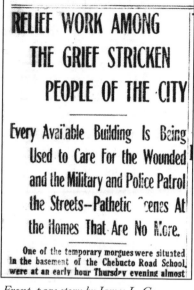

RELIEF WORK AMONG THE GRIEF STRICKEN PEOPLE OF THE CITY

Every Available Building Is Being Used to Care For the Wounded and the Military and Police Patrol the Streets—Pathetic Scenes At the Homes That Are No More.

One of the temporary morgues were situated in the basement of the Chebucto Road School. were at an early hour Thursday evening almost

Front-page story by James L. Gowen, Daily Echo 7 December 1917

Relief Work Among The Grief Stricken People Of The City
Every Available Building Is Being Used To Care For The Wounded And The Military And Police Patrol The Streets
— Pathetic Scenes At The Homes That Are No More

One of the temporary morgues were (*sic*) situated in the basement of the Chebucto Road School were (*sic*) at an early hour Thursday evening almost a steady stream of vehicles of all sorts were conveying the dead and despositing (*sic*) them in the basement in long rows.

The bodies were carried into the building and placed in long sheet covered rows. Practically none of them were recognizable in their blackened and in many cases burned condition.

Relief bands of military were covering the Common and the slopes of Camp Hill with a mushroom like growth of bell tents, which sprung into being with the passing minutes as if some magical force was behind them.

Military and police of all descriptions patrolled the streets, and in orderly grime stained gatherings worked among the ruins and loaded the people they recovered into waiting vehicles. Of those who were fortunate enough to escape with their lives practically every second person in the city was injured.

Medically (*sic*) men worked in an effort to render aid wherever it was needed and during the day must have relieved thousands who were not beyond their aid.

In the early morning after the collision, fire broke out and the department apparatus was rushed to the scene. They were preceded by the Fire Chief Edward Condon, Deputy Chief William Brunt and Peter Broderick in the Chief's automobile.[20] While on their way the explosion occurred instantly killing all of the occupants.[21]

The flame swept belt begins at what is known as the North Street Bridge and extends northward to Pier Eight Richmond on the water front and backward to a point running practically parallel with Gottingen Street. This embraces about two or two and a half square miles of territory. In this portion of the city there is nothing but rubble.[22]

John "Jack" Ronayne

Although *Echo/Chronicle* marine reporter John "Jack" Ronayne did not write about the Explosion, he merits mention as he died investigating the story. Born in Halifax on 24 August 1894, he lived at 34.5 North Street, technically where the district of Richmond started, with his mother Elizabeth and siblings Marjorie, Martha (Lil), Dorothy, Leo and Francis.[23] His father Ambrose died in April 1916, and John remained at home as the eldest, unmarried male. For several years prior to the Explosion he was a staff member on the *Chronicle* and *Echo*.

At approximately 8:30 a.m. on 6 December Ronayne was preparing to leave home for the Chronicle building when he saw smoke from a ship burning in the harbour.[24] Instead of reporting to work he phoned the paper to explain that he was going to investigate the story, unaware that it would be his last assignment. Accompanied by his sister's boyfriend, Roger Amirault, Ronayne hurried north on Barrington Street to Constant Upham's grocery store near Pier 6.[25] Given the distance from North Street to Upham's store on Barrington opposite Hanover Street, Ronayne and Amirault must have either taken a streetcar, flagged down a passing automobile or taken a cab in order to arrive before the Explosion.[26]

After talking briefly with Upham, Ronayne continued north on Barrington to the foot of Duffus Street, where he crossed the "heavy steel overhead bridge which spanned the yard at Richmond."[27] On the bridge there may have been as many as 150 bystanders watching the burning *Mont-Blanc* at Pier 6.[28] If so, they would have been scythed down when the blast occurred. When that happened Ronayne was "somewhere past the overhead bridge"[29] and was caught in the concussion "as he approached the pier."[30] Amirault, who miraculously survived the Explosion, found Ronayne "in the road, moaning, half his face as if scalded with steam."[31] He soon died from his wounds and his body was identified later that day in the Infirmary by his mother.[32] As for Amirault, according to family lore he returned home "with barely a scratch on him."[33] John Ronayne was buried in Mount Olivet Cemetery on 12 December.[34]

On 8 December the *Chronicle* eulogized twenty-three-year-old Ronayne under the sub-headline "Died Doing His Duty."

Daily Echo reporter John Romanyne was fatally injured near the railway footbridge that spanned the railway tracks from the bottom of Duffus Street to the head of Pier 7. The surviving abutment is on the far left of the damaged superstructure. A portion of "View From Pier 8," a panorama by W. G. MacLaughlan (courtesy of Joel Zemel)

Died Doing His Duty

Among the dead the City may well mourn is "Jack" Ronayne, a young man of splendid promise, of sterling worth, and high character. For several years he had been a member of The Chronicle and Echo staff and had endeared himself to all his associates by his unfailing courtesy and kindness, his enthusiasm for his work, his fine ideals and his clean living. Mr. Ronayne was assigned to the waterfront for his special work, and on Thursday morning telephoned to the Echo that he was going up to get a story of a munitions ship then coming up the harbor, before he reported at the office. After the explosion the Echo made enquiry and search for Mr. Ronayne but to no avail. Later in the day his body was found at the Infirmary by one of his former deskmates[35] and in every newspaper office in the City there was genuine sorrow over the loss of this bright young member of the profession. Mr. Ronayne met his death in the willing attention to the duties that characterized his brief career. The Chronicle and Echo, along with innumerable friends, tender their sincere sympathy to his family in their sad loss. Mr. Ronayne was only in the first flush of young manhood, nevertheless his death is a distinct loss to the City as well as to the newspaper profession.[36]

Editor, *Nieuw Amsterdam Courant*

Launched in 1905 the 17,000 ton Holland-America *Nieuw Amsterdam* completed its maiden voyage from Rotterdam to New York on 7 April 1907. The liner accommodated 417 first class, 391 second class and 2,700 third class passengers and remained in service until World War I began in August 1914. It resumed trans-Atlantic crossings when the United States declared war on Germany on 6 April 1917. On 30 June 1917 *Nieuw Amsterdam* sailed from Rotterdam to the Dutch East Indies via New York. However, after docking on 13 July the ship was held by American authorities until 24 November when it left for Rotterdam via Halifax under Captain Jan Baron. On board were 300 passengers and a crew of 350.[1] The ship was also carrying 10,000 tons of grain for the Belgian Relief Fund.[2] When *Nieuw Amsterdam* reached Halifax it was again detained, this time until the British government received additional guarantees from the German government that the ship would be allowed to proceed unharmed to Holland.[3]

When the Explosion occurred *Nieuw Amsterdam* was anchored among the many transports, freighters and merchant ships in the west side of Bedford Basin near Fairview Cove.[4] For several days Captain Baron had been awaiting clearance from port authorities to continue on to Rotterdam. The location of the ship, approximately three kilometres from Pier 6, provided a unique perspective for passengers and crew to experience the Explosion and its aftermath. Soon after the blast, Baron ordered a boat launched to check damage to the vessel and then row into Halifax. As the boat was returning, the onboard paper *Nieuw Amsterdam Courant* was going to press. The

Holland America liner S.S. Nieuw Amsterdam, *1909. Library of Congress LC-D4-22580*

Courant appeared a few hours later with an unattributed article about the disaster titled "Catastrophe in Halifax."[5] No copy of the original newspaper of 6 December 1917 is known to exist. The text below comes from the circa 1919 unpublished manuscript by Dwight Johnstone, "The Tragedy of Halifax: The Greatest American Disaster of the War."[6]

Catastrophe In Halifax

At about 9:10 this morning the ship suffered two shocks, succeeding each other within a few seconds, the last more severe than the first. Most of us thought that a nearby steamer had swung into us. It was worse, not for us, but for Halifax. Apparently an ammunition factory blew up, and the signs of damage, scarcely visible through the mist and smoke, are still enough to justify grave apprehension as to the loss of life and property.[7] Mr. Morris Drieblatt who was walking on the upper deck was blown off his feet, but landed without injury. Mr. Calman, apparently the only other person on the south deck at the time braced himself after the first shock and was not injured. Most of the passengers were at breakfast. The second explosion was accompanied by a fanlike discharge of black smoke in the channel leading to the entrance to the harbour. For two hours after the explosion, a huge white cloud mingled with brown poisonous looking vapors was rising in a vast cumulus into the otherwise clear blue sky. At the inner end of the entrance was a steamer with smokestack and bridge gone and the gun at the stern pointing into the air.[8] Later she was beached on the East side of the bay. At least four craft show signs of damage.

The damage to our own ship, two miles from the explosion, is limited to a few splintered doors. The heavy stairs to the upper deck are slightly damaged. A few cracks in the paint round the doors show the force of the impact. After the explosion a decided wave was observed over the bay, as the water was forced on by the expanding air.[9] One steward who put his head through a porthole upon hearing the first explosion, got a serious lump on the back of his head when the second crash came. Fewer breakfasts were served in cabins this morning than on any morning since we left New York.

There was a natural desire on the part of the passengers and crew to get on deck, but there was no panic or disorder. Within a quarter of an hour after the accident the ship's carpenter was placing a few necessary nails in woodwork, and soon thereafter our Captain had a boat lowered, made a tour of the ship, and was then rowed towards Halifax. The boat was returning as we go to press.[10] At 11:40 a column of dark smoke was rising from the hill directly South of us, and it was rumoured that this was an ignited oil tank. Our representatives, however, interviewed an oil specialist on board, and was informed that the smoke was not that usually seen when petroleum burns in mass. We are all right: but what of Halifax?[11]

As a postscript, *Nieuw Amsterdam* left Halifax on 17 December and arrived in Rotterdam on 28 December. Before it left the stricken city, passengers collected and donated $261 for victims of the disaster.[12]

Archibald MacMechan, Official Historian of the Disaster

> As I was reading the paper this morning in the dining room, a few minutes after nine, I heard a deep rumbling noise underneath me … I thought the boiler had burst in the kitchen.
> — Arthur MacMechan, 6 December 1917

Archibald MacMechan was a Canadian essayist, scholar and poet born in Berlin (now Kitchener), Ontario, on 21 June 1862. He started his education in 1880 at the University of Toronto and graduated in 1884 with a BA. Between 1884 and 1886 he taught school in Brockville and Galt, then entered Johns Hopkins University as a doctoral candidate in modern languages and received a PhD in 1889. The same year MacMechan was appointed professor of English at Dalhousie University, where he remained until 1931. During his years in Halifax he helped establish the Dalhousie University Marine Museum and served briefly as the University Librarian. Between 1907 and 1910 he was president of the Nova Scotia Historical Society and in 1926 was awarded a fellowship in the Royal Society of Canada (RSC). In 1932 he was awarded the RSC's Lorne Pierce Medal for achievement in literature. MacMechan died in Halifax on 7 August 1933.[1]

When the Explosion occurred, MacMechan was home at 72 Victoria Road reading a newspaper in his dining room. The blast damaged his house, but none of the occupants was hurt. On 15 December Dugald MacGillivray, inaugural chair of the all-important Halifax Rehabilitation Committee, asked MacMechan to begin the official history of the disaster.[2] The next day he engaged a room in the Halifax Chronicle Building as headquarters for the Halifax Disaster Record Office and on 17 December formally undertook the task of compiling material for the history of the Explosion and its aftermath.[3] Until 23 January 1918 MacMechan gathered information on events leading up to the Explosion as well as the days that followed, including individuals' experiences and survivors' personal narratives.[4] As the event's official record gatherer and preserver he wrote a report titled *The Halifax Disaster.* However, it was not published until 1978 as part of Graham Metson's book *The Halifax Explosion Dec. 6, 1917.*

Archibald MacMechan, Official Historian of the Explosion. Courtesy Archibald MacMechan, Notman Studio, photographer; NSA, Notman Studio Collection, 1983–310 no. 8631

On 22 December 1917 the *Canadian Courier* published "Halifax In Ruins," an account by MacMechan of the Explosion and its aftermath up to 9 December.[5]

Halifax In Ruins

Story By An Eye-Witness Who Lives In Halifax And Who Records In Haste What He Was Able To Focus Of The Tragedy Up Till December 9
By Archibald MacMechan

Because some one man or several blundered, or a piece of machinery broke down, because sheer misadventure steered two ships towards each other from the ends of the earth, the proud old city of Halifax was laid in ruins in an instant of time. A thousand of her people were slain and not with sword; as many more were maimed and wounded. Millions of money will not repair the damage. Nothing can make good the total of human suffering endured.

Halifax is a long, thin city, built on the western shore of a great harbour. The city is really two cities divided by the huge hill on which the citadel is built. The South End, as it is called, is the residential portion; the North End is industrial. There are the wharves, the dry-dock, the railway station, the factories, the main barracks, the naval department. This quarter was the home mainly of the working class. Their houses were of wood, cheaply constructed. Here is the wasp-waist passage between the outer harbour and the inner, which is known as Bedford Basin. This passage or strait has a deep, narrow channel. Here was the scene of the calamity which struck Halifax like a comet on Thursday morning, December the sixth, 1917.

It was a morning of unusual and surprising beauty. There was no snow on the ground. The air was kind and friendly as in summer. Nothing in sky or on earth portended disaster; but disaster was on its way. Men were getting down to their offices; the morning trains were coming in at the North Station; the children were assembled in their schools.[6]

Over the still, glassy surface of the harbour, a French ship, the "Mont Blanc," was proceeding cautiously towards the Narrows. She had four thousand tons of T.N.T. in her hold and a deck load of picric acid and benzol.[7] She was to anchor in the Basin out of harm's way. The Dock Yard officials had a special eye on her, as they must have on all dangerous visitors.[8]

At the predestined hour, the Belgian relief ship, "Imo," conspicuously lettered in red, as is the fashion of such ships, had left her anchorage in the Basin and was proceeding outwards to sea. Both were in charge of regular certificated Halifax pilots. As they neared and neared, those looking on noticed that the "Imo" was disregarding the old established, immutable rules of the road at sea.

About a quarter before nine, the two ships met practically in the Narrows, and the "Imo" rammed the "Mont Blanc" somewhere about the engine-room.[9] Some say the steering gear went wrong at the critical moment; others that the usual signals were misunderstood.

Almost immediately after the collision, the "Mont Blanc" was seen to be on fire. A tall column of smoke rose like a pillar of cloud through the still morning air. Onlookers remarked that there was a ship on fire in the Basin. The crew of the "Mont Blanc" well knowing what they had underneath their feet, took to their boats and rowed like madmen for the eastern shore, where the town of Dartmouth stands, opposite to Halifax. The abandoned ship, burning freely, drifted towards Pier 8, as it is called, a long double wharf, where the square-rigged ships load deals for the U.K. Long freight trains bear the sawn lumber from the mills to the wharf.[10]

One observer of the collision was the captain of one of H.M. ships in the harbor, for nothing takes place in the vicinity of a British man-of-war that is not noted and reported. He saw the danger and ordered his commander away in a boat, to board the derelict, anchor her, and get the fire under control. They never reached their goal.[11] Before they got near the "Mont Blanc" she drifted into Pier 8 and blew up.

An eye-witness on the citadel curiously watching the huge column of black smoke suddenly saw an immense upward spurt of red flame. And that was the last of the "Mont Blanc."

There came a burst of thunder sound. Those who have experienced earthquakes thought they were caught in another. The ground rocked, walls swayed and fell, roofs collapsed. There was only one explosion, but most Haligonians heard two reports; first a deep, awful, subterranean rumbling, for earth carries sound more quickly than air; the second was like the sound of an enormous blast, as when the engineers of the Ocean Terminals explode tons of dynamite in the cuttings.

Immediately all over the peninsula, in every dwelling, shop, factory, office, bank warehouse, there followed the sound of shattering glass, the splintering of wooden doors, shutters, as locks were burst and hinges smashed, where the whole fabric did not fall in a heap. The effect of the vast, sudden interferences with the air was practically the same as if an earthquake had shaken Halifax to the ground.

To those who heard those awful sounds two or three similar ideas occurred at once. Most thought, "At last" German ships were shelling the city from outside the harbor. One! Two! —When and where would the third fall? Or else it was "An air raid." Instinctively people ran into the open to look for the Zeppelins, or took to the cellar to escape the shells.

Then quiet reigned again. There were no more terrifying sounds. Neighbors began to confer in the streets and make inquiries as to damage and escapes. They also noted with surprise that everyone's house was wrecked as well as their own. In the South End, people were calm and unexcited; they were taken unawares, but they were not flurried. Annoyance at the inexplicable damage done was perhaps uppermost, and curiosity as to the origin of the trouble. Blasting at the Terminals and the roar of the big guns at practice have been so common here that it takes a great deal to put Haligonians in a panic.

The true story of the explosion soon spread mysteriously from lip to lip. Then practical people began to make repairs. They began to sweep up the broken glass and fallen plaster. If they were lucky enough to have some lumber they began boarding up their windows. If not they put up mats, rugs, blankets, roofing felt, cloth and battens — anything to keep out the weather. This was only true of the South End. It was some time before

the city realised the disaster which had befallen it.

Far different was the scene in what the local papers called "the busy North End."

There the incalculable force of the suddenly compressed air had blasted the whole quarter flat. Every house was level with the ground and every tree. The cheap, wooden houses, which covered the hillside simply collapsed in a moment like houses built of cards. In an instant of time, before the unfortunates could realise the peril, their houses had fallen on their heads. One poor man hunting for his wounded wife from hospital to hospital, said, "I was sitting at breakfast and the two ends went out of the house." Men, women and children were killed instantly by the concussion, and were thrown yards away from their homes. Others were torn to pieces, heads from bodies, limbs from trunk. Others were blinded by the pelting showers of broken glass, or strangely gashed and rent. In all conceivable ways was this poor human frame rent, and broken, and shredded and crushed. The houses collapsed, killing whole families at once, or heavy timbers pinned down living and injured. Their fate was the most fearful for — the wreckage took fire.

In an instant of time twenty thousand people, half the population of Halifax, were rendered destitute.[12] Those who escaped were homeless; they had only what they stood up in. The case of the little children was most pitiful. Richmond School came down and killed a hundred; the little white-crushed faces could be seen through the timbers.[13] Fifty more were killed at St. Joseph's School.[14] All but two perished with devoted matrons in the wreck of the Protestant Orphanage.[15]

Across the harbor the same things

happened, but the loss of life was much slighter. Perhaps forty Micmac Indians were killed on their reservation at Tuft's Cove. In Dartmouth itself, twenty-five were actually killed.[16] The flying fragments of the ammunition ship killed many. The plight of the aged, the sick, the infirm, the bed-ridden, the crippled, the nursing mothers, the pregnant, cannot be described.

In the immediate neighbourhood of Pier 8, the damage was greatest. The pier itself was simply abolished; hundreds of freight cars with their loads were upset, torn apart, and their contents scattered. The station roof came down, killing or injuring all but two. The road was completely blocked. Traffic was suspended. All through the city the trams and telephone service were at an end.

(Must send this to catch the 7:30 p.m. mail to-night, Dec. 9. Will send on conclusion to-night or to-morrow morning) –A.M.[17]

Perhaps nothing illustrates the inconceivable force of such an explosion as well as the case of the "Niobe." As guard-ship, she is anchored head and stern by heavy cables, and also moored in the wharf. Each link is of inch-and-a-quarter iron, in section. The explosion produced a miniature tidal wave, eight feet high, which tossed her sixty yards out of her place. The wooden deckhouses came down killing fifteen men. The same wave struck the wharves and put out many incipient fires. At least four steamers had their superstructures demolished and men onboard killed. The two steamers in the dry dock were badly injured. The dry dock itself was filled with debris. The old sugar refinery, a tall brick building near by, subsided into a shapeless rubbish heap, and the syrup-coated timbers burnt fiercely.

The Dock Yard suffered severely. The Royal Navy College with forty cadets in it had the walls blown in. A piece of the "Mont Blanc" weighing half a ton came down through the roof of the largest class-room and smashed the platform where the instructor stands. The floor of the "quarter-deck" buckled up in sharp angles. The new Y.M.C.A. hut just erected for the benefit of the sailor was smashed into a heap of kindling wood. The officers' quarters were broken open and the interiors ravaged as if by a tornado. All the water-front suffered damage from fire and water.

The sound of that awful rumbling had hardly died away before the work of rescue and relief began. Every private car, motor, lorry delivery van was soon in use carrying the injured to the hospitals, to chemist shops and to doctors' offices. Before long the Victoria General, Pine Hill, Camp Hill, the Infirmary, were full to overflowing. Then the injured were transported to improvised hospitals — the City Home, the School for the Blind, and such other public buildings as were fit to take them in. The Academy of Music and the moving picture places took in the waifs and strays. Some restaurants served refreshments gratis. Every house left standing was ready to open its doors to those in need. The motors flew screeching and hooting through the streets with extra men standing on the foot-board, and close swathed forms inside. The resources of the city were soon over-taxed, and aid came at the earliest possible moment from New Glasgow, Truro, Windsor, Lunenburg. Most efficient aid came from the American hospital ship lying in the harbour. Within fifteen minutes after the explosion she had two boats with landing parties, surgeons and appliances at the Dock Yard.

The work of collecting the bodies

also began at once. A young officer invalided from France who had charge of a party of soldiers said the bodies were lying as thick as on a battle-field. Many were found on their back without a bone broken or a mark of injury on them. These had been killed by concussion. Some bodies were naked, having been torn from their beds. Horrible human fragments had to be gathered up — children's heads — scorched limbs. The bodies were piled in tens, to wait for the lorries which were to carry them to the school which had been turned into a morgue.

The wooden smashed confusion had taken fire, and was burning in a dozen places. There were living and injured underneath. All the engines in the city were on the spot at the earliest moment. Unfortunately the Chief of the Fire Department and his Deputy were killed before they could direct the work. At the alarm of the burning ship they sped in their official motor to the scene of danger. The explosion caught them, flung their car high into the air and buried them both under a heap of earth. There was necessarily some delay and lack of direction at first, but the firemen worked heroically and were reinforced by brigades from neighboring points.

About eleven in the morning the only approach to a panic occurred. There was some danger of a second explosion, and the crowds of refugees and onlookers in the North End were warned to move south to the parks and open places. This order was run through the streets in the same mysterious way as the story of the collision, and there was a movement of the population southward, many abandoning their homes with doors and windows wide open. But time passed, nothing happened and everyone went back to his immediate and urgent task.

Almost as strange as the stories of the strange injuries are the stories of the hairbreadth escapes. Practically every survivor had a narrow escape from death or maiming. A man standing before his mirror shaving had the two large windows at each side driven in across the bed he had just risen from, daggers of glass stabbing it through and through. A woman in bed with her baby heard the heart-shaking rumble and instantly covered her face and the baby's with the bedclothes. The next instant the window frame crashed on them without inflicting a scratch. A telephone girl operator had just come off the night shift and had gone to bed. At the first noise she wrapped the bedclothes round her; the blast flung her out of the house unhurt whilst everyone else in it was killed. At the Naval College two cadets were skylarking on a table when the same thing happened. They were both hurled through a window and alighted on a bank outside, without sustaining the least injury. Indeed the escape of all the cadets is a marvel. They were cut with the flying glass, even got it in their eyes, but no one was killed, nor was the sight of anyone destroyed. The wife of a naval officer was at breakfast with her two children, while the baby was asleep in his cot upstairs. When the shock of the explosion was over she found herself in the middle of the room bending over the same two children, the only clear spot where heavy furniture had not fallen. The staircase was smashed. She called the first blue-jacket she saw to her aid; he climbed up the ruin of the house and found the baby still in his cradle, protected from harm by a closet door which had inclined across it. Forty-eight hours after the disaster a seven months' baby was dug out of a house in Richmond. He was semi-conscious but soon revived with proper treatment. He had been flung under the projecting front of the stove. Everyone else in the house was killed.

And so on, and so on. There are as many stories of escapes as there are survivors. Every one begins, "If I had been there ten seconds before," or "after," as the case may be, there would have been no story to tell.

What happened on December sixth is the worst calamity that ever befell Halifax. The material damage is estimated at thirty millions. The whole North End beyond Wellington Barracks will have to be rebuilt. The physical suffering, the mental anguish from wounds, blinding, crippling, bereavement, cannot be reckoned by human calculation. On Friday it began to snow, softly at first, but soon the wind blew with blizzard force. In the afternoon a pitiful little procession followed a hearse from St. Mary's, which looks like an old Gothic ruin. "We shall have many funerals now," said a sad woman looking on. There are hundreds of bodies blackened, charred, dismembered, awaiting selpulture (*sic*). "The visitation of God."[18]

Arthur Lismer, Principal, Victoria School of Art and Design

Had glass of house smashed and other damage done. Came into city [Halifax] as far as overhead bridge at Fairview [Fairview Lawn Cemetery], where he was stopped by military cordon.

— Personal narrative of Arthur Lismer, 8 February 1918

Arthur Lismer was a painter and art educator born in Sheffield, England, on 27 June 1885. At thirteen he was apprenticed to a photo-engraving firm attached to the *Sheffield Daily Independent*; two years later he was providing drawings for the newspaper, including cartoons and courtroom scenes as well as sketches of festivals and royal visits.[1] He studied at Sheffield School of Art between 1889 and 1906 and at the Academie Royale in Antwerp, Belgium, between 1907 and 1907. Lismer moved to Canada in January 1911 and worked as a commercial artist at the Grip Engraving Company in Toronto.[2] The next year he returned to England to marry and then come back to Canada. Between 1916 and 1919 he established a career in art education as principal of the Victoria School of Art and Design (later Nova Scotia College of Art and Design) and during 1918 and 1919 painted views of Halifax Harbour as a war artist for Canadian War Records.

In 1919 Lismer moved to Toronto to become vice-president of the Ontario College of Art. The next year he joined with six other Canadian landscape painters to form the Group of Seven.[3] In 1938 he left Toronto for stints at Columbia University and briefly at the National Gallery in Ottawa. In 1941 Lismer became principal of the Art Association of Montreal, a position he held until 1967. In 1946 he was elected to the Royal Canadian Academy of Arts and between 1948 and 1955 was also an assistant professor at McGill University. In 1967 he was made a Companion of the Order of Canada. Lismer died in Montreal on 23 March 1969.

When the Explosion occurred Lismer was at home about to eat breakfast with his wife Esther and daughter Marjorie. They lived on Cliff Street in Bedford at the head of Bedford Basin and mouth of the Sackville River. The house was nearly 20 kilometres north of ground zero and relatively untouched by the blast.[4] However, when he reached Halifax during the afternoon, Lismer found severe damage to his school, located at the corner of Argyle and George Streets. Over the next few days he drew sketches of the disaster's aftermath and, after a request from editor Augustus Bridle of *Canadian Courier,* sent eight drawings to the publication on or about 13 December.[5]

Arthur Lismer in 1920

On 29 December 1917 the high circulation Canadian magazine published a two-page, three-part article on the Explosion titled "When War Came to Halifax … As Seen by the Artist."[6] The first part was a description of the event and its impact on the city of Halifax, the second part outlined Lismer's experience on the day of the blast and preparation of his sketches, and the third part featured eight sketches spread over two pages (all but one captioned). While Lismer did not write parts one or two of the article, he likely supplied information for the text as well as the sketches' captions.[7]

Lismer's drawings provide images of the immediate aftermath of the blast, the snowstorm that followed and the shock experienced by survivors. The following are descriptions of the sketches, not the actual captions:

    1 – refugees fleeing the rumour of a second explosion on 6 December;

    2 – a damaged area surrounding the collapsed Acadia Sugar Refinery, with the *Imo* aground in the distance on the Dartmouth shore;

    3 – a man carrying a dead woman;

    4 – (the only sketch without a caption) a crowd outside a store waiting for warm clothing;

    5 – the skyline of a devastated part of the North End;

    6 – refugees in a church or college;

    7 – a smashed storefront window;

    8 – dead bodies on horse-driven carts being transported in a blizzard to morgues.

Arthur Lismer sketch 6 Canadian Courier *29 December 1917, p. 11. The lengthy caption provided by the paper indicates that Lismer provided some explanation of the sketch: "Evening in a Place of Refuge, says the Artist. He does not say whether it was a church or college. People who had never seen one another before were suddenly homed here. Children asked their mothers — what? The mothers knew not. The aged woman, somebody's grandmother, could not recall in all her readings of the Bible anything that seemed so like the Day of Judgment on earth as this. And because the Artist felt what he saw he flung down his impressions in quick, nervous lines and splashes more eloquent than the accurate lines of any camera, at a time when the eyes and ears and the very brains of people were in a State of Chaos in a City of Wrecks.*

Chapter 3

Visiting Canadian Journalists and the Aftermath

Alfred Coffin, *Truro Daily News*

> The public have not got over the shock of the Halifax tragedy, in fact the magnitude and terribleness of this disaster is only being realized as bit by bit the horror is unearthed.
>
> — Alfred Coffin, *Truro Daily News* 6 December 1917

Alfred Coffin was born in Port Clyde, Nova Scotia, on 7 April 1875. He was educated locally and at Mount Allison University. In October 1894 he joined the *Truro Daily News* and *Truro Weekly News* as a reporter. In December 1906 he and his father became ownership partners of the two newspapers, incorporated as the News Publishing Company Limited. At the time of the Explosion Coffin was the publisher/editor of the *Daily News*. In 1936 Coffin sold his interests in the printing end of the business and concentrated on publication of the *News, Weekly News, Guysboro County Advocate* and *Victoria Inverness Bulletin*. He continued to serve in the company as editor-in-chief until 1956. On 8 October 1954 he celebrated sixty years in the publishing business.[1] Coffin was awarded the Order of the British Empire (MBE) in 1946 and died in Truro on 21 April 1962.

When the Explosion occurred Coffin was in Truro. Soon after details of the disaster arrived at the paper from the Truro railway telegraph office, he was contacted by Canadian Press news service via Amherst, Nova Scotia, to obtain news of the event.[2] In response to CP's urgent request, Coffin hired a taxi and in three hours reached Halifax.[3] While in the city he visited newspaper and printing offices to place his paper's plant at their disposal. Coffin remained in Halifax until 11:00 p.m., when he left with a carload of injured people for Truro.

Between 6 and 8 December the *News* published three stories on the Explosion and likely exhibited them on a main floor bulletin board.[4] Two stories can be attributed to Coffin and the third to the paper's special representative in Halifax.[5] Coffin's accounts were published on 7 December. The first omitted a dateline and included a section headlined "Notes Of The Halifax Disaster."

No Change In Condition of Stricken Halifax Disaster As Great As Reported

Snow Storm Raging Interferes With Work — Loss Cannot Yet Be Given

Gloomy skies broke over the stricken city of Halifax, when a raging snow storm early this morning [7 December] came down interfering greatly with the gruesome work of trying to unearth the dead from the debris of fallen buildings and other wreckage.

Sad was the work of willing helpers, doing all in their power to unearth the dead, but sadder indeed was the position of those waiting and looking for lost loved ones amid the falling snows of winter storms.

There were scenes, that were simply indescribable; but amid falling snows — in this scene of desolation — this rescue work goes on.

The number of the dead is yet uncertain, as the work of the rescuers is not yet completed. It is heard that over 800 have lost their lives and this number may be increased.

The condition of things around North Street is the same except under the cloak of snow the grim horribleness of destroyed buildings is some-what hidden.

The C.G.R. [Canadian Government Railway] authorities have cleared away a lot of the immense wreckage and a train on the main line is now running to North Street Station.

No train (*sic*) cars are yet running in the city and last night the city was only partly lighted.

There has been no time so far to think of an investigation and nothing in this line will be done until the city recovers a bit from the disaster that has clouded everything with gloom.

Notes Of The Halifax Disaster

The public have not got over the shock of the Halifax tragedy, in fact the magnitude and terribleness of this disaster is only being realized as bit by bit the horror is unearthed

----

The evening newspapers of the city, Recorder, Mail and Echo, were not issued and this morning the Chronicle and Herald were unable to appear.[6] The difficulty is largely with the supply of gas for type-setting and other machines that so far cannot be supplied. Never before in the history of Halifax have the city newspapers been put out of business.

Hero Died At His Post

Telegraph Operator Vince Coleman stuck at his key at Richmond Station giving the news of the burning of the ammunition ship Mont Blanc but remained there nobly at his post too long — the flames reached the magazine, the terrific explosion took place and Vince Coleman died at his post: a Hero as brave as a soldier in the battle field.[7]

Grand Work By
D.A.R. Manager Graham

Geo. E. Graham, General Manager of the D.A.R. [Dominion Atlantic Railway], was in Halifax with his daughter at the time of the explosion. He rusht (*sic*) his car to Rockingham and gave information on the disaster to the outside world and was the means of organizing the help that poured into Halifax from every quarter. His work was simply invaluable in this sudden and appalling disaster.

Between Bedford and Halifax there is hardly a pane of glass in any residence or building that is not broken. The shock of the explosion was terrific all along the Bedford Basin.

C.G.R's Good Work

Unceasingly have the C.G.R. officials been working since the explosion yesterday morning. They have now many wrecking trains with big crews in Halifax assisting in removing debris from the devastated sections of the city. Their work as experts is invaluable and joined with them have been Chief Stewart and a band of Truro Firemen that are doing grand work.

The C.G.R. officials by this time have the main line open to North Street and trains can now run thru this heap of wreckage to their destinations. This is good work and men must have workt (*sic*) like beavers to have accomplisht (*sic*) this feat.

In Truro the injured ones, men, women and children, who arrived by train last evening from Halifax are resting on cots (collected in wonderfully short time by untiring Truro workers) at Academy Hall, Court House, Military Hospital, Firemen's Hall, [and the] Agriculture College.

Mr. James Yates, son of Mr. Alfred Yates, Victoria Street lost his wife in the Halifax disaster. She was burnd (*sic*) to deth (*sic*). Their one little child escaped with a slight injury over the eye.

Relief Train Special From Boston

A special Passenger Relief Train from Boston left St. John at noon today for Halifax with Doctors and Nurses and filled with bandages, medical supplies and other requisites.[8]

The Halifax Explosion Disaster
Whole North End Of The City Razed To The Ground,
About 2000 Died And 3000 Injured
From the Morning Edition

Halifax Awakened

Halifax Dec. 6 – Old Halifax had a rude awakening and today fifteen hundred families are homeless, scores of entire families wiped off the slate, about 1000 citizens and approximately 4000 more maimed or wounded.

At nine o'clock Thursday morning, business Halifax was having its usual morning nap, preparatory to getting to work about ten or eleven o'clock, and the labouring classes already two hours at their work, were toiling cheerfully when the blow fell with the almost instantaneous result scheduled.

French Transport Rammed

The French transport ship Mount (*sic*) Blanc, one of the large ones of the fleet, steamed into Halifax and, under pilot McKay (*sic*), moved on to take an anchorage in Bedford Basin. At the Narrows, the strip of Channel connecting the harbor with the Basin, there was coming out from the Basin a Norwegian ship, engaged in Belgian Relief work, under command of Pilot Hays (*sic*). It is alleged that the Norwegian blew wrong signals and in some, so far unaccountable way, veered around and rammed the Mount Blanc a port.[9]

Masses Of Flames Spread

The impact wedged the Norwegian for a few minutes in the great gap in the side of the Mount Blanc, but when she fell away, it was seen that she had been in the Engine Room and that masses of flames from the great Boilers had started.[10]

Great Ship Blew Up

The Norwegian headed at once for [the Dartmouth] shore and beached in a few minutes under her own steam.[11] The Mount Blanc, out of power, proceeded under her headway, and uncontrolled, swung around gradually drifted towards Pier No. 6, and in 17 minutes after the collision, blew up into atoms, with the greatest report and concussion known on this continent.

Loaded With High Explosives

The Mount Blanc had recently sailed from New York for France, laden with a quantity of munitions, and the highest explosives in the holds, and carrying a deck load of benzene.[12] There is no trace of the Mount Blanc. Those who saw the explosion report that the vessel was blown to atoms, and the minute parts of her steel plate picked up at all parts of the city bear this out.

Shock And Concussion Disastrous

The shock and concussion was so great that every pane of glass, plate or otherwise — in all buildings in Halifax and as far distant as Bedford is shattered into fragments. In the North End of the City and in Dartmouth, opposite and adjacent to the Narrows, the destructing death and injury is appalling. The Acadia Sugar Refinery, The Cotton Mills, Hillis Foundry and a couple of Breweries were razed to the ground, set on fire and practically all the employees at their work, killed outright or burned to death. In the Foundry not a single man escaped and the Proprietor himself is missing.[13]

The Acadia Sugar Refinery, The Cotton Mills, The Railway Station at Richmond, cannot be found, and the North Street Station is in a heap of ruins burying death in its fall.[14] Barracks were demolished, one or two churches blown to pieces and about 1500 houses in the sorely afflicted North End levelled to the ground by the shock or burned by fires started from the upsetting and breaking of stoves and lamps. In practically every one of the houses were victims, either in death or injury.

Great Loss Of Life

The great loss of life was caused by the people being killed outright in their homes, stores or factories, or pinioned under falling debris or being caught in the flames and burned to death.

The Casualties

The tabulating of the casualties is in progress. At time of going to Press the indications are that about 1000 men, women and children are dead, and approximately 4000 others more or less seriously injured.[15] The Halifax hospitals are overtaxed and hundreds were forwarded to outside points for hospital care. About 800 were given to Truro, and are being cared for at the Academy, Agriculture College, Court House Building and Military Hospital.

Voluntary Workers

A very large delegation of voluntary workers poured into Halifax chiefly from Truro, Windsor, Amherst and the New Glasgow towns and well for the sufferers it was so.

About 100 men under Fire Chief N.B. Stewart headed by all the town doctors and some eight trained nurses went from Truro. The Truro delegation was the first to arrive. The more fortunate citizens of Halifax, who got off with broken glass only and possibly a small scratch, were generally too taken with their own troubles that the aid of Truro and other towns came in good time. The greatest good sent to the poor North Enders was the detailing of all soldiers and mariners in companies to assist.

Rescuing Dead And Injured

The willing crowds proceeded systematically. Many Truro trains fell in to get the fires in control and at 6 o'clock all were out.[16] All workers went about rescue work, and as the dead were recovered from the debris they were piled in rows on the street sides to be called for by teams. The injured living were conveyed to hospitals on stretchers and in every conceivable way.

Heart Rending Scenes

The scenes were heart rending. Many bodies were crushed and broken into parts and unrecognizable.

Husbands would arrive at their homes to find in cases wife and 8, 9 and 10 children buried in the debris of a razed house. Children came looking for parents and one lad of 17 was pathetic — the sole survivor of a family of father, mother and nine children.

One man went into a drug store with one of his eyes held in one hand and the empty socket covered by the other to enquire stolidly if anything could be done with it.

Among the injured is a woman who while holding her babe had both eyes destroyed by flying glass.

The list so far compiled does not show any Truro people dead, but is understood there are several railway men missing.

Among The Dead And Injured

Supt. J.T. Hallisay of the C.G.R. and daughter, Miss Cumane of Truro had a narrow escape. They were in a private car near North Street Station. Both are badly cut and scratched, but not seriously bruised. The car was smashed, practically nothing but the frame being left on the wheels.

Among the dead are Mrs. Swetnam and little daughter, wife and daughter of Rev. J.W. Swetnam, at one time in charge of Brunswick Street Methodist Church, Truro.

Notes Coincident

The little daughters of Messrs. G.W. Edens, G.H. Vernon and Ira Thompson, were students at Mt. St Vincent, some four miles from Halifax. The parents went to the scene yesterday and brought home the little girls uninjured, though every glass in the large brick building was destroyed.

Capt. Johnson, brother of Dr. D.W. Johnson of Truro, was on the Dartmouth Ferry Boat, crossing the Harbor at the time of the explosion. All the glass of the Ferry was broken and fragments of the blown-up vessel fell all over the Ferry and harbour like hail. Capt. Johnson was uninjured.

Many small craft on the waters were demolished. The Warper B. was among them. Her Captain and Engineers, and one of the crew were saved. Engineer Charles Prest, on going to shore found his home destroyed, one boy killed, his wife in a hospital and a daughter missing.

Every man but one — of both the

Mount Blanc and Belgian Relief ships were saved.[17] The men had fifteen minutes after ordered to the boats to get away. They landed on the Dartmouth side, warning every craft they met and took to the woods.

An Investigation

There will be an investigation. It cannot come too soon. This is no time for sentimental suspensions of certificates. The party or parties responsible for such a needless collision with clear water, in broad day light should be hung in good old fashioned style at the yard's arm.

The Newspaper Offices

The newspaper offices fare the same as other business places, chiefly broken glass and wrecked frames. No papers were issued yesterday afternoon or this morning chiefly being unable to get the city gas plant in order to supply power. The News reporter visited the newspaper and printing offices in Halifax and placed its plant at their disposal if needed.

Business Houses

The business houses and hotels in the more fortunate section are boarding up their windows and all kinds of material are being used to cover up windows and breaches in standing houses. The largest supply obtainable of glass has been ordered from all points. The re-glassing of the remainder of the city will be a long job.

Financial Loss

No authentic estimate of the Financial loss is yet compiled and in the confusion it may be weeks before it can be compiled. A safe estimate is over $50,000,000. One feature of this is that the owner of the property will likely largely have to stand the loss themselves. Insurance is against fire and is the losses of the properties destroyed by fire, because of its origin some companies may hold off.

Truro Men Dead And Missing

Among the large number of Railway men killed is Driver Fred Hamilton, C.G.R Brakeman Wylie Canning of Truro was killed while sleeping in his van. Fireman Alex McIsaac, Prince Street East, is missing.

A special train from St. John passed through Truro last night with doctors and nurses. As some of Truro's doctors are still on the scene of the accident some of the St. John doctors stayed here.

Died In Truro

Since the patients arrived in Truro one man, one colored woman, and three children have died.[18]

George Yates, Former *Toronto Globe* Reporter, Private Secretary to Prime Minister Borden

> I begin to feel that I now know what war must mean.
> — George Yates, *Toronto Telegram*, 10 December 1917

George Yates was born in London, Ontario, on 29 May 1872. His newspaper career included work with the *London Free Press, London Advertiser, London News* and *Toronto Globe*. Upon the formation of the Union government on 17 October 1917, he became Prime Minister Robert Borden's private secretary and remained in this position until Borden resigned on 9 July 1920.[1] After leaving the prime minister's office, Yates continued in government service until 1 December 1942. During this time he served fourteen federal ministers and five deputies and was awarded the MBE on 3 June 1935. Described as a "kind, warm-hearted person, a dapper dresser and an excellent entertainer," Yates died in Ottawa on 16 April 1952.[2]

George Yates 1947. Courtesy Carol Eagles

Prior to the Explosion, Yates had survived one major Canadian disaster and witnessed another. On the night of 3 January 1898 he was covering municipal election results at city hall for the *London Free Press*. During the event the second floor of the building collapsed killing twenty-three, injuring many others and trapping Yates. He was rendered unconscious and awoke in a temporary morgue where he had been carried as dead. In 1911 Yates became secretary to Hon. Frank Cochrane when he became Minister of Railways and Canals in the newly elected Borden government. As Cochrane's secretary, Yates was on the official tug during the opening of the Quebec Bridge on 11 September 1916. All of the newspaper reporters had left when the main span was being raised and suddenly fell into the river, resulting in the deaths of thirteen workers. Upon returning to Ottawa, he wrote an account of the event for the Canadian Press Association.[3]

When the Explosion occurred Yates was with Borden in Prince Edward Island as the prime minister campaigned for the 17 December election. Upon learning of the disaster both abandoned the election campaign and left for Halifax. They arrived by train the next day at 5 p.m. in the midst of a tremendous blizzard.[4] Yates remained in the city with Borden until their departure on 10 December.[5] During his "early tour" of the devastated Richmond area on 8 December, Yates was accompanied by three relief committee representatives from Boston and a Boston journalist.[6]

According to family history, "The frightful picture of the catastrophe made sleep impossible for Mr. Yates that night. He relieved the mental strain by writing a story of the explosion. The next morning he left the account at the telegraph office with instructions to send it to the Canadian Press as soon as the service was restored."[7] Yates's "pen picture" of the aftermath of the Explosion for CP was published on 10 December in several Canadian newspapers, including the *Herald, Toronto Evening Telegram, Toronto Star,*

Montreal Gazette and *Ottawa Journal.*[8] Along with his story the *Toronto Telegram* included a blurb and photograph of Yates.

Whole Community Wiped Out Worse Than Bombarded Town
(*Toronto Evening Telegram*)
Merely A Flattened Heap Of Wreckage – Blizzard Raged For Fifteen Hours
Canadian Press Despatch

George Yates, who has written the following pen picture of the Halifax Disaster, is the private secretary of the Premier of Canada and is a trained newspaper man, having been on The Globe staff when he resigned to become secretary of the provincial Department of Crown Lands. Returning to the stricken city with Sir Robert Borden from Prince Edward Island, the day after the grim event, Mr. Yates had the advantage of an early tour of the ruined district.[9] Mr. Yates was among the casualties of the City Hall collapse in London, Ont. some years ago. He woke up after the event and found himself on slab No. 23 of the temporary morgue.

Halifax, Dec. 10 — The catastrophe is almost too dreadful to admit of description in coherent, matter-of-fact English, and yet too complete for adequate portrayal by means of the indiscriminating camera. To properly appreciate it one must be able to conjure up a picture of what once was in contrast with what no longer is. I have visited Halifax on many occasions, have seen the North street station area, Richmond and Willow park (*sic*) in normal times and when swollen with the normal flux of war. I have seen the panoramic beauty of the Dartmouth shore at all seasons, and always in restful contrast to the somewhat sombre, decidedly crowded and for the most part frame-constructed district that sloped back from the tracks up the hill on which this historic old city stands. It was the home district of the working classes with here and there an isolated, though stately, relic of other times.

Wiped Out

It was this hard-working, wage-earning community that Thursday morning's tragedy wiped out. Wiped out is exactly the proper phrase. In the hard-shelled towns of Flanders some walls do stand after the intense bombardments. Here a single devastating blast passed up the hill, and, in the twinkling of an eye, crushed the breath of life out of two thousand people and rendered twenty thousand homeless and destitute. This morning I walked over what had been a dwelling, among the debris of which an old man worked alone.

Flattened Heap

It was merely a flattened heap of wreckage, offering no obstruction to the eye and very little to the feel. What once had been a backyard looked out over the exact scene of the explosion. In the cutting below were the railway tracks, in the foreground the narrows, leading from the harbor proper to the seclusion of Bedford Basin, and, probably half a mile across the Dartmouth shore. In the railway yards scores of men labored to re-establish communications where the tracks had been washed out by the tidal wave that followed the explosion. And which left dead fish and other evidences of marine life embedded in the wreckage at the base of the cliff on which I stood.

The blizzard, which had raged for fifteen hours, had doubled the task of tired and disheartened men. Imagine, ye with intact rooms and snug double windows, the influence of a terrific gale of wet, clinging snow, sweeping over a city with scarcely a pane of glass intact, and carrying its chill contact in a falling temperature over thousands of beds of pain. But towards morning the gale subsided into a steady, though bitter, northeast breeze, and now the sun lit up a melancholy scene.

On The Water Front

On the shore, less than 200 yards away lay the war grey prow of a steamer — all that was left of the Mont Blanc, so I was informed.[10] To the right, over on the Dartmouth shore, hard aground, but seemingly not in bad shape, lay the Imo, the Norwegian Belgian relief ship, which collided with the French boat with its dreadful cargo. To the left a few sunken piles, and one distorted steamer, slammed bodily against a pile of wreckage, which had once been a dock, was all that was left of piers 6, 7, 8 and 9. To those piers had come the fire chief and his deputy and men when the alarm of fire was turned on, and to the same spot hurried reporter Ronayne of the Chronicle, who had gossiped cheerily with me at my room in the Queen's Hotel when the Prime Minister opened his campaign in Halifax the other week.[11]

Many Soldier Victims

Soldiers had hurried to the scene — how many I do not know, but I have talked with one man who told me he and others had found at one point a score of bodies of men, who though stripped of clothing and, in some instances, even of flesh were quite evidently military men, because of the scraps of khaki rags in their immediate vicinity. It was indeed, a rendezvous with death, and death overtook even the man who turned in the alarm.

But death was no respecter of persons in the neighbourhood of the explosion. A few blackened timbers along the track to the left represent the Richmond station where every employe (sic) was killed. The despatcher [Vince Coleman] phoned to a confrere up the line, "Ammunition ship is on fire in the harbour, and there is likely to be an explosion, but I am going to beat it." Just then the explosion occurred, and they found his body in the basement.

Trainmen Suffer

Of the yardmen not ten per cent remain; of seventy spare trainmen not two had reported for duty this morning. That mass of wrecked and twisted rolling stock in the Richmond yard represents some four hundred freight cars, and seventy or eighty passenger coaches have been temporarily placed out of commission.

All that and more was what the eye caught as it swept in semi-circle along the water front and railway tracks. But what lay behind and up from the hill? It is not necessary to move from the spot and supply details enough to convey an adequate idea of the scene as a whole. Less than a hundred yards away volunteers are searching the ruins of a house for bodies. With sledge-hammers, pickaxes, crowbars and levers of all kinds they tug at the twisted wreckage which they hurriedly throw aside.

Premier Visits Scene

A passing sleigh pauses and a man joins the little group of onlookers. It is the

Prime Minister Borden's 7 December 1917 Press Release

I am appalled by the terrible disaster which has overtaken the City, with which I have been associated in the strongest ties for more than half my life time. This morning [December 7] I cancelled my meetings which had been arranged and came to Halifax by special train for the purpose of conferring with the Civic Authorities and Citizens' Executive Committee, as well as my colleague, Hon. A. K. MacLean. The Federal Government is placing at the disposal of the Executive Committee all facilities and resources for the purpose of rendering such comfort to the sufferers as may be possible.

Prime Minister's Statement 8 December 1917 in the *Daily Echo*

The people of Canada are profoundly grateful for the generous sympathy of the people of the United States in the terrible disaster which has overtaken the City of Halifax, and they most deeply appreciate the splendid aid which has been offered and sent from so many communities of our great kindred nation.

Prime Minister of Canada gathering at first hand the intimate details of the appalling disaster of the city of his youth and early manhood.[12] Along the road comes another sleigh — an open cutter. The driver walks behind, and with him walk two downcast men. There are passengers in the sleigh, but they mercifully covered, though not sufficiently to hide the ghastly contortions of their twisted frames. Across the street is a heavy wagon turned upside down. In the shafts lie the remains of two horses, one completely cut in two, with what seems to be a plate from the ill-fated vessel. This team had reached the street from a roadway leading back about fifty yards to what had been a foundry.

Tomb Of Forty Men

There a jumble of bricks and a brightly burning pile of coal marks the tomb of forty men, who met death at the bench and lathe. None escaped. On the roadside the remains of two motor cars torn absolutely to splinters. The old man referred to is working aimlessly over the wreckage of what had been his home. He threw to one side an artificial limb. "That," he said, seeming to think that the incident required explanation, "belonged to the lodger downstairs. He won't need it any more. He was a railway man, and he lost his leg, and they put him on a crossing. He's gone. When my old woman heard that the boat might blow up she went up to the daughter's place on the hill there. You can see the place, still smoking, from here."

Six Burned To Death

"Did she escape injury?" I asked, as it seemed to me the old man had left the story unfinished. "Oh no," he answered simply, "She and the daughter and four were burned up. It's funny I should find that cork leg undamaged, don't you think?"

Two men approached. One had the usual bandages around neck and face that mark the hundreds of walking victims of flying glass, the other with hollow, lack-lustre eyes, and blackened hands and face, carried a sack on his shoulders. It was of sinister shape and blood-stained, possibly all that was left of his family.

Remains Of His Family

I was prepared for that by the story a railroad friend told me earlier to-day, about a man carrying a small box on his shoulder who was enquiring for a train. He seemed dazed and someone asked him what he had in the box. "That", he replied, "is all that is left of my wife and two children. I am taking them to Windsor to bury them."

On the other side of the street, a short distance from the dead horses, was what seemed to be a bundle of bedding. On the top, as a protection from the snow, was spread some frayed kitchen linoleum.

To prevent the wind from blowing this away was a piece of scaffolding. Instinct warned me not to seek the obvious explanation, but a compelling curiosity caused me to raise a corner of the linoleum. I was relieved to see nothing but some bedding, and turned to look at a camera man for a Boston paper, who was making a series of photographs in the vicinity.[13] At this I heard a cry of horror from my companion. He had pierced the veil and raised the blanket. I caught one quick glimpse of the bed's dead occupant, for which I shall always be sorry, as now my memory is indelibly seared by an impression I would gladly forget.

It was enough but not all. As we drove back past the diggers in the ruins by the foundry a man came forward and asked my companion if he was going down town, and if so, would he call at the undertaker's and have them send out a sleigh. "We have found two more," he said, pointing to two wrapped bundles, one pitifully small.

Coal Piles Burning

To-night they brought the car around from the new ocean terminals to North street. All the way in through the devastated area piles of burning coal, of which there is now an acute scarcity and still smouldering wreckage threw a ghastly light over a scene of wreckage more complete than star-shelled lighted No Man's Land. I write this on a siding alongside of the North street station, familiar to thousands on both sides of the Atlantic. The platform is sprinkled with splintered glass, and the building is roofless, windowless and doorless, while the interior is filled with confused masses of wreckage and drifted snow.

I begin to feel that I now know what war must mean. Close at hand is all of war's dreadful embellishment, but the sentry on the platform alongside spoils the illusion by singing, none too quietly, about his girl "In little ole New York" and the car porter has risen from his first sound sleep to put his head out of the kitchen window and ask him, more in sorrow than in anger, the whereabouts of the sergeant of the guard.[14]

Stanley Smith, *St. John Daily Telegraph*

> In the newspaper man's way, as I heard the mournful stories entering Halifax, and by hearsay at the hotels and offices visited the first evening, I weighed them carefully in my mind and some I believed and some I did not. But the second day convinced me that they were all true — as true as they were horrible.
> — Stanley Smith, *St. John Daily Telegraph* city editor, 10 December 1917

Stanley Smith began his newspaper career in 1908 as a reporter for the *St. John Daily Telegraph* and two years later joined the *St. John Standard*. In 1911 he returned to the *Telegraph*, where he worked until 1918 as a reporter and news editor. After leaving the *Telegraph* he first edited *The Business Review* (1919–22) and then *Maple Leaf* (1922–25).[1]

Following the Explosion, thirty-five-year-old Smith rushed to Halifax to cover the story for the *Daily Telegraph* as well as be "special correspondent" for the *Toronto Star* and *Montreal Gazette*. He left Saint John after 1:30 a.m. on 7 December 1917 and arrived in Halifax at 6 p.m. Smith remained in the city for two days and returned to Saint John during the evening of 9 December.[2] The *Daily Telegraph* ran his "personal experience" story on 12 December; the *Toronto Star* and the *Gazette* published it on 15 December.

Based on his experience covering the disaster's aftermath, in early 1918 Smith authored a 120-page book titled *Heart Throbs of the Halifax Horror*.[3] Published in Halifax by Smith's publisher/friend Gerald Weir, *Heart Throbs* is subtitled *60 Illustrations from Actual Photographs, Map of City Showing Devastated Area and List of Dead*. Chapter 7, "Covering the Story," is a reprint [with slight changes] of his 10 December 1917 *Toronto Star* story, and Chapter 8, "Pen Pictures," is a reprint of George Yates's 8 December 1917 CP despatch. *Heart Throbs* includes a picture

Stanley Smith, 1918, from Heart Throbs of the Halifax Horror *by Stanley Smith*

of Smith on page 7, advertisements for *Post Cards of the Ruins* from Cox Brothers in Halifax, the second edition of *Devastated Halifax,* published by Weir, and the publisher's public invitation for stories on the disaster.

How Newspaperman Got To Halifax And "Covered" Story Of The Disaster (*Toronto Daily Star*)

St. John Man Arrived Back Home Before His First Despatch Came Through — Fought Down Temptation To Quit Scene On Arrival — Found And Slept In Smashed Up Room — The Psychology Of It All

The personal experience of Stanley K. Smith city editor of The Daily Telegraph, St. John, N. B., and special correspondent of The Toronto Star, in the Great Disaster[4]

St. John. Dec. 10 — Tragic experiences, like honors, are often thrust upon us. When it fell to my lot to take the journey to the stricken city of Halifax I little thought what was in store for me. No sooner was I on board the night train than I discovered that the angels of mercy were already spreading their protecting wings over the homeless, the starving, the wounded and the dying.

By a fortunate coincidence H.A. Milburne, representing the Canadian Red Cross and Foster Rockwell and J.S. Fellsworth of the Military Relief Section, American Red Cross, were all in St. John at the time of the explosion. They were immediately notified by their respective organizations to proceed to Halifax and report the situation there.

The train was due to leave at 1:30 o'clock a.m. There was little delay in starting. A hastily organized St. John Committee had filled three cars with provisions and clothing. Some wholesale places had been practically cleaned out. A large north end pork packing plant gave every ham in the place.

The Conductor's Story

Quite soon I noticed the sleeping conductor, W. D. Ross, a manly little chap, was unusually pale and quiet. It did not take long to find out the cause. His wife and two children were in the ruined, fire-devastated region and he had no word from them. With considerably more men in the car than there were berths his was the task that required tact and forbearance. He went through it all bravely, and I cannot resist the temptation to leap ahead in my story to a little scene at Shubenacadie Station, some forty miles from Halifax. Mr. Ross had just alighted from his car when a woman's form catapulted itself into his arms. The world which to him but a moment before had seemed such a dark and forbidding place suddenly assumed a rosier hue, and when his wife — for it was she — sobbed into his ear that the two little children were also safe though the home was gone the sun broke through the clouds altogether and brought warmth and comfort once more to the anxious heart. The baby, she said, was seated on the floor in the kitchen and showers of glass, the ruins of the room, pieces of stove itself fell all about it but miraculously it was unhurt. Her brother had heard the explosion from Shubenacadie and had made a quick run to Halifax in his car to find his sister and family.

It was evident from the first that the train would be late. The heavy cars of supplies and provisions which made imperative an early arrival were the very things which mitigated against fast time. We were two hours late in coming into Truro and the blizzard which added untold horror to the suffering of the homeless in Halifax was then gathering in force. The confusion attending the disaster had extended to the town sixty miles away. Even here one met victims of the disaster. Several had slight cuts and all had that strange, dazed expression which I was to see on so many faces before the day was out. Breakfast here proved to be luncheon. As the storm grew in violence the long heavy train, which some thought should have been divided, kept losing time, and it looked for a time as if we would be stalled absolutely. At a little station along here I made my first effort at filing copy. A rotund agent held the key and he welcomed me cordially, but I am sorry to say his smile was a delusion and a snare. After two days in Halifax I arrived home about the same time this despatch came through from Stewacke (*sic*).[5]

First Signs Of Damage

In the early twilight, hastened by the swirling snow driven before a forty-mile gale, we ran along the shore of Bedford Basin. Ten miles from Halifax the windows were blown from the summer houses. Lying low in the water, close inshore some of them, we saw ship after ship in this natural anchorage all safely beyond the range of the explosion. By this time we began to meet people who had been through the hell of Thursday. One man with a strained face sat dumb and stricken as a friend who came out to meet him told him as gently as possible of the death of his entire family. His wife, five children and aged mother were all gone, the mother struck in the breast and mortally wounded by a flying piece of metal from the cooking stove over which she was bending to prepare the children's breakfast.

In all the time spent at Halifax, I saw nothing which brought home the tragedy more than my first sight of the refugees at Rockingham station, three miles out. These people had fled on foot from the Richmond section, had spent the night on the open and were now packed into a little station and overflowing out on the platform where the driving wind cut like a knife and the soft snow clung to their apparel in sticky dabs. Hopelessness was in their faces and their sufferings were intense. They were waiting for trains to carry them to points in the country where they had friends.

It was here I first noticed that strained, staring look which was on every face as I went about the ruined streets the following day. If I saw a normal, healthy face I was pretty sure to find out that the owner had not been in Halifax on the fateful Thursday, but had come in afterwards to render assistance or learn the fate of friends.

It seemed a gentle irony that those on a relief train bearing carloads of provisions should themselves be on the edge of hunger. A long delay at this little station aggravated the situation. A few fortunate ones had brought along supplies and these people were most popular. Some loaves of brown bread and white bread were produced by provident nurses, but it went very much against the epicurean tastes of certain doctors to lunch from the heel of a loaf without cheese or butter. I satisfied myself with one third of an apple.

Huge Crater As In Flanders

At last we were told we were to be honoured by being attached to a special train carrying to the scene Sir Robert L.

Borden, Premier of Canada, but I was unable to find out whether or not we actually trailed him in. At any rate we made the record of having been the first passengers carried to the south terminals by the new route skirting the western side of the city. Fallen houses could be seen lying by the track. The face of the embankment along the water's edge was gone and one mighty gash had all the appearance of a shell crater in Flanders with the effect heightened by the huge pile of earth and stones which had been heaped up several yards ahead, the lip of the crater itself extending to the harbour front. One railway close to the edge was badly damaged and before we left the waterfront vanished altogether, the protruding rails left dangling over nothingness.

It was now pitch dark and the blizzard had reached its height. At six o'clock — ten hours later — the train came to a halt, we were told, for the last time. There is no station here, the explosion anticipated the use of the new terminal from a passenger standpoint by a least one year. As I waited at one end of the sleeper for the porter to unlock the vestibule doors most of the St. John men made their exit from the other end.

When I stepped from the train I was caught by one terrific gust and turned completely around. No one seemed to know just where to go. Many had not been in Halifax before. As there was (sic) no street lights there was no guidance. For one awful moment I was completely alone. Then there was a decision to be made. We were told that the train from which we had alighted would return immediately to Truro. It seemed almost incredible that the wires from Halifax would be able to carry the load imposed upon them by the additional weight of the storm. In this case it would mean a

fruitless night so far as getting any story through to my papers was concerned. At Truro the chances for filing would be infinitely better and in ordinary circumstances the run to Truro would be made in two hours. Already I had seen and heard enough to fill a book, if necessary.

Overcame Temptation To Return

Turning I took two steps towards the warm comfortable train with the light showing like a beacon through the storm. Then came the thought of the seven hours spent on the train between Truro and Halifax and a rapid calculation told me it would be well on towards morning before the over-worked engine and crew could reach Truro again. I set my teeth and faced the blizzard again. Where the turn was made from the track into the main street northward stood a woman — outpost in the cause of humanity come to meet the nurses and direct them where to go. A few vehicles were standing there but they were rapidly filled by the official parties. I began the long walk of nearly two miles and believe I made it in record time. An occasional pedestrian with a lantern lighted the way but for the most part it was total darkness, going only by the sense of direction. The lighted refugee stations shone forth hospitably and it was a temptation to enter and at once begin the work of interviewing refugees, but there was always ahead the more important task of securing a general idea of the disaster for transmission on the wires that night.

At a little store where appatizing (sic) food was being served to the homeless I secured half a dozen chocolate nut bars, munching these as I went along I soon felt greatly refreshed and when I finally found the one remaining door of the Queen Hotel — the others being boarded up — I was not more than ordinarily hungry.[6] One of the wonders of the disaster is the fact that the Queen and its neighbour the Halifax [Hotel], kept their cuisine unimpaired with far fewer restrictions than the Food Controller had ordered. Soup, salmon, asparagus on toast, roast chicken, pork, plum pudding, and bread and cheese, made me feel happier.

Finding A Room

The hotels were not so well provided with sleeping accommodation as with food. The official relief party had rooms engaged, but the mere newspaper men had to shift for themselves.[7] I had visions of sleeping close up to the furnace in the Chronicle newspaper office with my snow-wet clothing slowly drying on me. Then an angel appeared, little R.A. Hirsch, special representative of the Imperial Munitions Board, had been on the train on an important mission and he had, while I dined, been searching for rooms. By chance he found two over a cheap café not far from the Queen's. The windows were blown from both but the proprietor had offered to allow us to "fix them up." Hirsch had taken both not wishing to have a possible spy in the next room and now he offered to share his with me, closing mine altogether. Much to my surprise upon entering the café, I saw a stooped figure and narrow face of one Schools, late proprietor of an all-night restaurant in St. John, where often I had breakfasted when a late edition went to press. He welcomed me as a former fellow-citizen and as a potential customer. I found I was greatly favoured in my room as a once haughty grand piano was one of the pieces of furniture nearly filling it. Folding doors opened between the two little rooms

and after moving all the mats from the floor and the bed clothes from the bed we closed these securely.

The next task was to take the hammer and nails which Schools provided and nail mats across the windows through which the snow was driving in. We made a good job of this and at a register in the floor gave forth a little heat. Arrangements made for the night, the next task was a visit to the newspaper offices and supplication to the wire wizards [telegraph operators]. The Western Union did not waste any time. They had not wires and did not expect to have any. No hope there.

Write Short, Snappy Bulletins

When I called at the Chronicle office men were at work boarding up the broken glass transom,[8] and water was pouring down in the lobby as if tons of water had been poured into the building to quench a huge fire. The composing room seemed a wreck, but work was going on, and I was told one linotype was working.[9] One lone newspaper man had also found his way there, and he informed me that chances for getting stuff through were pretty slim.[10] After a visit to the C.P.R. telegraph office in the Dennis building and an interview with A.C. Fraser, maritime superintendent, I had more hope.[11] There was but one wire just at that moment, he said, and that was loaded with the official messages regarding relief. No one wished to sidetrack these if they could but Mr. Fraser intimated that there would be a partial recovery during the night.

"Write some short, snappy bulletins," he said, "and they will go through."[12]

Later on his prediction proved true. At midnight, he said, there were four wires, and he loaned one to the C.G.R. for the operation of important trains. By that time I had secured something of a connected line and in fifteen minutes a despatch of 1,500 words — the first to come through apart from the routine Canadian Press service — was in the hands of the operators.[13]

In A Creepy Place

Just as a precautionary measure, I made an effort to get some outlying pieces by telephone and secure the filing of some bulletins at different points, the through telephone service to St. John having been interrupted for the last week as a result of a previous storm.

I entered the telephone company's building and found it like a huge clammy tomb. Groping my way forward, I found one telephone booth at the foot of a stairway. I figured the operating room must be on the top floor and tried to find my way up, but after two flights in the darkness — the only sounds my own footsteps and the rustle of the wind as it penetrated the windows and altered the papers in the deserted office — it got on my nerves a bit, and I gave it up. A short talk from the booth with the chief operator convinced me it would be hopeless to try to get any long-distance message through that night. I will remember that half-hour in the telephone building — the shadows were disconcerting as one thought of stories of ghouls who lurk on the outskirts of tragedy and feed upon the victims of disaster.

Going back to the café I was ready for my third meal in Halifax since arrival, and at 1 a.m. came the time for retiring.

Soldier Warmed The Bed

We found the door of our room locked, and when we knocked a soldier came out partially undressed. He had been warming our bed. An assistant, not knowing of the previous arrangement, had later rented him the room, which we had made comfortable. Here was a problem. One small single bed and two big men and a little man. As the French say, "One can refuse a soldier nothing," and this man had served his country and was going back the following day. We had my room to draw on, but here the snow was sifting softly through on the silent keys of the piano and there was no register — in the floor, I mean, not the piano. An effort to put the two beds in the one room proved a failure, as contrary to the simple rule of physics that two bodies cannot occupy the same space at the same time. What we did was to take the mattress, lay it on the floor, and then divide the bed clothes and overcoats. The soldier chose the mattress; it was an old story with him, and with the assistance of two quinine pills I was rather too warm than otherwise. Deep, refreshing sleep until 9:30 a.m. wiped out the rigors of the day which had gone before and prepared me for a day in which I walked steadily until 6:30 p.m., with but a few minutes intermission. The sun was shining once more, but the snow lay deep in the streets and no street cars were moving. It was impossible to secure a conveyance of any sort. If bribe or persuasion had secured one from the owner it was likely to be taken at the first corner by a member of the Relief Committee to transport a homeless family to some place which had been provided. What I saw on that strenuous Saturday I have written in a previous despatch published on Monday.[14]

How A Newspaperman Feels

Through it all I felt curiously detached and not greatly moved by those distressing scenes in morgue, in hospital, in the ruins and at the inquiry stations. I was there for a single purpose and that was to give to such as the outside world as might read my words a living picture of what had actually occurred. Until this was accomplished my own feelings were secondary. I could see and write of them unmoved but let me try to tell, new, to a circle of friends the stories so glibly written and I find that I must stop short. So much for the psychology of it.

In the newspaper man's way, as I heard the mournful stories entering Halifax, and by hearsay at the hotels and offices visited the first evening, I weighed them carefully in my mind and some I believed and some I did not. But the second day convinced me that they were all true — as true as they were horrible. Incidents related without names were confirmed later by my own observation and sometimes I found and talked with some of the people involved.

Just before I left Halifax a curious thing happened. In the days before prohibition a visitor came to my office in St. John and by soft speech and fair promises inveigled me into a loan which would take him to his home in Halifax. It was too much to expect that I should see the money again, and I didn't. In the rotunda of the Halifax [Hotel] that evening the same man accosted me. He did not recognize me and will never know if I recognized him unless he reads this. I found he had, since his St. John visit, entered my own profession and was looking for information, giving at the same time the news that his own home had been badly shattered and that he had escaped death only because he was a little late starting for the scene of the explosion when the fire broke out on the steamer. His competitor on the rival paper had been ahead in the sprint and died doing his duty.[15] The other man is welcome to the money.

"What You-All Want Here?"

I have also written of that train filled with refugees on which I made my journey home. I stayed in the cars with them for an hour, then I wanted to get away — far away. I dropped off the train into the snow and forward to the car next to the engine. The vestibules were closed and a blind baggage separated the car from the rest of the train.[16] As I climbed precariously up the window of the blind baggage and entered the car. I was greeted by a chorus of negro voices in the soft southern accent. "What you-all want here?" "Are you a railway man?"

I was forced to confess I was not a railway man and could not provide the magic which would stop the train and carry these boys back to New York — for they were porters who had come down with the relief train and this was a dining car in which the doctors and nurses had eaten. At the other end of the car the Boston and Maine official in charge informed me that I couldn't ride there, but I proved he was wrong by staying right there in the warm, lighted car with my head down on one of the tables until the train reached Truro at 4 a.m. Sunday and I was able to get a berth on one of the two sleepers added to the train there, making the tired morning newspaper man's nap by remaining snugly in the berth until 11 a.m.

Twenty-four hours the journey to St. John occupied and several times we passed splendid steel cars of the American relief trains rushing forward on their errand of mercy. A memorable journey this with memorable sights —— one that I shall never forget.

Eight pounds the scales say I lost in three days, but this is a paltry thing compared to the plight of those people over there.[17]

Thomas O'Leary, *St. John Globe*

I spent the night in a home with practically every window blown out; the curtains in two windows a fringe of silk and lace and in the other untorn. Every bit of furniture is scarred with flying glass, and in the wall is embedded a bit of glass, so deeply has it penetrated that it cannot be pulled out.
— Thomas O'Leary, *St. John Globe* staff reporter, 11 December 1917

The son of a ship's captain, Thomas O'Leary was born in Hoy Lake, England, in 1884 and moved to Saint John, New Brunswick, with his parents in 1887. He graduated from St. Joseph's University with a B.A. in 1903 and later attended the University of New Brunswick in Fredericton, where he pursued electrical engineering studies. O'Leary also studied law and in 1916 obtained a Bachelor of Civil Law degree from King's College Law School, forerunner of the present University of New Brunswick Law School in Fredericton.

O'Leary began his newspaper career in 1911 as sports editor of the *St. John Daily Telegraph*. In 1913 he joined the *St. John Globe* and for seven years was the official City Hall and later New Brunswick Legislature reporter. Beginning in 1921 he was the paper's barrister but in 1927 left for private legal practice. In 1942 he was appointed Registrar of Probate for the Judicial District of Saint John. For several years he was also secretary of the New Brunswick Liberal Association and from 1929 to 1943 editor of the *Fundy Fisherman*. O'Leary died in Saint John on 24 July 1943.[1] Upon his death, Saint John Probate Judge H.O. McInerney wrote, "Besides being a lawyer he was a newspaperman of rare capacity." New Brunswick Premier J.B. McNair commented, "During the years that he served the Legislature as official reporter he won the esteem and regard of all members for his fairness and conscientiousness in the discharge of his duties."[2]

St. John Globe publisher/editor Frank Ellis sent thirty-three-year-old O'Leary to cover the Explosion story.[3] He arrived in Halifax on 8 December and left on 10 December. On 9

Thomas E. O'Leary, 1904. Courtesy Archives & Special Collections, UNB

December O'Leary wrote two despatches for the paper. The first appeared in the *Globe* on 10 December and the second on 11 December.

Horrors Of The Situation

Conditions In Halifax Have Not Been Exaggerated
(From Globe staff reporter)

Halifax, Dec. 9 – Wreck and ruin and desolation on every hand is the scene in the area formerly known as the North End of this city. Beyond the most vivid flight of imagination has destruction been wrought, and the death, injury and suffering which have resulted from the period of explosion, fire and storm surpasses the most exaggerated pictures of a hideous dream.

This (Sunday) afternoon, at a time when the residents of Halifax normally enjoy Sunday peace, organized crews of volunteer workmen dig and pick in the North End ruins for the remains of former fellow citizens.

God! What a mess!! Oh! The pity of it all. A few scraps of homes are found at times — found in the ashes of the homesteads, and they are carefully and tenderly collected and placed in blankets, while a funeral pyre ascends from the embers of what was a happy home.

This afternoon, for instance, in a section of a block the bones of a man, woman and child were found together in one place, and in another place nearby a child was picked up.

"Here's another," is the murmur among the workers from hour to hour as bodies are brought forth.

The scenes are beyond description especially at the hospitals and other shelters.

The people are dazed. They have almost ceased to exercise sensation of pain. Yet, their fortitude is marvellous. There are no complaints.

Passing from street to street, the tragedy is brought home most sharply in the number of funerals which are taking place, and one learns that these must occur sharply on time — "there are so many you know," the undertaker explains.

Truck loads of coffins are hurried here and there.

There is a reign of death in the city and death rules here with a heavy hand.

Halifax is suffering a period of agony unprecedented in the history of America, and as the days pass, the limit of the great trial appears not at hand.

Thursday there was the stupendous explosion and a conflagration, in the concussion every home in Halifax and Dartmouth was damaged, and in the conflagration, an area two miles square was reduced to ashes.

Friday brought a blizzard and the work of rescue was interrupted and the people who needed warmth and comfort were exposed to one of the worst snowstorms ever experienced in the Nova Scotia capital.

Saturday the work of rescue went on. Think of it — men were found alive Saturday in the ruins of buildings which had fallen Thursday morning. Not only men, but little children and some were only scantily clad. In one instance a baby almost naked was located under a dog which had protected and warmed its playmate for two days. Only after considerable coaxing did the dog permit the workers to take the child. Hundreds of heart-rending stories are told.

Saturday at midnight, the general alarm of fire again sounded in the stricken city. People rushed in windows and doors and inquired what was wrong. Towards the North bells were ringing.

"God!" They said. "What is this?"

In that awful North, a reflection of fire glowed.

Then to add to the horror of it all lightning broke sharply and lighted brightly the snow-clad streets. It was bitter cold.

"What is the world coming to?" the people asked.

The rumble of thunder was heard in the distance and soon the city of Death was swept by a violent rain storm.

With the fury of a cloud-burst the rain patted upon the houses and as many houses were only hastily repaired after the wrecking of Thursday, water poured in and did further damage.

The wind howled fiercely and many window and roof coverings were torn away and hurled into the street. The storm continued until nearly noon on Sunday, and the streets were almost impassable in a sea of slush and running water. People wondered if there were any unfortunate human beings still alive in the wreckage. They shuddered to think of injured persons exposed to the elements and unable to escape or to summon assistance.

Dr. John Allingham of Fairville, who worked at the Camp Hill Hospital on Saturday, said on Saturday night that at least 300 more nurses were urgently required.

This afternoon hundreds of people were seen, some with bandages on their heads and others with their arms in slings.

Dr. Allingham stated that a large proportion of patients in the hospital had suffered about the eyes. Many had lost one eye and some were entirely sightless.

This is sadly understood from the description of the explanation.

"There was a tremendous crashing and clinking of breaking glass," he said. "It seemed as though thousands of shards — yes, millions — were being virtually agitated. Flying glass was everywhere. Splinters from windows and mirrors and lamps showered about, driven by terrific force. Walls were pierced.

The Globe may safely say that there is not a single person in St. John who can imagine the loss that has been wrought in Halifax to citizens and to property.

Thousands are dead. Thousands are injured, thousands are homeless, thousands are in poverty.

This is a city of death and destruction.[4]

Sunday In Stricken Halifax
People Brave And Courageous Beyond Words Awful Scenes Witnessed
Work At Hospitals And Relief Work Now Well Established
Magnitude Of The Disaster
(Correspondent of the Globe)

Halifax, N.S. Dec. 9 — Halifax blown to pieces, swept by fire, buried under a snow storm of unusual severity and deluged this morning by a driving rain, is a Halifax brave and courageous beyond words. Every other man and woman on the streets wears not one but several bandages; Red Cross cars and the always pathetic long box covered to-day from the rain with whatever was procurable at the moment are with the teams piled high with boxes marked Relief, the most notable feature of the traffic.

It is Sunday and in but one or two

churches are there congregations — many of the buildings having no glass and being in other respects too damaged to permit of the usual services. All stores are open, and those business houses dealing with transportation and supplies are working as they never worked before. About 4 sq. miles of Halifax are in a condition, said a returned soldier that resembles more than anything else a town in Flanders. The destruction of life is appalling and the total of two thousand is felt to be a conservative estimate.

The scenes at the hospitals, all of which are crowded beyond capacity, are heart rending. The children are terribly injured, torn and mangled; they are too many refugees whose parents are only appearing to-day, some of the fathers and mothers are lying in other hospitals, some are dead, and some are still looking for the children who are being tenderly cared for by nurses and volunteer workers. Many little children and babies that escaped death were not dressed and suffered awful wounds. The flying glass has injured the eyes of hundreds who otherwise are unhurt.

Halifax presents the appearance of a town devastated by a cyclone. Practically, as has been stated, every window in the city has been blown out but this has to be seen to be realized. I stood to-day and watched a man shovel out load after load of window glass mixed with the contents of the show cases, beautiful cut glass dishes — the whole representing hundreds of dollars — and all valueless. In a row of stores, all of which were badly damaged, stood one without a break or crack in any of its windows. Why no one knows. Not far from the City Hall, which has suffered severely, stands uninjured a big bill board with the poster "Slip Across Lad and Help Us, We Need You," dominating that part of the street.

I spent the night in a home with practically every window blown out; the curtains in two windows a fringe of silk and lace and in the other untorn. Every bit of furniture is scarred with flying glass, and in the wall is embedded a bit of glass, so deeply has it penetrated that it cannot be pulled out. On one instance, a woman struck by just such a bit was almost decapitated. And in that house where happily no one was hurt the mother of the children in her thankfulness was making night gowns for the babies of the hospitals.

Only to-day has relief work assumed definite organization. This does not mean that the work of relief has not been effectively administered. Far from it. An hour after the disaster, and while many were anxiously waiting to know what had happened, relief work began. The City Hall, which is the centre of information, has under its roof medical, food and clothing bureaus. To-day 3,500 persons were served bread and cooked food; yesterday food was supplied to 9,000 persons from the food depot at the City Hall and at the armory and St. Joseph's there are also depots doing similar work. The clothing depot under the care of the Woman's Council, recalls the days of the fire from which St. John suffered.[5] And at the Canadian Red Cross depot the demands for surgical supplies are unprecedented. Imagine what it means to have three thousand wounded men, women and children all at once needing immediate assistance! Some critically ill, some seriously wounded, and others suffering from hysteria. It has been found necessary to establish a maternity hospital and to provide for many new babies. The assistance has come from all over

Canada, from the United States, whose flag flies over a Red Cross station, and from the people of Halifax, who worn and tattered are standing at their posts like heroes.

Yesterday two hundred and fifty bodies were picked up in the harbour, and every moment some fresh tale of suffering is added to the terrible story. The belief grows that it was not accidental, this disaster, and so no man feels safe. "We died a thousand terrible deaths," said one woman, "and with but one thought in our minds — the Germans." The nervous shock and the terror was as hard to bear as have been the wounds, and to-day the city is only recovering.

Many St. John men are met with and rumors that a St. John hospital was to be established heard, but no definite information could be obtained. The St. John relief has been unpacked and distributed and everyone is doing a great part. The magnitude and awfulness of the disaster has not been exaggerated but Halifax is meeting it with a thankfulness that it was not greater and a determination to do the utmost for the stricken men and women.

I never saw such a kindly, friendly feeling and much tender sympathy one for another. In a day of strenuous endeavour and heart breaking conditions I have never heard an impatient word. To appreciate this one wants to work with man and women who are covered with bruises, whose hearts are heavy and who have not had a moment's rest and who go all day without a thought of a break so that the homeless and (sic) in the hospitals may be fed.[6]

Grattan O'Leary, *Ottawa Journal*

> Freedom of the press is limited to the right to print truth; the truth is its own justification.
>   — Grattan O'Leary *Recollections of People, Press, and Politics*

Grattan O'Leary was born in Percé, Quebec, on 27 February 1888. After working two years for the *St. John Standard* he joined the *Ottawa Journal* in 1911 and soon became the paper's Parliamentary correspondent. Fellow reporter Frederick Griffin described him as "quick, clever, [and] smart."[1] If O'Leary had one shortcoming as a journalist it was his typing skills. According to *Citizen* editor I. Norman Smith, O'Leary used the "two-fingered hunt-and-peck system…and beat the hell out of it [typewriter] at a terrific clip."[2]

The Halifax Explosion was not O'Leary's first disaster assignment for he had covered the 1912 *Titanic* story.[3] O'Leary remained with the *Journal* for over fifty years, becoming associate editor in 1932, vice-president in 1949, president in 1957 and editor emeritus in 1962, the same year he was appointed to the Canadian Senate by Prime Minister John Diefenbaker. In 1967 O'Leary was inducted into the Canadian News Hall of Fame and in 1968 awarded an Honorary Life Membership to the Canadian Parliamentary Press Gallery. He died in Ottawa on 7 April 1976.

Prior to his newspaper career, O'Leary had spent several years at sea. In December 1908 he was part of the crew on board the *Lady Eileen* en route to Philadelphia from Saint John, New Brunswick, with a cargo of pulp. The vessel encountered heavy seas and was tossed onto its side. The captain gave the crew the choice of remaining on board or taking to the lifeboats. O'Leary chose to remain on board. *Lady Eileen* miraculously righted itself and was able to complete the voyage to Philadelphia where it went into dry dock for repairs.[4] O'Leary also escaped the burning Parliament Buildings during the fire of 16 February 1915. When the fire started he was attending a dinner given by Minister of Militia Sir Sam Hughes at the Chateau Laurier Hotel. O'Leary raced back to retrieve his typewriter in the Press Gallery; soon after the bell in the tower came crashing down.[5]

On the day of the Explosion, the Ottawa paper's front page informed readers that O'Leary was on his way to Halifax.

Journal Man On Way To Scene Of Disaster

Mr. Grattan O'Leary, of The Journal staff, is now on his way to Halifax. He will wire exclusive descriptive stories of the disaster and tell of his experiences of Ottawa men in the wrecked city.[6]

Journal editor John Crate sent twenty-nine-year-old O'Leary on special assignment to cover the disaster. He arrived in Halifax at 4:00 p.m. on Saturday 8 December 1917 and remained in the city for five days during which he wired two stories on 9 December and a third on 12 December. His initial two stories appeared in the *Journal* on 10 December. The first was published on the paper's front page with his photograph and a boxed blurb.[7]

Grattan O'Leary's Despatches Have Special Value To The People Of Ottawa And Capital District

Mr. M. GRATTAN O'LEARY, The Journal's staff representative at Halifax, succeeded last night in getting through a despatch of the utmost importance to the families of several score Ottawa people who were awaiting news of relatives in the stricken city. Mr. O'Leary was confronted with the greatest difficulty in securing clearance for his despatches for a flood of emergency business had been launched on the telegraph companies such as they could not care for. But Mr. O'Leary's copy is now coming over the wires freely, and today The Journal Newspapers present a story of the great disaster, with special reference to the Ottawa people and the capital's direct angle of interest.[8] Mr. O'Leary has also the advantage of having worked on Halifax city newspapers for several years before coming to Ottawa.[9] He has been for several years, one of the best known of Ottawa Parliamentary correspondents.

Two Ottawa Men Head Rescue In City Of Halifax

Lt.-Col McKelvey Bell And Major Canaan Had Big Task On Their Hands, Ottawa Cadets Saw The Ship All Ablaze, Flying Glass Came Like Snowflakes, One Cadet Tells A Journal Reporter

Special to The Journal by Mr. Grattan O'Leary of The Journal Staff

Halifax, Dec. 10 — Two Ottawa men, Lieut.-Col. McKelvey Bell and Major Canaan led the work of medical rescue and brought order out of chaos when the first blast of death struck Halifax on Thursday.[10] Col. Bell is adjutant of the Medical Service here, and Major Canaan is his chief assistant. Col. Bell was at his hotel preparing to leave for his office when the explosion shook the building to its foundation breaking glass and knocking down plaster all about him. He escaped without a scratch.

Major Canaan was in the elevator of the Dennis building going up to the Medical service offices located on the sixth floor, when the explosion came. The building is the largest and the most powerful in Halifax, but the elevator jammed and could not budge. Practically every pane of glass in the building was shattered.

It Was A Heavy Task

Less than an hour later Col. Bell and Major Canaan were directing the work of

rescue, commandeering teams of all kinds, rushing the wounded and dying to the hospitals, sending the dead to the morgues, arranging for temporary hospitals, issuing instructions to the people where medical attendance could be secured and otherwise directing medical work of succor and rescue.[11]

GRATTAN O'LEARY'S DESPATCHES HAVE SPECIAL VALUE TO THE PEOPLE OF OTTAWA AND CAPITAL DISTRICT

MR. M. GRATTAN O'LEARY, The Journal staff representative at Halifax, succeeded last night in getting through a despatch of the utmost importance to the families of several score Ottawa people who were awaiting news of relatives in the stricken city. Mr. O'Leary was confronted with the greatest difficulty in securing clearance for his despatches for a flood of emergency business had been launched on the telegraph companies such as they could not care for. But Mr. O'Leary's copy is now coming over the wires freely, and today The Journal Newspapers present a story of the great disaster, with special reference to the Ottawa people and the Capital's direct angle of interest.

Mr. O'Leary has also the advantage of having worked on Halifax city newspapers for several years before coming to Ottawa. He has been for several years, one of the best known of Ottawa Parliamentary correspondents.

Mr. Gratton O'Leary, of the staff of The Journal Newspapers, who has been in Halifax for several days.

HELP HALIFAX

Journal Fund Meets With Quick Response—List of Those Giving Today—Dominion Theatre's Generous Offer.

Grattan O'Leary, Ottawa Journal, 10 December 1917

O'Leary's second and much longer despatch appeared on page sixteen of the *Ottawa Journal.*

Hint That Pilot Not On Bridge As Ships Collided

That Is Story Told By Pilot Of Munition Ship, So Journal Reporter Hears, How Relief Came To Halifax On Saturday, Seafaring Men Can't Understand How Vessels Should Come Into Contact

Special to The Journal by M. Grattan O'Leary, of The Journal Staff

Halifax. Dec. 9 – (Sunday night) – Four days of toil and endeavor in a herculean task of succor and rescue have only served to bring out in more terrible relief the awful extent of last Thursday's tragedy.

Words are but feeble things to picture the tragedy and the horror and the pity of the scenes that are hourly being enacted. Today a Journal representative was permitted to walk through the districts where the suffering is greatest and the destruction most severe. Everywhere there were pictures to crush the heart with their pathos, crowded hospitals, morgues overflowing with mangled unrecognizable dead, tear-stained faces of men and women piteously seeking missing loved ones, long lines of sombre vehicles conveying their own grim message of death, and whole blocks of once happy homes, an absolute barren waste. Four days and four nights a well organized army of soldiers, sailors, and civilians have toiled without ceasing at the work of rescue but despite all their endeavors it will be days perhaps weeks before the full reality of the disaster can be known, and apart from the staggering toll of dead and wounded the havoc wrought throughout the city is almost beyond calculation.

An Almighty Blow

To-day in the entire city there is not a single building that has not suffered; great churches are wrecked to an extent of many hundreds of thousands of dollars; some of the finest, most modern offices are battered into debris; the largest hotels are considerably damaged and practically every bit of window glass within a radius of ten miles is powdered into dust. The explosion and havoc and what it wrought in its wake seem beyond human comprehension. Men aboard ships lying in the harbor were instantly killed by the terrific concussion; powerful structures crumbled like a deck of cards; freight cars weighing many tons were lifted from their tracks; huge pieces of iron and steel were hurled as far as two miles through the air; parts of the ill-fated French steamer were showered throughout the city, killing scores and crashing through roofs; street cars were overturned and their occupants killed or maimed; and houses were flattened as if by a blow from Jove's own mailed fist.

The Thought Of The Germans

The mighty roar of the explosion followed the sound of toppling buildings and the hideous crashing of glass struck terror into the hearts of the people. The very earth itself seemed to tremble and sway under the force of the shock. "The Germans!" was the cry from every lip, and many a soul must have departed this life in the bitter belief that the sackers of Louvain and the murderers of London children were the authors of this terrible tragedy.

The hours which followed were hours of terror. Appalled and staggered, the people at first were incapable of responding to appeals for organized aid. On all sides were the maimed and dying, and the authorities, unprepared for a catastrophe of such colossal magnitude, were powerless to meet the demands of the situation. Night only added to the horrors of the day. With the gas and the electric supply gone the city was in darkness, street car traffic was hopelessly broken, fire swept through the ruined districts mounting the toll of death, the homeless were exposed to a bitter wind that drove through the darkened streets, and many died from wounds and exposure. Friday morning brought little relief. A gray leaden sky soon broke into a terrific blizzard and snow, as if anxious to hide the hideous spectacle of the dead, began to fall.

Relief Came Saturday

The suffering that followed baffles description. The homeless, many still unprovided (*sic*) with tents, were exposed to the pitiless elements, vehicle traffic became more and more difficult, and the work of the heroic rescuers was retarded. Saturday brought a measure of relief with an end to the storm and the arrival of doctors, nurses and medical supplies from all points throughout the province, as well as from the generous hearted State of Massachusetts. Tents sprang up all over the city, the homeless were fed, given medical care and otherwise provided for, temporary hospitals were secured, and the work of rescuing the bodies of the dead greatly advanced. But again on Saturday night it seemed as if Providence was visiting wrath and tribulation upon the stricken. Rain, driven in gusts, swept through the now distressed city, tents were levelled; the snow turned into torrents of water, thoroughfares became almost impassable, and the plight of the homeless already terrible, became almost unendurable. Human capacity for pain and suffering and terror had all but reached the limit.

Worse Than Incompetency

What of the cause? Who or what was responsible for this catastrophe, so gigantic in its proportions, so appalling in its results? Was it the result of criminal incapacity or stupidity or was it something immeasurably more criminal? Was it the result of calculated endeavor at murder and destruction? Thus far the authorities, only now adequately grappling with a situation at first beyond the ken of human efforts, have been able to pierce through the mass of conflicting rumors and reports, some of them terribly disturbing, as to how the collision of the two steamers occurred. The truth is that in the minds and hearts of the dazed, half-stricken survivors, there is fear and belief that not incompetency but something worse was responsible for what has befallen Halifax.

The fear is given expression to by the [Halifax] Herald which under the caption of "Fix Responsibility" boldly demands that the authorities find out if there were "any Germans amongst the crew of the Belgian relief ship."

"If men higher up or men lower down through incompetency or duplicity are to blame", says the Herald, "let it be known, if this was the work of the arch-enemy, whose methods do not stop at killing women and children, then the people want to know it. Halifax is deeply concerned in this. All Canada is deeply concerned, and the people will not rest satisfied until the truth is known. We owe this much to the dead, the suffering wounded and to the friends who are left to sorrow. Let justice be done though the heavens fall."

Clear Day In The Harbor

Had it been night or had the day been

foggy there would be some glimmer of excuse for a collision. But it was neither night or misty. It was a clear, bright morning, with a cloudless sky and a fresh breeze blowing across the harbour. The French steamer Mont Blanc, with a benzene cargo on deck, nitro-glycerine (*sic*) in the forward compartments, T.N.T., the most deadly explosive known, in the middle and aft compartments, and oil in her ballast tanks, had come up from the entrance to the port at slow speed under instructions to join the ships in Bedford Basin. A Halifax pilot and former sea captain, Frank Mackie (*sic*), had her in charge. The Norwegian steamer, the Imo, with a cargo of relief for the sufferers in Belgium, and with the words "Belgian Relief" blazoned on both her sides in letters three feet deep, was coming down under slow speed out of the Upper Harbor or Bedford Basin. The steamers were seen by numerous spectators to approach each other as they drew into what is known as the "Narrows," only a short distance above the Canadian Government Railway passenger depot, and directly opposite a very thickly populated residential portion of the city.

There was ample room for the vessels to pass each other without the slightest danger of collision, but to the amazement and horror of the spectators on shore, the Norwegian ship drove almost squarely amidships into the French one. It is said by competent seamen that the Norwegian vessel kept over to port, when, according to the rules of navigation, she should have kept to starboard. Pilot Mackie, who was in charge of the Mont Blanc, and whose life was saved, at first made a statement that he had given the necessary signal and that only a confused signal was returned from the steamer in charge of Pilot Hayes

and that the vessels by that time were so close together that the rolling of the wheel hard over on the French ship was unable to put her clear of the on-coming relief ship.

Not On The Bridge?

Pilot William Hayes has gone before a higher judge and will never tell in this world of what occurred aboard the Belgian steamer, but those in Halifax who knew him as a man of ability find it hard that he could be to blame. A comparatively young man, conscientious, sober and with a record as pilot unmarred by a single mishap, he was regarded by seafaring men as at the top of his profession. How could this man, it is asked, be responsible for what would have been an unpardonable blunder on the part of the most seafaring novice? Since it became known that Hayes had lost his life, Pilot Mackie has steadfastly refused to make a statement. Preferring to wait for an official inquiry but the Journal correspondent is reliably informed that Mackie has confided to his fellow pilots here that neither before nor after the collision did he ever see Pilot Hayes on the bridge of the Norwegian steamer. If this statement is true, and its truth or falsity will be established at the enquiry that is to come, then the terrible suspicion is heightened that there was something more sinister than carelessness behind the awful tragedy.[12]

But whatever the immediate cause, whether carelessness, incompetency or murderous design be responsible for hurling two thousand souls into eternity within the twinkling of an eye, Halifax has felt the tragedy of war. Today a thousand times more it realizes the pity and pathos of Belgium and the hearts of its people cry out with pardonable desire for vengeance upon the monster of Prussianism.

Showing Its Heroism

But although it is suffering as no community on this continent has suffered, its people are showing a heroism in the face of desire that challenges admiration. Halifax, in truth has been British and when the full story of these terrible days comes to be written there will shine out from a record of calamity and death deeds of heroism as noble as any in the annals of our race. For the present, everything, business, politics, elections has been swept from the public mind. Today there is no distinction of religion or creed, or social caste in Halifax, but two things remain, one the call of grief, unspeakable from a section of the city, once prosperous and happy, but now a blackened waste; the other an eager cry from all the rest. "How can we help? In days of peace we lived together, tell us how we can make less terrible for our people this tragedy of death and ruin that has fallen upon them?"

And so Halifax bears its cross with Christ-like faith that all is for the best.

Tonight it is a city of death, of nameless graves, ghostly phantoms, but from the blackness of the shadows there emerges something bright and holy, the faith and the heroism and the human brotherhood of man. Halifax is prostrate in agony, but she does not despair. Her mental gaze cannot pierce the cloud but her Christian faith and moral vision tell her that its lining is of silver. M. GRATTAN O'LEARY[13]

O'Leary's 12 December 1917 despatch ran on the *Journal's* front page.

A Field Of Snow Where Sir Robert Spoke At Halifax

Reporter Who Listened To Premier Before Disaster Visits The Spot Again, Dash And Generosity Of The Boston People, Quick Aid And Organization Of New England City Wonderful In Itself

Written specially for The Journal by M. Grattan O'Leary

Halifax, Dec. 12 — This stricken place needs three things: money, clothing, and building material.

The sooner these are given the greater their capacity for relief, but whether sooner or later, the merest instincts of kinship and chivalry make their contribution imperative.

Today in Halifax, upwards of 15,000 people are absolutely homeless and but poorly clad, and the homes of 5,000 more are all but wrecked.

So sudden was the devastation of the explosion, so complete the destruction by the conflagration that followed in its wake that even those who were fortunate enough to escape death LOST EVERYTHING IN THE WORLD THEY POSSESSED. Many millions of dollars, scores of millions of feet of lumber and an enormous quantity of all kinds of clothing are required; but the need will not end there. It will be at least a year before Halifax can possibly be restored to anything approaching the conditions which obtained before the disaster.

The Quick Aid From Boston

The people of Halifax may be pardoned if it is the great-hearted State of Massachusetts that is among the first on their lips when they speak of what has been done for them. And no citizen of Canada who was in this city and witnessed the unspeakable misery and suffering of the first terrible days could fail to be profoundly moved by the sheer brotherhood, and dash, and enthusiasm of these spirited Americans. News of the catastrophe had barely reached the consciousness of the outside world, and the people of the stricken city had barely recovered from the stunning effects of the calamity when Halifax was literally invaded by Americans — American doctors, American nurses, American Red Cross workers, American engineers and American architects. How they managed to get such a start on everybody else, can only be explained by an enthusiasm and a dash absolutely contemptuous of details and intolerant of delay.

Infused New Courage

Their arrival infused new heart and courage into a dazed and stricken people. At a time when the crying need was for medical aid, when, in truth, hundreds were dying because they lacked a physician's care, train-load after train-load of American doctors — some of them eminent physicians — came pouring into the city, bringing all kinds of medical and surgical supplies, medical tents and staffs of nurses. It was one of the few bright pages in a story of death and disaster, and it will be long before Halifax will forget the helping hand of this great and generous people.

Still There Is Distress

But despite all that has been done in the way of relief during the past week, Halifax is still in sore distress. No one who has not seen the city's obliterated streets extending not alone for blocks, but for actual miles, can have the slightest conception of what

the devastation was like. So complete was the destruction in what was known as the Richmond district, that there is scarcely evidence of the ruins.

About a month ago the writer heard Sir Robert Borden open his campaign in the Halifax arena — a large, powerful, concrete structure.[14] ON SATURDAY LAST HE STOOD ON THE SAME SPOT AND IT WAS SCARCELY MORE THAN A SNOW-COVERED FIELD. What before the holocaust had been thickly populated streets could be traced only by rows of small fires, the burning coal bins of the various houses. Huge trees that had borne the storms of years were not only torn up from their roots but cut squarely off by flying pieces of iron and steel. Three hundred Intercolonial cars and twenty-five of the heaviest engines were simply battered beyond recognition; the big dry-dock was turned into a heap of debris; and pieces of metal actually weighing tons hurled, miles through the air.[15] IMAGINE THE EFFECT OF SUCH TITANIC FORCE UPON MILES OF WOODEN RESIDENCES IN THE DISTRICT RIGHT OPPOSITE THE EXPLOSION. Some of the smaller homes not only collapsed, they were simply blown away, and three miles of desert were created in the twinkling of an eye.

A Mystery Of Mercy

Just why many more thousands were not killed must ever remain a mystery. In more than two-thirds of the buildings still standing in which death did not occur, destruction of life would not have been remarkable. In fact there were instances of escape from disaster which were nothing short of miraculous. Among these none were more notable than the case of the Naval College, which, though not more than five hundred yards from the scene of the explosion, did not record a single death, while hundreds, miles further away, were instantly hurled into eternity.

Material Damage Great

The material damage while, of course, not so appalling as the loss of life, is staggering in itself. Eight splendid ships, all the more precious at the present time, were wiped out. Hundreds of thousands of dollars worth of Government Railway rolling stock were turned into useless bits of twisted debris; the huge Halifax dry-dock is ruined; the Naval College will have to be rebuilt; the North Street station is obliterated.[16] And apart from the Richmond district, which is nothing but a black waste, the business portion of the city is wrecked to the extent of millions of dollars. In short, it is estimated by some competent observers on the spot that the material loss may even reach $50,000,000. While immediate relief is imperative, the situation also calls for a permanent relief committee, and it will be probably a year before this committee will have concluded its work.

Lumber Is Needed

If the writer were asked how Ottawa citizens, or this city as a corporation can best render assistance to this permanent committee, he would say that a generous contribution of lumber and other building material would constitute the most effective aid.[17]

Thomas "T.P." Gorman, *Ottawa Citizen*

> They finally advised me that they had found a room in one of those old waterfront hotels. Anything, I had told them, would do, because I was wet, cold, tired and hungry. "Just wait until we remove the dead man and you will be quite comfortable there," the desk clerk assured me.
>
> — Tommy Gorman, *Ottawa Citizen* staff reporter

Tommy Gorman was born in Ottawa on 9 June 1886. His first job was a page boy in the House of Commons in 1905. Soon after he joined the *Ottawa Citizen* as an office boy and remained with the paper until 1921, when he left as sports editor. Although primarily a sports reporter, he was also given general reporting assignments. For example, in April 1912 he covered the *Titanic* disaster in New York City. *Citizen* editor Joe Finn described Tommy as "the greatest reporter the *Citizen* ever had."[1]

As previously indicated, both Gorman and the *Ottawa Journal's* Grattan O'Leary had been assigned to the *Titanic* story. However, after Gorman was scooped in New York by O'Leary, the *Ottawa Citizen* accused O'Leary of rehashing stories in New York morning papers to produce his own "eye-witness" account of events involving *Titanic's* survivors. As a result, the *Journal* and O'Leary commenced legal action against the *Citizen*, but when O'Leary was able to authenticate his scoop, the *Citizen* printed an

Tommy Gorman, 1908. Courtesy Diana Zimber

apology and the *Journal*/O'Leary lawsuits were dropped.[2]

Gorman was interested in sport as both a player and manager. He won an Olympic gold medal in 1908 as a lacrosse player, and in November 1917 was one of four founders of the National Hockey League.[3] Also, between 1920 and 1935, he managed four different NHL teams to Stanley Cups. He died in Ottawa on 15 May 1961 and was inducted into the Hockey Hall of Fame in 1963.

Soon after the Explosion occurred, thirty-one-year-old Gorman was assigned by *Citizen* editor Joe Finn to cover the story. Finn's decision once more made Gorman and O'Leary rivals reporting a major disaster, one which Gorman would later describe as "my toughest newspaper assignment."[4] Two sources provide details of his trip to Halifax and first days in the stricken city. They also reveal he was an ingenious and persistent journalist. The first source is Gorman's unpublished private journal.

An hour or so after they [his bosses] received word of the dreadful explosion at Halifax, Gorman and his little brown suitcase were on their way. Standing next morning [7 December] on a CPR platform at St. John, I saw a smart-looking American train steam in and inquired concerning it... "That is the Red Cross Special from Boston" they informed me. "Only doctors and nurses are carried on that one." I had to get to Halifax as quickly as possible, so just as the Red Cross Special started to pull out I left other reporters, dashed across the tracks and jumped aboard. Conductors and trainmen not only threatened to have me tossed off but they promised to find me a nice cool cell when the non-stop journey to Halifax ended. There was so much death and destruction at Halifax, however that they completely forgot about their unexpected passenger. Accordingly I was one of the first travelling scribes to reach the stricken city... [After arriving downtown] I appropriated a typewriter from one of the nearby stores whose windows had been shattered to smithereens and left a note saying where I could be located and guaranteeing payment for the machine.[5] I also located a telegraph operator who appeared willing to be subsidized and was soon back in business. By noon [8 December] my stories were being ticked off to Ottawa. Before retiring that night I had filed over five thousand words... Next day I had to face some sort of an Army court for allegedly violating censorship regulations and for refusing to submit my stories to the temporary commanders. However, I managed to survive.

Given the extent of the damage to hotels, another challenge for Gorman was to obtain accommodation.

They [city officials] finally advised me that they had found a room in one of those old hotels along the waterfront. Anything, I had told them, would do, because I was wet, tired, cold and hungry. "Just wait until we remove the dead man and you will be quite comfortable there," the desk clerk assured me. Any port in the storm... When I returned to my hotel they had fortunately taken the poor dead man away.

The second source is an article written on 1 February 1947 by Joe Finn headlined "Meet 'Tommy' Gorman, Reporter. He Beat 'Em All In His Day."[6]

In his hey-dey (*sic*) as a "headline hunter" Tommy was a tall, blonde package of dynamite with a ready smile and an equally ready wit. His tremendous energy kept pace with his almost uncanny "nose for news" and these things, combined with a complete and utter disregard for barriers and obstacles, which would have stymied a less rugged soul, made him the greatest reporter the Citizen ever had.

It is extremely difficult to single out Tommy's most spectacular exploit in the old days — simply because most of his exploits were spectacular. But, the one I personally got the biggest kick out of has to do with the Halifax explosion and how "T.P." beat the stuffings (*sic*) out of the opposition by several fast moves.

Sent out on a mad dash when word of the explosion reached Ottawa, Tommy got to Montreal, boarded a Halifax-bound train there and arrived at St. John, New Brunswick when the trip was halted abruptly. All traffic to Halifax from that point was being held up temporarily to clear the way for non-stop mercy trains into the stricken city and there he was, stranded, with some 20 or 25 other newspapermen.[7]

A hospital train was being hastily loaded with doctors, nurses and much-needed medical supplies and as he stood on the platform Tommy saw a glimmer of hope. He waited patiently carrying on an innocent conversation with his fellow scribes until the hospital train began moving out. At the last moment Tommy suddenly made a leap for a handrail, swung up onto a car-step and waved a smiling farewell to his bewildered and completely baffled confreres.

But his troubles were by no means over. Apparently mistaken for a doctor (a small black satchel increased the illusion) little attention was paid to him until someone finally discovered the deception. A consultation among the train crews and medical men immediately took place and there were some suggestions such as "toss him off", "have him arrested" and sundry other "helpful hints." But, stopping the train would have cost precious time and, in due course — and hours ahead of other outside newspapermen — he got to Halifax.

In the meanwhile The Citizen had published in its news columns the fact that Tommy Gorman was en route to Halifax. Anyone having relatives down there was invited to send the names of the relatives in at once and they would be forwarded to Tommy so that he would discover whether they were among the thousands of casualties.

Finn continued the recollection with a description of Gorman's first hours in Halifax.

When Tommy stepped from the hospital train a long telegram containing numerous names was awaiting him and, within the space of a few hours, The Citizen was able to publish an authentic casualty list based on the names sent from Ottawa. And it was a clean "scoop."[8]

Describing his arrival at Halifax, Tommy told me in a chat I had with him recently. "I finally found a hotel and talked my way into the good graces of the clerk. 'We'll have a nice warm room for you in about ten minutes,' the clerk told me. 'A man just died from shock

and we'll have him right out'."

After taking over the room for the "departing guest", Tommy got down to the business of getting a story together. He told me. "I finally found a store in which the plate glass window had been blown out. And there, right in the midst of the shattered glass and rubble were a number of brand new typewriters. I picked out the best one and left a note pinned to the wall. The note read 'Please send bill for one Remington typewriter to D. Finn, The Citizen, Ottawa.' Maybe that machine didn't catch hell for the next few days!"[9]

While in Halifax, Gorman wrote five despatches. They appeared in the *Citizen* between 10 and 13 December. The following are his stories of 10, 11 and 13 December.

Amazing Scenes To Those Arriving In Capital N. Scotia

Citizen Reporter Tells Of His First Impressions Reaching City Of Dead On Proceeding Through The Stricken City One Is Gravely Impressed By The Scenes Of Desolation On Every Hand — Distressful Sights Greet The Eye On All Sides

(By Staff Reporter)[10]

Halifax, N.S., Sunday, Dec. 9 — Nineteen Seventeen will always be recalled as one of the darkest days in the history of Canada. Reeling under the shadow of one of the most disastrous

calamities that has ever taken place, Halifax, after heart rending sorrows, consequent upon Thursday's explosion, which entailed a death list of about two thousand and property losses which run into the millions, awoke this morning to a grim realization of what extent the holocaust had reached.

On Friday a blinding snowstorm had set in turning the entire city into one of chaos and demoralization and multiplying ten-fold the difficulties connected with the work of rescue. Trains were snowbound from Montreal, Boston and many other points. Provisions bound to the Halifax of death and desolation were delayed in transit and for hours the Nova Scotian metropolis was completely cut off from communication with the outside world.

Gale Hindered Rescue

Last night a heavy gale drove up from the south, followed quickly by a blinding rainstorm, that soon transformed the heavy snow into water and slush, blocking the sewers, submerging the sidewalks and rendering the more pitiful general conditions in the already stricken city. In many ways, however the storm descended as a blessing in disguise as it aided heroic bands of workers in their gallant efforts to extinguish the still blazing fires and facilitated to some extent the work of digging out the unfortunate victims who lay in helpless heaps beneath masses of debris,

Hence as daylight broke over what was a few days ago one of the most prosperous seaports in the world, transformed by the crash between the Belgian relief ship Imo and the French munition transport Mont Blanc, into a center of death, desolation (*sic*), suffering and sorrow. It was with mingled feelings of poignant grief and relief that the workers resumed their grim tasks. Further danger from fire had been alleviated and hopes were held out in view of the remarkable rescues of the previous days that it would still be possible to

extricate from the wreckage of factories, warehouses, schools, orphanages and buildings, persons in whom the breath of life still remained.

Relief Trains Arrive

For the first time since Friday trains began to reach the city. The relief special from Massachusetts delayed at several points on account of the heavy snowstorm, reached Moncton last night and was immediately given the right of way. Crowded with doctors, nurses and supplies for the wounded and injured, it arrived in Halifax late last night. Shortly afterwards the regular Ocean Limited reached the city and it was followed early this morning by Intercolonial and Canadian Pacific trains, which left Montreal Friday evening.[11] The Thursday expresses were nearly 24 hours late. Lines between St. John and Halifax have been finally cleared, however and it is thought that barring another heavy downfall of snow, the transportation difficulties are, for the present at least, over.

Telegraph communication with the outside world has been re-established though the cable stations are still crippled, and the parts of the city which by reason of their location were not seriously damaged are beginning to resume their normal appearance.

Bring In Rations

Morning trains from the east and west brought in additional ration supplies. Doctors and nurses registered from all parts of Eastern Canada and the Eastern States and work of succoring the heart-broken afflicted ones is being greatly facilitated. Military authorities have matters well in hand despite the crushing realities which are striking deep into the hearts of those who have lost their loved ones. There has been no disorder of any kind. Messages of condolence continue to arrive from various points and the officials of the city have made excellent progress with their magnificent work of relief. Rain is still coming down in torrents and a slight mist hangs over the ill-fated city, adding a dull grey obscurity to the sombre appearance it has already assumed.

Vast Devastated Area

Though the cordon had been drawn tightly about the devastated district which khaki clad engineers, infantrymen and artillery soldiers still encircled, carrying loaded rifles as a silent warning to trespassers, a party of newspaper men were permitted, shortly after their arrival this morning [December 8], to visit the heart of the sorrow stricken of Halifax, now a grey panorama of shattered buildings, smouldering heaps of coal and furniture, twisted telegraph and telephone wires and huge poles that had been snapped in two by the unimaginable force of Thursday's explosion.[12]

Friday's train from Montreal was delayed at St. John owing to the snow trouble and again at one or two other places along the Intercolonial route. It was due here at 11 o'clock last night, but did not reach the outskirts of the city until an early hour this morning. The Intercolonial Railway station is, of course, absolutely ruined and cannot be used as terminal for many months. All trains, consequently, have been stopped at the southern limits and their passengers discharged there.

As soon as the Limited pulled into the environs of Halifax naval police boarded her and notified all passengers they would be obliged until the relief committee had interviewed every one, their aim being to allow into the city only those who had legitimate business.

Exceptions were made, of course, in the case of those holding military or naval passes and scores of people who came down to seek out relatives supposed to have lost their lives were also given the right to enter. Some of the American and Canadian newspaper men succeeded in getting through immediately.[13]

Amid Terrible Scenes

Halifax was just beginning a new week as the party detrained and wended its way through the snow covered sidewalks some places knee deep in slush to the relief headquarters. Vivid mind pictures of the actual conditions had of course been visualized and scarcely had The Citizen representative and his companions stepped off the Pullman than the nerve wracking details surrounding the tragedy begin to make their actual impression. On a siding near the temporary terminus eight or ten white pine coffins were heaped beside a box car, awaiting shipment to the former homes of those now lying silent and peaceful within the roughly made boxes, unfortunate victims, men, women and children, whose lives had been snuffed out instantaneously in Thursday's terrific explosion.

Other Cities Pay Price

Each coffin had been labelled for shipment by rail and one glance was sufficient to convince that St. John, Truro and other maritime cities had also been called upon to pay a heavy toll in the greatest disaster of modern times. That unfortunately served only the beginning.

All Coffin Laden

As the party trailed up Hollis Street and toward the harbour, two or three sleighs passed the newspapermen all loaded with coffins. They were coming from the temporary hospitals, where during the third night after the catastrophe more names had been added to the long list of victims.

By this time the streets were almost impassable, so high was the snow and slush. Scores of men working day and night since the fatal crash between the Imo and the Mont Blanc sought with success to clear the streets so as to make traffic possible. To their strength had been added a corps of husky blue jackets from one of the American battleships harbored here.

U.S. Seamen At Work

Up to the knees in slush and water these young sons of Uncle Sam labored tirelessly, determined to do their utmost to aid their neighboring city in its hour of distress and pathos. Canadian troops helped in clearing the way and within a couple of hours fair conditions had been restored. On both sides of the street one could see further evidence of the heartrending extent of the explosion.

Hardly a plate glass window remained unshattered, while in many cases residences had been hurriedly boarded up to stop the dangerous inrush of the damp atmosphere. Fortunately the mercury had gone up and indoors, conditions were really better than they had been since the crash. Water poured down from the steep incline that rolled up toward the west part of the area and in the blinding rain the task of restoring the city to its former appearance was carried on.

In The North Sections

Further north appalling conditions were soon brought to the attention of the new comers. Men and women with bandaged heads and faces, the majority victims of flying glass and or splinters of

wood were met by the score, hundreds of houses had been practically ruined by the force of the explosion and in scarcely any cases was glass visible. Nearly all the stores were open, as Deputy Mayor Coldwell had declared the usual Sunday observances unnecessary, but they were indeed strange looking structures — boarded up in such a way that not a bit of daylight streaked through. For a time the street cars endeavored to operate but it was a forlorn service and at periodical intervals the electric lighting system also failed.

Station A Total Wreck

On Barrington Street as far as North Street, tragedy could be noticed on all sides, but it was past the intersection of North Street that the real damage had occurred. Standing grim and gaunt, roofless, and fairly trembling before the heavy breeze, the Intercolonial Railway station was a total wreck. Its red brick walls alone had withstood the destructive shock though the loss of life within it is said to have been remarkably small. Across from the station the Revere House was also found a total wreck, while on the opposite corner the King Edward hotel was likewise demolished, though its main walls and parts of the roof had withstood the impact.

Navies Side By Side

Out in the harbour, where the water lashed about by the stiff wind crashed back and forth between the Halifax and Dartmouth shores, small boats puffed slowly up and down in midstream. A giant British cruiser, rushed to the scene when her commander had heard of the disaster, lay at anchor, the red and white ensign of John Bull's indomitable navy flying proudly from her stern.

A short distance away an American

cruiser, likewise a new arrival, also lay at anchor, while over on the Dartmouth side, her nose pushed firmly into the beach, though keeled over on her starboard side, lay the Belgian relief steamer, the Imo. One side had been stove in considerably, but under the circumstances, the immediate cause of the Halifax calamity seemed to have come through miraculously well.

Might Be Bravery

Stray bits of wreckage from boats which had been seriously damaged in the explosion floated about but nowhere was there any sign of the Mont Blanc, which appears to have been literally blown to pieces. Causes for the great disaster have of course been enumerated and the general supposition appears to be that the Imo and Mont Blanc crossed signals, with the terrible results, but the one story in which some credence is placed, was to the effect that the Imo, knowing that the Mont Blanc was ablaze and hoping to avoid the calamity, had purposely rammed the muntion boat in a brave, though unsuccessful attempt to sink her before the flames had reached the deadly explosives.[14] This, of course, will be thoroughly sifted when the government investigation gets under way.

Are All In Ruins

Past the Intercolonial station and down Barrington Street stood a business section, fine residences and factories. Today, these are but smouldering ruins. At one place, a Halifax resident pointed the wreck of [a] sugar refinery, where many had gone to their death. Further north was indicated the former headquarters of the Richmond Printing Co., whence only five of about seventy are known to have escaped.

100 Orphans Killed

On one side of the hill further on was shown an orphanage, where over a hundred helpless little tots met their doom, and at another point the newspapermen were shown a house from which only the father from a family of seven had escaped.

Out in the vicinity of Richmond rescue workers labored away in their grim task, every now and then extricating something that was at one time a human form.

Desolation And Sorrow

Desolation, ruin and sorrow was (sic) indelibly stamped everywhere, all contributing to a scene of pathos never before realized. Men and boys worked tirelessly to secure possible trace of their loved ones, sympathetic friends were present to assist and condole, civic and officers military aided to the utmost in the heartrending struggle, and charitable women workers passed to and fro, all engaged in the one task, that of relieving those, on whom Thursday's lamentable calamity had imposed physical or mental torture. In many cases suspense was relieved this morning by the discovery of clothing that would convince one that for her or him for whom he sought was beyond all earthly aid.

All up outside of the caldron of suffering humanity there arose series of individual heroism, possibly the few bits of glow in this an hour of pain and grief. Miraculous escapes, brave rescues and gallant attempts at the saving, which in many cases cost the existence of those so engaged have added to the story of the great calamity. In some instances only one out of large families live to tell the tale and in others but one or two escaped. One babe who lay since the explosion under wreckage was taken out yesterday with a good chance of surviving, and there have already been reported many remarkable feats of surgery which have literally pulled back from the grave people for whom no hope at first had been entertained.

Families Mourning

One youthful member of the Engineers Corps, a chap named Elliot, lost his mother, two brothers, two sisters and his grandmother, while another veteran of Vimy Ridge, David Heffler, is mourning the loss of his parents and four brothers, three of whom fought with him in France.[15]

Practically All Victims Were Killed Instantly, Boston Physician Asserts

Thinks The Few Who Perished Later Mainly Lost Lives By Going Back Into Ruins — Many Thrilling Stories Of The Disaster Continue To Come In

(By Staff Reporter)

Halifax, Dec. 10 — A Boston physician, who has made a specialty of relief work, gave an indication of the terrifying force of the explosion, when he stated that practically all the victims had been killed outright.[16] He believes they were nearly all beyond earthly suffering when the fires broke out, though a number, having survived the concussion, lost their lives in rushing back among the crashing debris, to rescue their loved ones.[17] He said today that many of the women and children were without a mark of any kind on their bodies, the majority having been spared the worldly knowledge of what had really happened.

Thrilling Incidents

From the huge columns of stories concerning the greatest disaster in the history of Canada, there continue to arise stirring tales of heroism, such as that of the telegraph operator who flashed "Good Bye" to his friends and went to his doom, sitting at his key. The fire chief and his deputy and other flame fighters fought gallantly to extinguish the blaze of piers six, seven, eight and nine, though they knew that an explosion was inevitable.[18]

There are people who substantiate the narratives dying to save their little ones and the bravery of sailors and soldiers who rushed into the heart of the danger zone to succor those in peril will add another page to the glorious history of the army and navy.

These stories in some cases, almost beyond belief, continue to reach the ears of the officials, all testifying to the remarkable heroism and fortitude with which Nova Scotians are bearing their staggering burden.

Will Be Prosecutions

What the investigation will reveal remains to be seen. Certainly there will be prosecutions. It is too late however to recall the poor lifeless creatures who now lie amid the dull tolling of church bells in pitiful rows in the various morgues, the school houses and the armouries. But is not too late to prevent a repetition of the heartbreaking occurrences of the past few days, and steps in this direction have already been taken.

"This is war, and we Americans must prepare for it," commented a Boston photographer, after admitting that Belgium and France offered nothing more cruelly penetrating or pathetic.[19]

Grossly Inhuman

"War plus its horrors when women and children are the innocent victims," commented one of the New York physicians, "but God spare us from anything so inhuman as this." He had surveyed the smouldering area where a few days ago the working class of Halifax had dwelt, in supposed peace and security. He had stood at the corner of North and Barrington Streets and had contemplated in amazement the terrible damage done to the warships, the relief boats, the Naval college, and the docks themselves. Over across to the Dartmouth side he had focussed his field glasses on shell-riddled buildings in which men and women had been struck down without warning and he had gone with a friendless Italian woman through two of the temporary morgues where she gazed tearfully from one to another for several hours until finally she had sobbed out in grief and fallen prostrate over the slightly disfigured remains of one who had been dearer to her than life itself.[20]

Touching Scenes At Burial Soldier And Sailor Heroes
Internment Of Score Who Died In Performance Of Their Duty During The Terrible Disaster At Halifax
(By Staff Reporter)

Halifax, Dec. 12 — With dignified, though simple ceremonials, the funerals took place this morning of about twenty soldiers and sailors who were killed in the shipping district. Their bodies, practically all of which had been recovered out of the harbour lay for several days in the Admiralty building, as it was impossible to get coffins and all the city ministers were engaged in urgent relief work.

Soldiers' Funerals

Today several expeditionary force chaplains took charge and conducted the funerals. Hundreds of sailors gathered within the big building to pay the last respects to their dead comrades, a pathetic picture of heroism and grief as they gathered closely about in their picturesque blending uniform of khaki and grey. There was no funeral dirge, no muffled drums, no gun carriage and no solemn military pomp, though in a few cases friends had covered up the rough coffins with Union Jacks.

Eulogy Of Soldiers

Rev. Capt. Veach of Truro spoke briefly in eulogy of the lamented men of His majesty's forces, except for their companions in arms, with no loving relatives to claim the bodies. He took for his theme the Biblical text: "greater love hath no man," and his trembling voice rose softly above the low whisperings of the sobbing group of mourners as he referred to the noble sacrifice the victims had made and expressed his sincere belief that were they in a position to they would again show no hesitation in laying down their lives that those in the city whom they had sworn to protect might be spared.

Borne To Graves

Capless sailors and soldiers, here and there a sprinkling of women and civilians listened attentively to the grey-haired Nova Scotia chaplain consigning the bodies to the earth and their souls to God, after which there followed a slow shuffling of feet and companions of the unfortunate victims lifted the coffins and carried them through tear-eyed throngs to the waiting trucks outside. All the admiralty flags flew at half-mast as a mark of respect. The many unclaimed bodies were driven out to St. John's [Anglican Cemetery] and lowered into big graves where scores of conspicuous white crosses and one big monument mark the last resting place of the unknown victims of the Titanic, whose bodies were washed ashore nearby after the memorable steamship disaster of 1912.[21] The burial of the soldiers and sailors all of whom had died like heroes in the performance of their duties, constituted one of the most impressive of the many sad features of the greatest of American disasters which plunged both Canada and United States into grief.[22]

William Stuart, *Montreal Standard*

> Were I possessed of the pen and power of a Dante I might hope to set down here some adequate account of the inferno into which the thriving modern city of Halifax was plunged and hurled in the twinkling of an eye.
> — William Stuart, *Montreal Standard* staff correspondent,
> 13 December 1917

Montreal Standard editor Fred Yorston sent staff correspondent William Stuart to report and obtain pictures of the Explosion for the popular Saturday weekly.[1] Stuart left Montreal on the *Maritime Express* at 11 p.m. on 7 December 1917 and arrived in Halifax at 4 p.m. the next day.[2] He remained in the city for several days and wired his account of the disaster on 13 December.

On the front page of the 17 December 1917 issue, the *Standard* published a large box-notice headlined "The Standard And The Halifax Disaster."

On Page 32 of this issue will be found a descriptive account of the Halifax disaster from the pen of a Standard staff representative who journeyed to the stricken city. The pictures in the Art Section of this issue were taken under the personal supervision of The Standard's correspondent and the material for his article was gathered at the time these pictures were taken. The Standard's pictures taken in conjunction with the article on page 32, form the most comprehensive account of the great disaster yet issued to the public.[3]

On page 32 of the Standard the banner headline announced:

If Explosion Which Wrecked Northern Portion Of Halifax Had Occurred On Land Nothing For Ten Miles Around Would Have Been Left Alive

Standard's Correspondent Tells Of Sights Seen In Stricken City Of Halifax Graphic Pen Picture Of A Journey Through The Devastated Part Of Halifax — A Visit To One Of The Temporary Morgues — With The Bread Line And On The Common Where The Tent City Housed The Refugees — The Stricken Water Front — Many Wonderful Escapes And The Courageous Spirit Of The City — Nothing Like It Before Ever Seen In The History Of The World

Written Specially for The Standard by W.M. Stuart, Staff Correspondent

Halifax, Dec. 13 — Were I possessed of the pen and power of a Dante I might hope to set down here some adequate account of the inferno into which the thriving modern city of Halifax was plunged and hurled in the twinkling of an eye.[4] But lacking the descriptive powers of the great Italian it is only possible to present herewith in a fragmentary and sketchy way some of the many vivid pictures which have burned their way into the storehouse of memory never to be effaced in this world.

Where horror is piled on horror, ruin on ruin, desolation on desolation, destruction on destruction till the mind reels and faints under the strain it is only possible to point out the major tragedies in the succession of sensations and leave the rest to be filled in by the imagination of the reader.

A City Of Desolation

When I arrived in Halifax at 4 p.m. on Saturday afternoon, 17 hours late from Montreal, it was to find a mantle of virgin snow covering the city of the dead as a beautiful shroud. It was as if nature had paused a moment, aghast at the havoc wrought by the carelessness of man, and then moved by the awesomeness of the spectacle had greatly dropped her cover of snow over the stricken scene to blot it out if only for a few hours, from the gaze of those who still quivered and cowered under the shock.

My first visit to the temporary morgue, one of the many alas to be found throughout the city, in the Shebucto (*sic*) school. Two hundred and sixteen bodies had at that time been conveyed to this school where the cement cellars had been turned into a habitation for the dead. Outside the building a placard was nailed there.

Bring Your Dead Here

It was as if one had been suddenly transported back to the plague days of Old London when the dead carts made their mournful rounds of the streets, their drivers dismally calling "Bring out your dead."

The scene inside the morgue was one that would have brought tears from a demon of the lowest regions. Here in a corner was a pitiful pile of what had once been human beings, human now only in that they bore traces of clothing about the torn, mangled and burned bodies.

Laid out in long, pitiful rows were the bodies of those, whose features were still recognizable, while soldiers, with tender hands and trembling lips, washed from the dear, dead faces the dirt and grime so that they may be more easily identified. It was a strange commentary on what the city and its people had passed through, to see delicately raised women and girls, still dazed by their losses, walking through the ghastly place, glancing hurriedly from face to face, and then, with never a tear, turning away with a "No he's not here, let's go to the next place." The living people of Halifax were shocked into a state where they had almost as little feeling left as the dead themselves.

No Tears In Halifax

In all the time I have been in the stricken city I have never seen a tear shed. The horror has been too deep for tears; it has dried up the very spring of feeling.

From the morgue I moved on to the Armouries. Here the chief of the many relief stations was located and a bread line of men, women and children several hundred yards long was standing in the snow waited their turn to secure the precious bread and other necessities of life. Little children were in the line, each with his basket or box and most of them with their heads, or hands, bandaged, where the flying glass had cut them.

In the entire Richmond district of the city, a territory of some two and a half miles square, there was not one of the population of approximately 30,000 people who was not either killed or injured in some manner.[5]

A majority of those wounded were of course struck by broken glass and terrible, indeed, were the cuts inflicted.

The relief stations, which sprang into being as if by magic, were scenes of many pathetic and touching incidents. Persons thought dead or dying were often found lined up in one of the bread lines waiting for something to eat, and too dazed to do anything towards aiding themselves.

One man standing in one of the bread lines suddenly threw his hands over his head and screaming at the top of his voice "God kill all Germans. I'll have to go over there myself." He rushed down the street, poor fellow, his nerves shattered by the sights and scenes around him and by his own experience, his wife and four children had been instantly killed, his mind had given way and he fled insane through the streets until taken in charge by several soldiers and taken to a hospital.

Volumes could and should be written of the heroic work performed in these same hospitals. Never in the history of healing have braver men and tender women worked more devotedly than they did and are doing in Halifax, the city of heroes as well as the city of horrors.

The doctors for miles around the stricken city appeared on the scene as rapidly as possible, bring stores and stocks of drugs, bandages, sprints etc. A special train was rushed from Moncton with a complete unit of doctors and nurses and was the first of the many relief trains to arrive.

The American hospital units who came on special trains did magnificent work, how great can never be expressed in words but only in the prayers of thankfulness that rose from the suffering so carefully tended.

The Tent City

From the Armoury it is only a few steps to Common Hill and here some 600 tents had been erected by the soldiers who evacuated their barracks so that homeless women and children might find some shelter. The great snow blizzard of Friday night was followed by a terrific rain and wind storm on Saturday night so that the plight of the soldiers sleeping in these tents can be better imagined than described.

The Devastated Area

Leaving Common Hill the real devastated area was soon reached. For the first

I saw houses completely demolished, flattened out, close to the ground as if crushed by a gigantic weight. While every house in Halifax has broken windows, it was the Richmond district, from the water front back to a distance of over two miles, that experienced the, full relentless force of the devastating blast. The St. Joseph Roman Catholic Church was noticeable on one corner, noticeable by reason of the fact that it had three walls standing. Other buildings close had but one, or two — or none.

The Slaughter Of The Innocents

The Richmond schoolhouse on Thursday morning at nine o'clock was a fine building where, daily, over 600 children learned their lessons, and in their spare moments romped and played. At seven minutes passed nine it was a charnel house with over 400 children pinned beneath the mass.[6] One boy was blown through a window and landed among a pile of soft snow — uninjured. It is not believed that another child in the building escaped and only the fact that school did not begin until 9:30 in the morning prevented some 200 others from sharing their fate. Of all the tragedies of this tragic event the fate of these youngsters is perhaps the most heart-rending. These little men and women of the future, engaged in their innocent childish play and prattle, hurled into eternity in a fraction of time is something that touches the innermost cords of the most hardened heart. Surely if Halifax had to be sacrificed, its children might have been spared.

The slaughter of the innocents has another and even more terrible side. In one family of three small children not one of them has retained the sight of even one eye. Totally blind they will grope their way through a world

darkened in a flash as if by a giant hand.

One woman, the mother of eight, was found in a dazed condition wandering in a side street shortly after the explosion. She was carrying a baby, wrapped in a blanket, close to her breast. Seven of her brood, she stated, had been killed before her eyes. She had grasped her baby and run. To a question whether the baby was hurt or not, she unfolded the blanket, screamed and fainted. The baby was headless.

Great Buildings Damaged

Leaving the scene of the massacre of the children, I made for two of the largest buildings in Halifax, or what was left of them. One was the great factory of the Dominion Textile Company. The bare walls were standing and the water tower. Nothing else remained — not a sign to show that one of the busiest hives of Maritime manufacture had hummed on the spot. What the explosion failed to ruin fire had finished.

Across a vacant field from the ruined factory is the Halifax exhibition grounds. The great dome on the top of the principle (*sic*) building is cut in two as with a knife, the wings of this fine building are torn and tumbled round like a pack of cards., while the great new grand stand is tossed here and there as if the sportive play of a band of giants had played with them.

Into The Gates Of Hell

When the observer leaves the top of North Street and walks down the hill towards the North Street Station of the I.C.R. he leaves behind him all sense of peace, of prosperity, of civilization. It is as if he has entered the portals of the infernal regions. The I.C.R. depot is marked by several posts and twisted girders. The Maritime Express from Montreal, due in Halifax at a few minutes past nine, was ten minutes late on the fatal morning. Had it been on time a hundred more victims would have been added to the list, for the roof of the station fell with a crash a few seconds after the explosion, killing instantly everyone in the station.

Three hundred I.C.R. cars of various kinds and twenty engines were blown into more or less "nothingness" and the bodies of the men working on the water front were found, some of them, half a mile from where they had been working.

Worse Than Ypres

The scene along Barrington street, both on the river front side and the Richmond side, baffles description. It is not destruction or ruin — it is obliteration. On the left there extends for about two miles a slope, inclining back for perhaps 400 or 450 yards. Here was a whole district in itself. There were streets, houses, stores. There is now nothing. In the other parts of the city there are instances of the tremendous concussion. Here there are no "Instances." A reporter from a local paper who accompanied me on my trip tried in vain to find where a certain street had been.[7] The very curbstones had vanished.

On the river side, a shorter distance from the railway station, there stood the prosperous business of the Richmond Publishing Company. Thirty girls, employes (*sic*) of the company, were underneath the ruins as I gazed at them. Further along on the river side is the Naval College and the pier where the Canadian training ship, the Niobe, is moored. Thirty-five young boys, their ages ranging from 14–17, were in the college. They watched the fire on the Mont Blanc after the collision with the Imo, with curiosity and speculation.

Not one of them was killed when the explosion took place, but every one of them carries the marks of flying glass, while their beautiful college building is a sight to make the angels weep.

The Niobe Takes A Trip

The Niobe took her first trip in three years. The explosion moved her thirty feet along the dock, her great chains snapping like threads. One, which had considerable cable left to pay out, managed to hold or she would probably have drifted out into the channel.

Thirteen men who were on the Niobe were killed instantly and many injured, while a pinnace and cutter with full crews, who, with other crews from the Canadian vessel Highflyer, were attempting to tow the Mont Blanc to safety are missing and certain casualties.

Next comes the dry dock. In it at the time of the explosion was a vessel named the Hevlon (*sic*).[8] Today she looks as if she has just come through a naval engagement of the first magnitude.

Not far from the dry dock a large vessel was lying being loaded for a trip across the ocean. Fifty-six stevedores were busy as bees. Not one survives.

The Acadia Sugar refinery, close at hand, was a reality prior to the explosion. Today the visitor looks in vain for any sign of a building in the smouldering mass of ruins which meets his gaze.

Across the street from the remains of the sugar refinery I saw five poor, mangled bodies taken from the ruins of a house. As the last beam was raised a black cat which had been caught under it screamed like a human being in pain. A soldier caught it and placed it under his coat. It was the only thing in all that dreadful Richmond area, that city of the dead, that I saw alive.

Across the channel at this point on

the Dartmouth side lies the Imo, the Belgian relief ship, which collided with the Mont Blanc. She lies, visible to the gaze of all, a sad reminder of what fate was pleased to visit on the city of Halifax.

For perhaps a mile on the water front north from the Acadia Sugar refinery there extends a series of Railway tracks each loaded with freight cars. If a boy took a large box of burned matches, crumpled them up, stamped on them and smashed them in every conceivable way he would achieve, in a miniature way, a very good imitation of what these freight cars look like today.

The Force Of The Explosion

The force of this explosion can be judged by the fact that a doctor, Doctor White of Moncton, took a piece of boiler plate out of a man's leg in which it had lodged at Bedford, some five miles from the scene of the explosion.

The 4-inch cannon on the forward deck of the Mont Blanc was found 2 miles and a half from where the boat blew up.

Scenes Of Bravery

As can readily be imagined scenes of the greatest bravery were to witnessed (sic) on every side and many exhibitions of courage that deserved to go down the lists with the best traditions of the British Empire were recorded throughout the stricken city.

The magazine in the Naval Arsenal close to the Royal Naval College caught fire soon after the explosion. In it at the time were many aeroplane bombs, shells and much T.N.T. the terrible weapon of warfare that had wrecked the city like a flash of lightning when the flames reached it on board the Mont Blanc. The Jackies on board the Canadian

vessel "Canada" stunned and wounded as they were themselves in the tremendous blast of a few moments before saw and recognized the danger that faced what remained of the city if the magazine ever caught fire. The roof was already burning when these devoted men rushed into the magazine, secured the aeroplane bombs and threw them into the harbour, and then flooded the remainder of the magazine. The fire was then an easy matter to subdue, but the citizens of Halifax should know what a debt they are laboring under today to the men of the Canadian navy.

The behaviour of the boys in the Royal Naval College was also altogether admirable and upheld the best traditions of the great service to which they will one day belong. Not one of them but bears the marks of flying glass or falling timber and two of them at least had narrow escapes from losing their eyesight. But a wonderful piece of good fortune none of them were killed while all around them men and women were falling like leaves in a forest.

An Act Of Heroism

Then came an act of heroism worthy of the best traditions of the British mercantile marine. A former sea captain, now head of the marine department of the Halifax branch of a well-known shipping firm, agents for the ship, knew what the ship contained.[9] Practically unaided, he cut at the ship's steel cables until she was adrift and floating out into the stream. The fire on board was still making headway. Fortunately it had started where the progress could not be very rapid. The captain boarded the ship and as she drifted outward he was able to completely extinguish the blaze and then to get help to manage the steamer. Had the ship been allowed to burn following her desertion, the explosion that would have come would have levelled every building in the City of Halifax, and the whole city would have been a mass of ruins as is the north end today with a death list of probably thirty or forty thousand persons.

The Spirit Of The Stricken City

Never, however, did a stricken city rally from the terrible calamity which had overtaken it in a more heroic manner than did Halifax.

I saw a man greeted in the street by his friend who asked him how it stood by him, and he replied cheerily:

"Great, great. Of course, I have lost my house and all my furniture, but it is going great. I have my wife and family left, never even scratched."

That is the spirit in which Halifax has awakened from the great disaster that has overtaken her. It is the spirit in which she is going out to meet the future and to grapple with the tremendous problems which now confront her.

Over the city has swept like a devastating cloud a tragedy of its kind never before equalled in the history

---

Letter from Reporter William Stuart to *Montreal Standard* Editor Fred Yorston

Dec. 21 [1917]
Mr. Yorston

With reference to your request for a report in connection with the letter from the Chief Press censor regarding our pictures of Halifax, I beg leave to state that I have read his letter carefully and with interest and that in this connection I report as follows: -

No attempt was made to conceal the taking of photographs published in the Montreal Standard. As you can doubtless understand when I arrived in Halifax at 4 o'clock on the Saturday following the explosion, and immediately after a tremendous snowstorm which had practically tied up everything, there was considerable confusion all over the district. I inquired at the various newspaper offices as to what arrangements had been made for taking photographs, and was informed that photographs had been taken on the day of the explosion and shipped out to St. John, from which point they were distributed all over. I was also informed that it was not necessary to secure any special permit, other than the permit used by the reporters of the various papers, to obtain admission to the devastated area.

The photographs secured by the Montreal Standard were taken simply with the aid of the permit and at no time was an attempt made to conceal the taking. There was no attempt to avoid contact with any official at the time, and numerous officials, both naval and military, were passed and repassed (*sic*) without comment.

As you are certainly aware, we had no intention of doing anything that would conflict with the laws laid down by the censorial department of the government, and I did not think that such was being done, especially in view of the fact that many military and naval officers saw the actual taking of these pictures.

Yours very truly
W.M. Stuart

of the world and Halifax lies smitten almost to the very heart. But it is bearing its cross of pain with a Christ like fortitude, and from the ashes, the ruins, the agony of the dead, it will rise again supreme to prove that the spirit which has built up the Dominion of Canada and the Empire of Greater Britain is a spirit that disasters cannot crush or calamities subdue.

Halifax has gone through Hades. She will rise, stronger, better, greater and more perfect to the proud position that yet awaits her.[10]

Toronto Daily Star Reporters

> Get there, get the story, get it written, get it on the wire — those were the cardinal principles. Their very essence was speed, but there was a demand for quality of feeling and interpretation.
> — Frederick Griffin, *Toronto Daily Star* staff reporter[1]

Toronto Star city editor Harry Hindmarsh sent two reporters to cover the aftermath of the Explosion.[2] Neither was permitted a byline and to this date their identities remain unknown. The male correspondent arrived in Truro from Ottawa on 9 December 1917 and was in Halifax the next day; by 10 December the paper's woman reporter was also in Halifax.[3] Between 9 and 13 December they sent fifteen despatches to the *Star*: twelve by the male reporter and three by his colleague.[4] As well, in the paper's attempt to provide comprehensive coverage of the event, on 10 December the *Star* also published the 8 December story written for CP by George Yates, on 14 December, Joseph Sheldon's 8/9 December narrative and on 15 December a 10 December account by Stanley Smith. Finally, the paper "issued some ten extra editions."[5]

The following are three despatches wired by the *Star's* male reporter. The first, datelined from Truro, was sent *delayed* on 9 December and appeared in the paper the next day.[6]

Explosion Blew Hair Off Halifax Woman
Men Were Lifted Through The Air Long Distances Without Injury
— Man Seeking Brother Found Only Ruins
— Truro Sorrow Annex To The Capital City

Special to The Star by a Staff Reporter

Truro N.S. Dec. 9 — (Delayed) — Very often the first reports of accidents are much exaggerated. This is not so of the Halifax disaster. The reports grow worse with each new train arrival. Since arriving here a short time ago I have talked to over 20 of the wounded, as well as to many unwounded refugees. All have the same story to tell. "It is terrible beyond words, it is so bad it cannot be exaggerated."

And the trains of passengers other

than wounded are just beginning to get through. Five train crews were killed to almost a man when the railway station was destroyed.

"Were there many burned?" I asked a pale young man leaning against a wall in the fire hall, one of the temporary hospitals here. He had come from Halifax only about an hour ago to visit wounded relatives who were in that building. "Why yes," he replied. "I saw the corpses lying by the side of the street, in what seemed to be hundreds, some with their hands and arms burned off."

The same young man said, "My father saw the collision. He was coming into Halifax on the milk train. The explosion was not for 17 minutes after the ships struck."[7]

Truro Annex of Sorrow

But three days ago Truro was a peaceful little town of some 7,000 inhabitants, somewhat famous as a railway town and the centre of a fairly good agricultural district, pursuing the even tenor of its way. But it is only 62 miles from Halifax. So on Thursday morning the whole town received a shock lasting for some seconds. Women ran to the windows looking for aeroplanes, thinking the Germans had come. Employes (*sic*) from one of the factories fled across the street thinking it was an explosion in their own factory, never dreaming it was over 60 miles away.

Now Truro has become a sorrow annex to Halifax. Its fire hall is no longer just a fire hall. Downstairs are the fire engines, but upstairs are three large rooms filled with homeless people with maimed and wounded children, men and women, 52 people in all. The floors are covered with mattresses about a foot and a half apart. Truro is now building a hospital for the almost 200 wounded

who have come in. Not only the fire hall, but the Academy of Music and courthouse had to be utilized.[8]

Worse Cases Still

"Come with me and I shall take you to the courthouse and the County Academy, the worst cases are there," kindly said Mr. Putman, whose wife is the president of the Red Cross here.

"I have all I can stand for tonight, thank you," was my answer.

Oh those poor cut mangled faces and pale crying little children! One man had his face all the eyes hidden by bandages. His nose had been smashed, his face cut and bruised almost beyond recognition. He was in bed when the accident came. The bed was smashed in and all manner of stuff piled on that.

One woman had her face terribly scalded. She was getting ready to do her washing. The kettle full of boiling water was blown from the stove its contents coming on her face. She had been blown into a corner of her kitchen.

Only Foundation Left

A young woman had her face one mass of cuts and bruises; her eyes were blood-shot. "My name is Dwyer," she said. "We lived opposite Pier 8 on Barrington Street. Just across the railway tracks and right by the water, so near we could hear the sailors calling for help in the water. Our roof blew off and away ever so far. I was pinned between the bureau and windows with broken glass all about me. My brother never got out of the house. He was killed there. My other brother went to find him afterwards but nothing was left only the foundation of the house."

Another woman, Mrs. Driscoll, was sitting on one of the mattresses on the floor. Three pale little children were about her. "One of my little girls, ten years old, was playing on the street when it happened," she paused — "and we have never seen her since."

Nearly all had the same story to tell. "We did not know what had happened, it was so sudden. Of course, we thought the Germans had come."

Blown Clean Through Air

One of the refugees here had almost every hair blown from her head.

Mr. Frank Walsh, clerk, was blown from the A.R. yards right into Musgrave Park, a considerable distance away, and was almost uninjured. There were many other similar cases. One woman told me of relatives blown a good quarter of a mile into the park and only receiving a small cut.

"Could a city so far away as Truro do anything? I know the women there and the whole city would love to help," I said to Mrs. Putman, president of the Red Cross here. "Of course, they can help," was the answer. "There will be lots of money needed. Many of the ruined homes were in the poorest part of the city, now they have nothing.'"[9]

The next day the *Star's* reporter was in Halifax, where he would remain until 13 December. The following are his 10 and 11 December despatches.

Toronto Men Slightly Hurt, But All Escape In Halifax
Lieut. Harold Parkes Was Hurled Through A Solid Wooden Partition — Harris Abattoir Office Four Miles Away Was Badly Smashed Up — B.J. Donovan Thought Howitzer Went Off
Special to The Star by a Staff Reporter

Halifax, N.S., Dec. 10 — Although some of them were in the midst of the explosion not one of the dozen or more Toronto men, mostly representing big business firms here, were seriously injured in the disaster.

Many of them interviewed by The Star at the Queen's Hotel last night told graphic stories of their experiences when the first shock of the explosion was felt.[10]

Mr. B.J. Donovan, whose parents reside at 414 Ossington avenue [in Toronto], is here representing the William Davis Co. "I was in my room in the hotel when the first explosion occurred," he said. "I was thrown in a heap onto the floor and my windows went smash as if a big howitzer had just been discharged from the windowsill. I got up thinking the Germans had really come and rushed to the street. The scene before me then was one I shall never forget. Women and children ran from their houses, their faces streaming with blood and hair dishevelled. It was a pitiful sight. The streets were strewn with glass and masonry and other debris, and in their anxiety to escape from the holocaust people went tumbling over each other in sickening heaps of dead and dying."

Harold Parkes' Lucky Escape

"I then rushed to the dockyards about a mile and a half away to look after my cars. Here the destruction that had been wrought simply baffled description. I picked up two little kiddies on the way and ran with them to the Commons where we were told it would be safer in the event of a second explosion. On the way down I met Harold Parkes, a

Toronto boy, he was all right although he was quite near the explosion. His was a lucky escape."

Door Blown Across Room

Joe L. Aldridge, who rooms at 31 Homewood avenue, when he is in Toronto, was staying in the Queen's hotel during a visit to Halifax on business for his firm, The Gilette Lye Co.

"I was in the basement at the time, the door was simply torn from its hinges and blown right across my back, knocking me down pretty hard, but I was not hurt much." Mr. Aldridge is leaving Halifax for Toronto.

Blown Through Partition

Naval Lieut. Harold Parkes, whose home is on Margueretta street, had a remarkable escape from death. He was on his ship not 100 yards away from the Mont Blanc, when the explosion occurred.

He was lifted bodily and blown several yards clear through a thick wooden partition. His side was badly cut and bruised and required six stitches. Several men around Lieut. Parkes were killed outright. Lieut. Parkes has had many narrow escapes and thrilling experiences. He enlisted in the navy when the war broke out August 4th, 1914, and has seen service in many parts of the world. Twice he was torpedoed, first while on the way to Saloniki when near Hong Kong. "I would certainly rather be torpedoed than have this experience again," he said in answer to The Star. Lieut. Parkes' father is at present in St. John and his mother is on the way south to Florida. He is now permanently stationed in Halifax.

Brother On Star Staff

Mr. Joe Harper, 36B McDonnell avenue, who is examiner of neutral shipping, had his window blown in on him, but he escaped practically uninjured. He has a brother on The Star staff.

Mr. S.W. Levack, of 55 Bousted (*sic*) avenue, was in the act of opening his room door when he was blown back with terrible force, but was fortunate to escape uninjured. The windows of the bedroom were smashed like all the others in the Queen's Hotel. "We are lucky to be alive," he said, glancing at the barricaded windows of his apartment, and recalled with a shudder the fierce blizzard which followed in the wake of the explosion.

Hands Over Supplies

Speaking of the relief work Mr. Levack, who represents the Harris Abattoir, said there was plenty of meat stuffs in the city [and] immediately [after] the distress among the homeless was discovered he handed over to the military authorities twenty-two cars of bacon, butter, etc., which was ready for export and later received permission from his firm to deliver any further cars en route for Halifax. Mr. Levack has been here since September 10.

Smashed Four Miles Away

Mr. F.S. Smiley, of 100 Humberside avenue [in Toronto], another representative of the Harris Abbatoir Company, was four miles from the scene of the explosion at the company's branch office at 18 Mitchell street. The office was badly smashed.

Rev. Huddleston's Church Wrecked

Rev. A.L. Huddleston, pastor of First Baptist Church, and his wife, both Toronto people, who moved here late March are safe.

"I was in the study when the explosion occurred. The windows were smashed, but I escaped with a few scratches."

His church was partially wrecked, and no service will be possible for several weeks.[11]

A City Of Stopped Clocks Keeps Strange, Sad Sunday
Not A Bell Rings Out For Worship, Save Two — People Gather In Temporary Shelters In The Shadow Of Crepe And Coffins And Death
A Sabbath In Golgotha Is Halifax's
Special to The Star by a Staff Reporter

Halifax, Dec. 10 (delayed) — Broken and emotionless, struck dead as it were on the post of duty, stand the hands on the southern face of Halifax town clock pointing like two ghostly fingers to the hour of 9:04 — the hour of the greatest tragedy in the history of Canada. Half the dial on that side is gone. Inside, open to all weathers now, may be seen the mechanism of the great clock itself, broken and motionless too. Dial and hands on the other three sides of the City Hall tower are almost unrecognizable as such. When that blast of death rolled up from Tuft's Cove on the morning of December 6 every public clock in the city was shattered, but that on the Customs House has since been repaired. Other clocks, far removed from the immediate scene of death, stopped dead as if overwhelmed by the immensity of the catastrophe.

In the City Hall itself every window and sky light was blown out. Doors were wrenched from their hinge. Employes (*sic*) were tossed about like leaves. Deputy Chief of Police Northover, as he stood in the corridor near his office, was thrown beneath a falling window and fanlight, but was only slightly bruised.

The big stone building in the heart of the city, with the debris of destruction still strewn on its floors, is to-day a vast clearing house wherein relief committees keep records of the living and the dead, direct the hungry to food and the homeless to shelter, issue transportation and perform a thousand other charities. It is a place made almost sacred by the spirit of helpfulness and self-sacrifice everywhere revealed.

City Officials Suffer

Many of the city fathers have themselves suffered. Ald. J. Goodwin lost his child. Controller J.J. Hines of the Fire Department was prevented only by accident from taking that fatal journey with Fire Chief Condon when the first alarm was turned in.

In the records of duty none surpass those of the Halifax police force. Six out of the 43 regular constables are in the hospital. None have escaped wounds or affliction. Chief Hanrahan and his deputy have scarcely closed an eye since Dec. 6th, but with an atlas weight of responsibility on their shoulders they do not refuse any reasonable service to anyone. A pass from them is safe-conduct through all military lines except in fortified areas.

Shots Were Heard

Police Magistrate Fielding has not convened court since the day of the disaster. Shots were heard yesterday in the devastated area, and wild rumors spread that the American Naval patrol had been forced to deal with looters, but it was only the civil police destroying prowling dogs.

Seven city aldermen, including Fire Chief Condon and Deputy Chief Brunt, have been killed. They met their doom when they responded to the fire alarm that a ship was burning. A team and horse wagon were blown to atoms, but the big motor engine, the only one of its kind in the department, withstood the shock, losing only its fender and moveable parts. Yesterday it was hauled back to the fire station. A new engine ordered by the city has been delayed in transit.[12]

The following are the three despatches written by the *Star's* woman reporter.

Send Them Trucks Instead Of Money
Halifax People Would Like Substitutions Made
Special to The Star by a Woman Staff Reporter

Halifax, Dec. 12 — Halifax is delighted with Toronto's money offer. No more food and clothing are needed at present.

The following is the urgent need. Can you substitute these for the money? Col. Robert Low's order is one dozen Smith (form a) trucks, with shake bodies similar to the ones supplied to Colonel Bob Low at Leaside Camp; one dozen two and three-ton trucks, also experienced chauffeurs and spare parts; three dozen sloop sleighs for hauling; enough double harness, heavy with the breeching necessary on account of the hills, ready for operation.[13]

Committee Rooms Used As Relief Stations — Even Date Almost Forgotten
Special to The Star by a Woman Staff Reporter

Halifax, Dec. 13 — One week ago to-day men talked of the election about the street corners of Halifax. Some were against Union, Halifax had not to wait for an election to bring Union. Sorrow has brought it and sympathy.

Four days I have been here and never heard an election mentioned until this morning at the hotel breakfast table. One man asked another in a dazed, abstracted way, as though, he had just remembered it, "What day is election day?"

"Help" replied the other, "is all Canada should think of now. We cannot think of politics with 25,000 of our people homeless and suffering and mourning all about us."

Last week the respective candidates, except Mr. MacLean, left to conduct a series of meetings along the eastern shore, and all were in a country village in the eastern shore district when news of the explosion arrived. At first it was thought that it was only a minor affair, and all the candidates addressed meetings on Thursday evening. When fuller details of the catastrophe were learned, however, Mayor Martin and his friends left at once for the stricken city, taking over forty hours to reach their destination, only some thirty miles distant, because of the blinding blizzard which swept the countryside during their journey.

Although the political machine is in

a quiescent state and the headquarters of the candidates have been converted into relief stations, no preparations for the election have been cancelled. The indications are that even amid the horrors of death, human misery and suffering an election fiasco will be held — a melancholy contest in which coffins will pile higher than ballot boxes.[14]

Halifax Like Vimy Ridge

Chaplain Home For Rest Suffers In Disaster — Found In Hospital By His Major

Special to The Star by a Woman Reporter

Halifax, Dec. 14 — Major Rudland, recently returned from overseas seeking rest, as well as his chaplain, Father Thornton, compares the appearance of the explosion swept district with its snowy ridges to Vimy Ridge.

Much to the major's surprise he finds Father Thornton in hospital a sufferer from the disaster.[15]

Eldred Archibald, *Montreal Star*

> The editors of newspapers, the heads of the great relief organizations, none of those who are in a position to be the most accurately informed will even guess at the loss of life or property. It is a cataclysm.
> — Eldred Archibald, *Montreal Star* staff correspondent, 8 December 1917

Born in Dickson's Landing, Ontario on 18 October 1881, Eldred Archibald attended Clinton High School and in 1905 graduated with a BA from University of Toronto. He joined the *Toronto Star* and in April 1912 reported the United States Senate's investigation of *Titanic's* sinking. In 1917 he joined the *Montreal Star* and eventually became an editorial writer and the paper's executive editor. Archibald died in Saint-Lambert, Quebec, on 16 February 1958.

Archibald arrived in Halifax on 8 December 1917 and remained in the city until 12 December.[1] During this time he wired six despatches. The following are his stories of 8, 10 and 11 December.

Citizens Dazed By Calamity

Special to The Star from our Staff Correspondent

Halifax, Dec. 8 — The old city of Halifax is dazed with a sense of appalling immeasurable calamity. Ask any citizen of Halifax today and he will shrug his shoulders and say, hopelessly, "I don't know." The editors of newspapers, the heads of the great relief organizations, none of those who are in a position to be the most accurately informed will even guess at the loss of life or property.[2] It is a cataclysm.

Last night the stricken city was in the grip of a driving "north-easter." The wild weather the Atlantic Coast winter can produce and a thick pall of snow covered the black ruins of the north end. Trains were late and relief work was impeded, but, fortunately, thanks to the whole-hearted hospitality of the people, none of the survivors from the ruined portion of the city faced the wild weather without shelter. Every private residence in Halifax was opened to those who had lost house and home.

Loss Falls Heaviest Upon Children

There is not a single building in the city that has not suffered damage from the tremendous explosion. There is hardly a home indeed, that is not in mourning. The estimate of dead runs all the way from 1,500 to 2,000; the roster of injured is up to the 5,000 mark. No attempt has been made seriously to estimate the financial loss, but it will run to many millions. A finance committee of citizens last night estimated that from $25,000,000 to $30,000,000 would be required for immediate relief.

The extent of the loss cannot be known for many days, perhaps will never be known, for fire swept the area affected chiefly by the explosion, and wiped out the wreck of hundreds of buildings. But it is a sad fact that the loss falls heaviest on the children. Whole schools, filled with pupils, were demolished, leaving but one or two survivors. In many other schools every single pupil was injured by splintered glass.

To-day Halifax is a city of hospitals and morgues. Telegrams are pouring in from all parts of America asking for information concerning persons believed to have been in the city at the time of the disaster.

Every train brings its quota of relatives racked with suspense for some loved ones. The hotels are crowded with sad-faced seekers. Everywhere there is devastation, everywhere mourning.

Force Of Explosion Appalling

It is probable that there has never been an explosion of such force, even in the war zone. To begin with, the vessel contained 4,000 tons of the highest explosives known, three times as powerful as fulminate. A powder expert has since reckoned that had the cargo had a solid foundation under it there would have not been a live cat or rat left. Debris from shells, steel plates, and shrapnel have been found within a five mile radius within an area of ten square miles.

Something about the scope of the explosion has already been reported.

At Orangedale, Cape Breton, 150 miles distant in an airline, and at Sydney, 200 miles away, the shock was that of a severe earthquake. At Truro, sixty-two miles distant, the windows of the Learmont Hotel were broken and the clock was shaken from the walls of the train despatcher's walls.

Two American vessels were making port, one, a cruiser was forty five [nautical miles] miles off Halifax, and when the shock came the chief officer believed that his ship had struck a mine. Then, seeing another vessel on the horizon, he concluded that he had been fired on.[3]

Tour Of City Shows Appalling Nature Of Catastrophe

Special to The Star from our Staff Correspondent

Halifax, Dec. 10 — The scene of the area most affected by the disaster is one of appalling desolation. Sir Robert made a tour through the ill-fated north end Saturday morning, and the Prime Minister was deeply shocked by the scenes he encountered. The heavy fall of snow had softened the aspect to some extent, but it rendered doubly difficult the work of hundreds of soldiers who are engaged in picking over the ruins in search of the dead. As Sir Robert passed along the desolate streets several bodies were taken from the wreckage and laid by the roadside, tarpaulins being thrown over them pending the arrival of vehicles to take them to the morgue.

An area over two miles in extent is absolutely wiped out. The buildings were shaken down, and for the most part burned up later. Beginning at the scene of the actual explosion, the whole water front is practically wiped out. Four piers are ruined, and in fact wiped out of existence. These are piers 6, 7, 8 and 9.[4]

At the spot where one of these piers stood, a large freighter is aground, having been carried up by the tidal wave that followed the explosion. The twisted and shattered prow of a vessel, probably that of the Mont Blanc, the ill-fated munition ship that caused the disaster, remains to mark the former location of pier 8.[5] Fortunately, the new pier 2, part of the great terminal scheme remains intact, so that shipping operations can be carried on without undue interruption.

Railway Yards Wrecked

The railway yards extending from the ruins of the north station are a mass of wreckage, although on Saturday afternoon two tracks were laid up to the old station site to allow of trains entering. The station building itself is largely in ruins. The railway loss in men was tremendous, as was the loss in rolling stock already described in The Star.

Of a gang of 75 special men working in the city on Thursday, only ten have so far been accounted for. Fifteen yardmen were at work in the Richmond yards at the time and all but one were killed. Mr. Graham, manager of the Dominion Atlantic, was in the station when the explosion occurred. His wife and daughter were in a private car in a part of the station where the roof did not collapse, and escaped death by a veritable miracle. Mr. Graham himself jumped on a yard engine and backed out to Rockingham station, from which he sent to the outside world the first news of the catastrophe. On the way through the yards he passed the bodies of between sixty and seventy men.

Back through the so-called Richmond district and the rest of the north end the scene is one of indescribable horror. The whole district has been laid flat, an absolute desert. It is not possible in many cases to identify the places where dwellings stood. It is hard to believe that here, prior to last Thursday morning, was the home of a large population. Debris, charred and twisted, is piled everywhere, blocking many of the streets. On the roads are bodies of horses, killed by the explosion, and the twisted remnants of automobiles. Here and there, even now, may be seen dead bodies, hastily covered. On the day of the disaster the dead were lying about in the streets in all postures.

Even when found it was extremely doubtful whether many of these bodies can ever be identified. The fire has wiped out possibility of identification. The clothing has been stripped from many even the flesh from the bones. One body was pronounced to be that of a soldier from the fact that it bore the remnant of a khaki shirt.

The heavy storm of wet snow, freezing hard on the ground, has rendered extremely difficult the work of recovering the bodies. It will in many cases be days before the entire area can be searched over. It may be next spring before the last of the dead are found. Nobody here believes it possible ever to get the full roster of the dead. There will be many in the missing column. In many cases charred trunks alone are found. In some cases arms and legs are dug out of the wreckage.[6]

Halifax Sufferers In Sheltered Places Now And Relief Organized

Looters Will Be Shot — Arrests Of Germans Continue — All Necessary Supplies For Immediate Requirements Now To Hand — More Searchers Of Ruins Are Required, However

Special to The Star from our Staff Correspondent

Halifax, N.S., Dec. 11 — The ghastly ruins of the explosion swept area at Richmond are still yielding up their dead. The grim work of the searchers went steadily on during yesterday until the furious blasts of a blizzard made further effort impossible.

Up to last night 720 bodies had been recovered, and although many believed that the earlier estimates of the casualties will be reached when the whole devastated area is raked, Mr. Barnstead, chairman of the mortuary committee, estimated that the loss of life will not exceed 1,200 or 1,500. The wounded will run into the thousands, so that the estimate of 5,000 casualties, dead and injured, will probably be found to be not far astray when the final tally is made.

Mortuary Work Well Organized

There are at present 280 bodies at the Chebucto school mortuary. Some of these have been identified, but there is still a large number unidentified. The work is now under the supervision of Prof. R.W. Stone and A. Schrelter, who have been sent here by the city of Toronto to assist in looking after the dead, and they have been appointed mortuary supervisor and assistant. Since their arrival they have done splendid work.

At Chebucto school mortuary the rooms have been cleaned up and bodies placed in order and numbered. A number of those who have been identified have been taken away by relatives. Of each identified person, a survey of the remains has been made and all the effects taken account of. These facts are included in a list, which can be seen by anyone visiting the mortuary in search of missing relatives or friends.

Hope To Find More Living

The finding as late as yesterday afternoon of living persons buried in the ruins of the Halifax North End has caused a sensation in the city. There is the disquieting feeling that were there sufficient men to go over the entire devastated area, thoroughly and quickly, a number would yet be found.

The situation in Halifax as regards the building of houses one thing greatly in favor is the so-called basement kitchen, in which the housewives performed most of their tasks. It has been in these basement kitchens that the living have been found the last two days.

Of firm construction, and below the level of the ground, these kitchens have in many cases resisted the shock, and while the ruins of the houses are heaped over them, the space within remains. Not only protection from the flying debris, but warmth as well is afforded.

The force at present engaged in searching the ruins is wholly inadequate and as Col. R.S. Low pointed out today, the men are jaded as is almost every man in Halifax, as a result of many nervous shocks and ceaseless labor since the explosion. A trainload of soldiers coming here from Toronto to help was turned back yesterday at Truro, but it is felt by many that they should have been allowed to come through and take up a part of the work.[7]

Chapter 4

Visiting American Journalists and the Aftermath

> But words are things, and a small drop of ink, falling like dew
> upon a thought, produces that which makes thousands, perhaps,
> millions think.
>
> — Lord Byron, *Don Juan*

During the early hours of 8 December 1917 five American journalists arrived in Halifax on the first Boston relief train.[1] They were Anthony Philpott, *Boston Daily Globe*, Jerome Keating, *Boston Herald-Journal*, Roy Atkinson, *Boston Post*, Richard Sears, *Boston American*, and Richard Simpson, Associated Press. Within hours Prime Minister Borden arranged accommodation for them at the Halifax Club; some remained in Halifax for up to a week.[2] Given they were Boston-based colleagues, travelled on the same relief train for two days, were accommodated collectively and shared the same assignment, they in fact constituted a press club. On 9 December internationally famous photojournalist and war correspondent James "Jimmy" Hare of *Leslie's Weekly* arrived in Halifax from Long Island, New York, and the next day a *Providence Journal/Bulletin* staff correspondent arrived on board the Rhode Island relief train.

Why so many Boston journalists? First, Boston was the nearest major American metropolis to the disaster. Second, Boston's daily newspapers had large enough budgets to send reporters on assignment to Halifax. Third, the ties between Massachusetts and Nova Scotia were profound and filial with approximately 45,000 Nova Scotians, excluding their children, living in Massachusetts in 1917.[3] Readers in Boston and Massachusetts therefore had a special interest in the Explosion and the city editors of the *Boston Globe, Post, Herald-Journal* and bureau chief of Boston AP capitalized on this knowledge by providing credential letters for their correspondents to the public safety and state guard commission on the relief train.[4] Hare was sent to Halifax by *Leslie's* to obtain material for photo-stories, and the *Providence Journal/Bulletin's* reporter was sent to provide news of the disaster and learn the fate of 150 families in Halifax with relatives in Rhode Island.[5]

Besides the Boston reporters, Hare and the *Providence Journal/Bulletin* correspondent, no other known American journalists were sent to Halifax to cover the disaster's aftermath.[6] Reasons for this included the challenge of reaching Halifax by train due to severe winter weather conditions in Nova Scotia between 6 and 10 December, low staff levels and financial impediments for many newspapers while the war was in progress, and the presence in Halifax of Associated Press reporter Richard Simpson, whose despatches could be taken off the AP wire by most American newspapers.[7]

Anthony Philpott, *Boston Globe*

Born in Ireland in November 1862, Anthony Philpott was a member of the *Globe* for fifty-nine years, serving as reporter, desk editor, art editor and feature writer. Prior to joining the editorial staff of the paper in 1893, he worked on dailies in Philadelphia, Chicago and New York. For his fund-raising efforts for Belgian relief during World War I he was decorated by King Albert of Belgium. Philpott died "in harness" at age ninety on 29 February 1952.[1]

While en route to Halifax on 6 December, fifty-five year-old Philpott wired two despatches to the *Globe*; once in Halifax he sent five more.[2]

Relief Train Plans 22-Hour Run To Halifax
By A.J. Philpott

Portsmouth, NH — On board Relief Train for Halifax, Dec. 6 — The relief train from Boston, speeding toward Halifax tonight, is expected to reach Halifax in 22 hours.

The regular run is 27 hours. All tracks have been cleared for this train. In addition to the relief workers on board, the train carries four railroad men and five newspapermen.

Mrs. William H. Lothrop, head of the Red Cross civilian relief, mustered the entire party over the phone during the afternoon.

W. Frank Perons of the Red Cross War Council at Washington ordered the New England division of the Red Cross to take up the Halifax work. Another train will follow in the morning with supplies

The first train will be used as the headquarters of the party in Halifax.[3]

Halifax Horror Grows As Details Are Learned
By A.J. Philpott

Amherst, N.B. (*sic*) On Board Red Cross Relef Train From Massachusetts, 7 P.M. Dec. 7 — As the train progresses into Canada the horror of the situation at Halifax seems to grow, especially since the stop at St. John N.B. where refugees had already arrived from the stricken city.

In fact, a few moments after the relief train rolled into the station a train came in from Truro carrying 50 or more persons from Halifax, some with heads bandaged, others limping with canes, but none who were seriously injured. And few of these could talk of the horror they had left.

Survivors Dazed

One would say the whole city is destroyed; another that the dead are everywhere on the streets and that there are 25,000 injured in the city.[4]

Lieut. Col Good of the Canadian Army, who arrived in Halifax on a train about 10 minutes after the explosion, said that it was worse than any battlefield in Flanders. He never put in such a night. He and all the other people on the train began rescue work at the North-st (*sic*) station and the district around the station.

They broke into houses in which they heard people groaning or screaming and found the people either huddled together in terror or prostrate and wounded and many dead.

They quickly filled two sleeping cars with wounded women and children and had them taken to a hospital. He said all of the hospitals and available public buildings are overflowing with the wounded.

Storm Fells Wires

What has made the situation worse even than it should be is the terrible storm that prevailed all over Nova Scotia for days before the catastrophe.

The storm had already paralyzed the telegraph and telephone systems in and around Halifax, and the explosion completed the ruin, and also paralyzed the street railways and wrecked some of the steam roads.[5]

It also wrecked the gaslighting (*sic*) so that the type machines could not be worked in the newspaper offices.[6]

And finally, besides wrecking more than two square miles of the city it shattered practically every pane of glass in the city. The demand for window glass is so great that Mr. Ratshesky wired from St John for an immediate supply of glass, putty and beaver board.

Calls Aid A Godsend

At every station since we left St John the crowds were out to see the relief train go by.

At Moncton the American consul, Mr. Richardson, boarded the train with a number of railroad officials. He said the people of Halifax would consider the relief train a veritable godsend.

One of the railroad officials brought a message from General Manager Hayes of the Canadian Government railways at Halifax to Mr. Ratshesky asking that another Red Cross train be sent from Boston at once, as there is great need of medical supplies, blankets and clothes.

Sergt Robert Arseneault of the Royal School of Infantry boarded the train at Moncton. He was in Halifax when the explosion occurred in 45 Wellington barracks. A sergeant, a bandman and two corporals were killed. Many were injured. He was unhurt. He was engaged in relief work all through the day and evening and he saw some terrible sights.

Hugs Headless Babe

One mother had walked around for hours with her baby wrapped up in a shawl in her arms. The baby was taken from her. It was found to be headless.

Some of the stories that are told are too terrible to repeat.

At Fredericton earlier in the day, Mrs. F.H. Sexton, vice president of the Provincial Red Cross, asked to be taken on the relief train to Halifax. She was welcomed and her knowledge of the situation has made it possible for John F. Moors to make his plans for relief.

Mr. Moors has been notified from Washington to take entire charge of Red Cross work in Halifax. He had charge of the Red Cross work in San Francisco, Chelsea and Salem. With him are C.C. Carstens, William Pear, W. Prentiss (*sic*) Murphy and Katharine MacMahon.

Mr. Moors believes that the first thing that will be required after the hospital work is attended to is the matter of promptly providing warm clothing and shelter for the homeless population. James Jackson, manager of the New England division of the Red Cross, notified Mr. Moors at Moncton that another relief train was being forwarded from Boston.

Doctors Board Train

The surgeons on the train, under Maj. Giddings, added materially to their stocks of medical supplies at St John. Four additional surgeons and six nurses were taken on the train at St John.

Mr. Ratshesky, in charge of the train, is receiving telegrams at every station from Halifax, from railway officials and from military officials, all urging haste and thanking Gov. McCall and the Red Cross for the relief.

We had one hot box delay of about an hour beyond Moncton. The snow is falling very heavily. A man who was in the North-st station at Halifax described the explosion as something that sounded like "the crack of doom."

The first refugees to arrive at St John consisted of a group of eight girls, students from the Mount St Vincent Academy. They were all slightly injured.

To Work As Unit

All of the surgeons and physicians on the relief train are in the uniform of the Massachusetts State Guard. Dr. Peter O'Shea of Worcester rode in an automobile from that city to catch the train. He caught it.

Maj. Giddings has just announced that Mr. Ratshesky has wired the Governor General and the Mayor of Halifax for permission to work as a unit and that he expects a favorable reply.

Mr. Ratshesky, addressing the physicians and nurses, said that Gov. McCall expected all present to uphold the honor of the State of Massachusetts.

Maj. Giddings said there had been an epidemic of measles in Halifax before the explosion and an unusual number of cases of pneumonia.

The doctors on the relief train are: Dr. E.A. Supple, Dr. E.F. Murphy, Dr. John W. Dewis, Dr. Donald Baker, Dr. Harold G. Giddings, in charge of surgeons and physicians; Dr. Robert G. Loring, Dr. George M. Morse, Dr. Dewitt G. Wilcox, Dr. Thomas F. Harrington, Dr. Peter O'Shea, Dr. Nathaniel Morse.

The nurses are: Elizabeth S. Fedeen (*sic*), in charge; Charlotte J. Naismith, Marion Nevers (*sic*), Florence MacInnis (*sic*), Jessie MacInnis (*sic*), Mary Davidson, Caroline Carlton, Nellie Black, Edith Perkins, Elizabeth Choate.

The Red Cross officials are: John F. Moors, Katharine MacMahon (*sic*), Marion Rowe, C.C. Carstens (*sic*), William Pear, W. Prentiss (*sic*) Murphy.

The Governor's committee consists of A.C. Ratshesky, Capt. B.D. Hyde; Capt. H.G. Lapham.

The railway officials are: C.F (*sic*) Sturdee of the C.P.R., G.V. Worthen of the B. & M. and G.R. (*sic*) Howard of the C.G.R.[7]

Second Relief Train Arrives

Borden Praises Work Of Bay State Party
10,000 Tons Of High Explosives At Halifax Damaged

By A.J. Philpott

With Massachusetts Committee, Halifax, N.S. Dec. 9 — The Red Cross train from Massachusetts and Maine with 40 doctors and more than 100 nurses and orderlies, arrived in Halifax in charge of Roger Wolcott at 3 p.m.

The train, the second from Massachusetts, was met by A.C. Ratshesky and headquarters was established at once in the Church of England Institute beside the City Club on Barrington st. St. Mary's College on Quinpool road has been turned over to this unit for a hospital and it will be equipped with 350 beds.

In the unit were 25 doctors and 65 nurses from Massachusetts, the balance being from Maine, in charge of Gen. George McL. Presson. Besides medical supplies of all kinds they brought about 8000 blankets which were much needed.

The people of Halifax, who have been deeply impressed by the work of Massachusetts, were further cheered by a telegram which Mr. Ratshesky received from Henry B. Endicott announcing that the steamer Calvin Austin would be sent at once with Collector Billings, a corps of glaziers and engineers and a supply of glass and putty with which to repair some of the damage done by the explosion.

Wholesale Smashing Of Glass

It is estimated that $3,000,000 worth of window glass was broken in the city in less than two minutes. The breaking of this glass resulted in more damage to eyes and faces than any other feature of the explosion.

The reason for this was that there were two explosions about a minute apart. The first one caused the city to shake, but broke very little glass in the section outside of Richmond.[8]

People naturally rushed to their windows in houses and stores and office buildings and were caught in their faces close to the glass when the second explosion came and smashed practically every window in the city and with such force even three miles away as to topple people over.

Then the streets were filled at once with people whose faces were steaming with blood, and the result is that there are probably more eye casualties in the city than any other kind. Many of them are horrible, especially in the cases of children whose faces were pressed close to the window panes.

Morgues Filled With Bodies

The Massachusetts physicians say they never saw anything like the awful character of some of the eye casualties.

Soldiers who have been in the trenches on the Western front say that the face wounds seen there were, as a rule, very mild compared with the wounds they have seen in the hospitals here and the hospitals are all crowded, as are the hospitals of the nearby towns and cities.

More than 500 were sent to Truro

and of these eight have died. The morgues are filled to overflowing with unrecognizable bodies and more are coming from the ruins in Richmond at the north side of the city every moment.

There was a terrible rainstorm last night, but the weather has moderated, and a good deal of the snow has been melted, making it easier for the hundreds of men who are working in the devastated district.

Premier Borden has been directing much of the work the past two days, and he has been deeply affected by the work which Massachusetts has done.[9]

He dined with Mr. Ratshesky and John F. Moors at the home of Gov. Grant, and with Mayor Martin and other officials. He expressed a wish to see the Bellevue Hospital, which was prepared and outfitted by the Massachusetts committee inside of 24 hours.

Premier Borden In Tears

Tears streamed down the Premier's face as he went through the hospital and recognized many of the inmates. He shook hands with all of them and took the babies, of whom there are about 25 in this hospital, in his arms and kissed them.

He turned to Mr. Ratshesky and thanked him, saying that it seemed unbelievable that such a complete hospital should have been whipped into shape in so short a time.

The physicians under Dr. Harold F. Giddings have been working night and day since they have been here, and have besides the hospital work, done a large out-patient work. Dr. Barker was called out of his bed at 2 this morning to perform an urgent surgical operation.

These physicians in the khaki uniforms of the Massachusetts Home Guard, have made a deep impression on Halifax. Among the nurses under Miss Edem, Miss Elizabeth Choate, daughter of Charles F. Choate, famous Boston attorney, is one of the hardest workers, but every one of these nurses has been doing heroic work. Friday afternoon and night they aided in the Pine [*sic* and Hill] Camp Hospital, where there are more than 200 patients.

Estimate Dead At 3000

According to estimates of those in charge of the work in the devastated district, at least 3000 are dead.[10] Several hundred bodies were recovered today.

The deaths are confined to the old, native population of Halifax in Richmond, mostly working men and mechanics and their families. One of the oldest colored free communities on the American continent is just beyond Richmond, on the edge of Bedford Basin, and suffered very little damage, with few casualties.

Admiral Chambers R.N., commander of the fleet at Halifax, told Sir Robert Borden today how the entire crew of a pinnace from one warship, except one man, lost their lives in an attempt to save the Belgian relief ship Imo from destruction. The warship was only a mile away, around a bend in the harbour, when the crash occurred.[11]

The pinnace was sent to the assistance of the Imo and was towing her toward the Dartmouth shore when the explosion occurred.[12] One member of the crew of 10 men in the pinnace was picked up alive, but hasn't recovered sufficiently to answer any questions. The huge wave caused by the explosion washed the Imo ashore on the Dartmouth side, where she lies a wreck. The warship escaped injury.

Bad as the situation is in Halifax, and strange as it may seem, it might have been worse, for it was only by a miracle that some 10,000 tons of high explosives which at the time were not much more than a mile distant escaped.

An official of the Department of Munitions told the writer today that if this mass of high explosives had been affected Halifax would have been wiped off the map.[13]

On 16 December the *Globe* ran Philpott's final despatch from Halifax.

Second Explosion Wrecked Halifax
Globe Man Explains Why Two Blasts Occurred After Crash In Harbor
By A.J. Philpott

The idea that the explosion of the French munitions Mont Blanc in Halifax Harbor was due to a plot, that it was plotted by Germans or German emissaries, was naturally prevalent in Halifax and in Canada generally until the investigation by the Government had begun.

Since then, however, it has become more and more apparent that the crash was the result of an accident.

Another thing about which there is much mystery and on which the investigation had shed light is: why there should have been two explosions — one about 30 seconds after the other.[14] It was the second explosion that did the real damage.

Pilot's Nervousness Fatal

I went to Halifax for the Globe with the first Massachusetts relief party and interviewed C.H. Henry, counsel for the Canadian Government in the investigation. He is a noted legal maritime expert in Halifax.[15]

After studying the main facts which Mr. Henry has obtained from a variety of sources it is reasonably clear that the crash was due to the momentary nervousness of the two pilots who were very much in the position of two men walking toward one another, neither one of whom is certain which way the other wants to pass, until finally they bump into each other.[16]

The Mont Blanc was going up the narrowest part of the harbour, merely a channel at the particular point or about 300 yards wide, when the Belgian relief ship Imo came out of the Bedford Basin, into which the Mont Blanc was going for anchorage. The captain of the Mont Blanc signalled that he was going to keep to starboard and the captain of the Imo signalled that he was going to keep to starboard, which is according to pilotage rules. In other words the vessels have to keep to the right.[17]

Swings To Avoid Shore

At the moment the Mont Blanc signalled she was pointed out slightly to port to avoid a bend on the shore, but to make the position clearer to the Imo, the Mont Blanc steered a little more to starboard.

Pilot Mackay (*sic*) on the Mont Blanc, however, brought the Mont Blanc back a little to port as he did not wish to get too close to the shore, where the current runs strong.

This second pointing of the Mont Blanc to port, slight as it was, confused Pilot Hays (*sic*) on the Imo and he concluded that the Mont Blanc was going to cross to the Halifax shore, so he headed in toward the Dartmouth shore a little and both boats were then head on toward each other and only 300 yards apart.[18]

The pilot of the Mont Blanc then

signalled his engines to stop and he went a little more to port to avoid a crash.

The Imo signalled to reverse, but as she was light and without freight she swung on the reverse slightly to starboard — that is to her right coming down.

Benzol Casks Broken

The vessels were practically on each other then, but the pilot of the Mont Blanc put the helm hard aport so as to catch the blow on the starboard side as far as possible.

The crash was not a severe one, but it crashed in far enough to break some of the benzol steel casks on the forward deck which ran into the forward hold where the picric acid is stowed.

The picric acid flamed up and a great cloud of smoke issued from the Mont Blanc.

The captain of the Mont Blanc ordered all hands to take to the boats and flee to the Dartmouth shore. This was accomplished in about 10 minutes and [in the next 7 minutes] all hands ran through the woods to a depression in the hill.[19]

In the meantime the headway on the Mont Blanc was sufficient to keep her moving in a diagonal line toward the Halifax side.

The Imo tried to back to the Dartmouth shore, but the current was against her and she couldn't make it.[20] A pinnace from one of the British warships tried to help her but without avail, and this effort cost the crew of the pinnace their lives, all but one.[21]

About the time the Mont Blanc reached Pier 8, on the Halifax side,[22] the fire and heat in the picric acid compartment was so intense that it exploded the T.N.T., in the next compartment. A thick steel bulkhead was between both compartments, but the steel yielded to the heat.

Two Explosions Caused

There was not a great quantity of T.N.T. in the second compartment, however, and the explosion though loud, only damaged the buildings on the water front in the vicinity.[23]

But the shock was great enough to break the second and third compartments. In the latter compartment was most of the T.N.T. and in less than 30 seconds this exploded and then disaster broke loose for Halifax.

The people rushed to the windows after the first explosion and were close to the windows when the second explosion came and broke practically every pane of glass in the city, hence all the face and eye injuries.

The scene which followed the second explosion beggars description. People rushed from the houses and stores in the part of the city not actually wrecked by the explosion and ran about with faces from which blood was streaming and with terror in their eyes.

Smoke Cloud Over City

A pall of smoke hung over the city, buildings were falling, fires were breaking out all over the devastated district of Richmond where the houses were levelled, and for a half-hour the people were almost crazed with terror.

Then something happened which has never been described. A cry was started and ran through the city that a magazine near Richmond was about to explode and the people all started to run to the Commons and the citadel.[24] The city was quickly depopulated of all that could move and there in the parks and in the snow these thousands of people stood, many of them wounded and bleeding, for nearly two hours. Then it became noised among them that the danger had passed and they returned to the city, nervous, to take up the thread of their lives in a city that had been wrecked in less than a minute on one of the finest December mornings ever known in Halifax.[25]

Richard Simpson, Associated Press

Born in 1875, Richard Simpson served as city editor of the *Richmond* [Virginia] *Times* and editor of the *Greenville* [South Carolina] *News* and *Raleigh* [North Carolina] *Evening Times*. After joining Associated Press he represented the wire service in the White House during the administrations of Presidents Wilson, Harding and Coolidge. Following World War II he left Washington and worked for the *Virginian Pilot* and *Tampa Tribune*. Simpson retired in 1947 and died in Pasadena, California, on 31 May 1953.[1]

On 8 December forty-two year-old Simpson joined other American and Canadian reporters on a tour of the devastated Richmond district. His bylined story of the experience was published in the *Halifax Chronicle* on 10 December.[2]

Richmond District Worse Than Battle Fields Of France

By The Associated Press Correspondent

Through roads three feet deep in snow a correspondent of the Associated Press on Saturday [8 December] went over a strip of Halifax more utterly demolished than any section of Belgium or France. The ruin is complete. The Richmond district in the North End extends along the Narrows, a channel rightly named. It was in these waters that the French munition ship Mont Blanc, inward bound with a Government pilot aboard, was rammed amidship by the Norwegian steamer Imo, proceeding outward with a cargo for the relief of the Belgians.[3]

How this crash, not of itself serious, ripped open tanks of benzene on the deck that trickled down to the engine room and started a blaze that wrecked part of Halifax, never will be explained to the satisfaction of the people here, still dazed by the horror of it.[4] But the giant blast that came when tons of high explosives sent a wild roar far out to sea, shook the very foundation of an area of two and a half square miles and stripped it bare.

No Chance Of Escape

Nearly every house in the district fell with a crash. In nearly all of these fires started, and men, women and children — mostly children — were crushed to death or mangled under debris which a moment later was a roaring flame. There was no chance of escape. The horror surrounding the burning to death of hundreds who were unable to move is realized here but this town has not yet awakened to the enormous loss of life. Estimates of fifteen hundred dead accepted heretofore as high, seem far below the mark after traveling over the Richmond district, where the brunt of the blow fell.

Some idea of the powerful havoc of

the explosion was gained as the correspondent viewed scores of trees, burly of trunk, that literally were snapped in two, ten feet from the ground. Big brick structures frame (*sic*), but it was in these modest dwellings that the greatest loss of life occurred.

School Children Caught

Fortunately it happened before hundreds of children had gathered at the big school in the heart of the district, which was wrecked.[5] But most of these same youngsters were caught while playing about their homes.

The steamer Mont Blanc, a name never to be forgotten here, lies across the stretch of water from the section it laid low, a crumbled blackened heap landing.[6] Nearby, hard on the beach where it was driven by the explosion, lies the crippled relief ship, and nearer still the Canadian cruiser Niobe stands with no apparent sign of damage. Other, and smaller hulks, offer mute evidence of the disaster, while fourteen hundred freight cars on the waterfront were burned to the base.[7]

All over this wide area the story is the same. There is a sloping hill that runs down to the water and at the top a church still stands, with every window gone, its walls cracked, and its steeple leaning like the tower of Pisa.[8] Around and about on every side are the black and charred ruins where most of the congregation live. Further to the edge of the devastated area another church escaped, but every window frame was ripped out clean.

It was almost impossible to make progress over the streets because of the great drifts of snow. It lay deep upon the wreckage and tonight it had turned to a solid mass of ice that defied the attempt of searchers to dig with picks.

How long it will take this ice to thaw nobody knows. In any other time the blizzard yesterday would have caused as much suffering as any here in years, but coming on top of the great disaster it simply stunned the thousands of volunteers, not personally afflicted, and demoralized all effort for concerted searching. Even the sunshine, which had brought some comfort, failed to bring relief, for a cold north wind chilled the bone of men and women.

Will Never Be Found

And that one thing may account for the high loss of life, without one finding of bodies to bear out an estimate of four thousand dead.[9] They will never be found. There was no accurate census of the population of Richmond district. Families came and went and when an entire family was lost there was no one left to search the ruins and the long columns of names printed in the papers here. The Halifax man who has not looked upon that (*sic*) can no more approximate the death toll than the Boston man. Picture two and one half square miles of homes torn down by an explosion and then left to the fury of the flames, and the persons a thousand miles away can grasp its meaning.

There are dismantled buildings in the rows of streets that have not yet been dragged. The walls lean at dangerous angles, and window blinds, coated with ice, kept up an all day flapping as the wind swept through. There are piles and piles of ruins that no available force at present here can clear away in weeks. Not much will be found to help solve the maddening riddle as to the number gone.

Snow Covered Tents

Going out from the business section the newspaper correspondents obtained the first vivid impression in passing a wide snow-covered park with six hundred tents in which part of the homeless were being supplied with food and heat.[10] There were not houses enough to shelter them, but the fact stands out that while the city was stunned on Thursday [6 December], it provided quarters for every person in distress. The tent quarters were comfortable without doubt.

Between the tented park and Richmond district are the morgues. A four storey school building, badly damaged by the jar, is the main morgue into which hundreds tramped today in search of the missing.[11] But the view was heart-breaking to those who feared the worst, for the bodies burned and blackened to such an extent that the only chance of identification lay in the possible finding of a trinket. Of the three hundred in this morgue more than fifty bodies had been claimed tonight. One thousand have been recovered.

Estimates Of The Dead

Various reports regarding large numbers killed in certain buildings have been accepted generally as correct. Many of the injured died at relief stations, while being removed to hospitals, and elsewhere. Heretofore it has been more or less guesswork, but the officer in charge of the morgues fixed four thousand as the number, this being based upon reports from officers, who had made a general survey of the burned section.[12]

With everything burned under the snow, the search today was delayed, while the main forces were devoting attention to the injured. All vehicles have been commandeered. An aged man on his way to search for his wife was held up and the pung taken from him.[13] An officer explained in a kindly way that it was a life and death matter to take care of the wounded. Without protest he gave up the rig. This merely illustrates the wonderful spirit of the entire community. Guards stood all around the ruined part of Halifax, but this was form rather than for fact.

"There never is any looting in Halifax in time of trouble like this," the authorities announced today in disposing of inquiries concerning looting.[14] There has been absolutely none here."[15]

R.W. Simpson

Jerome Keating, *Boston Herald-Journal*

Jerome Keating was born on 20 December 1887 in Fitchburg, Massachusetts. He began his journalistic career as a reporter for Boston papers, including the *Boston Herald-Journal*. After moving to New York City he worked as a copy editor on the *New York World* and *New York Post*. In 1934 he became the *New York Times*'s national news copy editor, a position he held until retirement in 1962. Keating died in New York City on 7 March 1974.[1]

While in Halifax, thirty-year-old Keating sent several despatches to his paper.[2] The most significant story provided a description of events leading up to and following the Explosion by *Mont-Blanc*'s Captain Le Médec on 10 December. Considering Le Médec had already filed an official Note of Protest and would soon testify at the Wreck Commissioner's Inquiry, one explanation for his 10 December statement was to counter the public's growing discontent towards him and Pilot Francis Mackey.[3] Keating's despatch containing Le Médec's statement was published in the *Herald-Journal* on 11 December and picked up by American as well as Canadian newspapers.[4]

Says Something Wrong On Imo
Skipper Of The Mt. Blanc Declares Ordinary Rules Were Ignored By Craft Will Testify Tomorrow
By J. V. Keating

Halifax, Dec 10 — The explanation of the explosion which wrecked this city last Thursday morning as obtained by the Herald and Journal reporter this afternoon from the lips of Capt. Lamodec (*sic*), commander of the French munitions ship Mont Blanc, is the same story he will tell at the inquiry which opens Wednesday, and is the first public statement by the master of the vessel which caused the most utter destruction of history.[5]

Dr. Thomas F. Harrington, who is here as a member of the Bay state "minute man" relief expedition, will appear at the inquiry to testify as an expert on explosives. As chairman of the Massachusetts board of labor and industries, he delved more deeply into the study of all kinds of explosives and particularly T.N.T. than any public official in the United States. He was in charge of the investigation of the T.N.T. explosions at Woburn. Capt. Lamodec's story is as follows:

Loaded With Explosives

"I was on the quarterdeck of the Mont Blanc with pilot Capt. McKay (*sic*), last Thursday morning, going up the harbor, north to Bedford Basin, where I was to anchor and await convoys.

"We had on board the Mont Blanc nearly 500 tons of freight mostly explosives. The ballast tanks were filled with water. In the forward hold was stored picric acid, then came a steel bulkhead, and in the next hold was trinitrotruol (*sic*), a high explosive. We also had T.N.T. in the third hold.

"On top of the forward deck were stored about 20 barrels of benzol, over the picric acid, with a steel deck in between.[6]

"It was a clear morning. The water was smooth and we were proceeding at half speed on the starboard side, toward the Bedford Basin. There were no vessels in our course until we sighted the Belgian relief ship Imo, coming out of Bedford Basin and headed for the Dartmouth shore. She was more than two miles away at this time. We signalled we would keep the Mont Blanc to the starboard going up to the basin, where we were to anchor and await convoy. We headed a little more inshore so as to make clear to the Imo our purpose. She signalled that she was coming down on the port, which would bring her on the same side with us. We were keeping to our right, or starboard, according to pilotage rules, and could not understand what the Imo meant. But we kept on our course, hoping that she would come down, as she should, on the starboard side, which would keep her on the Halifax side of the harbour and the Mont Blanc on the Dartmouth side.

Imo Kept To Port Side

"But to our surprise the Imo kept coming down on the port side, so we signalled again. We saw there was danger of collision and signalled to stop the engines at the same time veering slightly to port, which brought the two vessels with starboards parallel when about 300 feet apart.

"Then we put the rudder hard to port to try to pass the Imo before she should come on us and at the same time the Imo reversed engines. As she was light and without cargo, the reverse brought her around slightly to port. This brought her now pointing toward our starboard and as a collision was then inevitable, we held the Mont Blanc so she would be struck at the forward hold, where the picric acid was, substance which would not explode, rather than have her strike us where the T.N.T. was stored.

"We were in the Narrows, where the harbour is about three-quarters of a mile wide. The Imo cut into us about a third through the deck and hold and the benzol poured into the picric acid, igniting it and causing a cloud of smoke to rise from the vessel forward. I saw there was no hope of doing anything more and knew that an explosion was inevitable, so the boats were lowered and all hands got aboard them and rowed for the Dartmouth shore. Pilot McKay went with us.

"In all there were 41 men aboard the Mont Blanc. She was headed at the time for the Halifax shore and toward Pier 8.[7] She was making very little headway, as we had to push the boat away from the side. This was about 20 minutes before the explosion but the picric acid was in fumes. It did not explode.

"In the meantime the Imo had backed away toward the Dartmouth shore. We landed and ran into the woods. About 20 minutes after we left the ship we heard the explosion. It knocked every one of us down and we were struck by steel and other things, but only the gunner was seriously injured. He has died."

The first officer Jean Glotin makes practically the same statement. Both statements make clear the fact that something was wrong on the Imo. Although she had on board Pilot Hayes, considered one of the best pilots in Halifax.

In talking of the matter today, Admiral Chambers of the convoy fleet said

"The whole thing seems to have been due to imperfect pilotage regulations."

Capt. Lamedoc says that the stopcocks were not drawn before the crew left the Mont Blanc, as that would have been useless because the ballast tanks were already filled with water.[8]

Roy Atkinson, *Boston Post*

Roy Atkinson was born in Brunswick, Maine, in 1883. He moved to Farmington, Maine, as a youth and began his newspaper career as a correspondent for the *Lewiston Journal*. He then worked as a reporter for two weekly papers: the *Lincoln Chronicle* and the *Millinocket Journal*. His first full-time job on a daily newspaper was on the *Kennebec Journal* in Augusta, Maine. In 1908 he became a reporter on the *Boston Post*, remaining a year. After a brief time as editor of a weekly paper in Phillips, Maine, he returned to the *Post* and remained there continuously until his death in Boston on 24 December 1938.[1]

While en route to Halifax, thirty-four-year-old Atkinson wired two despatches to the *Post* and once in Halifax sent four more.[2]

Boston Rushes Relief Special
Trainload Of Physicians, Nurses, Red Cross Workers And State Guard Officers On Way To Halifax

By Roy Atkinson

On Board Relief Train En Route To Halifax, Dec. 6 — With the hope of breaking all speed records between Boston and Halifax this train laden with physicians, nurses, and Red Cross workers is speeding to the assistance of stricken Halifax.

The usual running time for passenger trains is about 27 hours, but it is hoped to cut this down to about 22 hours. If this schedule is adhered to the train should arrive in Halifax about 8:00 p.m. tomorrow.

All tracks have been cleared for this train which pulled out of the North [Boston] station shortly after 10 o'clock. There was a good-sized crowd of people present at the gates to see the relief party start on its errand of mercy.

A.C. Ratshesky, representing Governor McCall and the Massachusetts Committee on Public Safety, and a director of the American Red Cross, heads the party. He has had wide experience in such work, having served during the Chelsea and Salem Fires.[3]

Extraordinary precautions were taken by those in charge of the party to see to it that no alien enemies or unwanted persons boarded the train. As each man and woman appeared at the car entrance his or her credentials were carefully vised by Benjamin Felt and others, who were down to help the party get off to Halifax.

On board this train are 11 physicians and 10 nurses and they were summoned from many places this afternoon by urgent telephone calls, and one and all responded with alacrity. Major Peter O'Shea of the Massachusetts State Guard was at a banquet table in Worcester when called. He left at once for Boston in a taxi, and arrived after a fast run, in ample time to connect with the train.

The women workers, including those sent from the Boston Metropolitan Chapter of the American Red Cross, are well provided with warm garments, many of them having fur coats.

From the Greater Boston department of the State Guard is Captain H.G. Lapham and Captain B.D. Hyde, and all the State Guard officers are in uniform of their rank.

Colonel William H. Brooks, surgeon-general of the State Guard, was at the station to help the party get away. He does not accompany the relief train workers, but checked them up and gave their names to the newspaper men before he left for home.

One of the first things Mr. Ratshesky will do on arrival in Halifax will be to learn the exact needs of the people. Then he will proceed to use the funds and the people placed at his disposal by the Commonwealth.

The Boston Metropolitan Chapter of the Red Cross is well represented. John F. Moors, chairman of the civilian relief committee of the Red Cross, heads the Red Cross contingent.

Miss Elizabeth Peden, head nurse at the Brook Hospital, heads the dozen nurses. Major Harold G. Giddings of the State Guard, heads the physicians on the train.

The list includes:

Captain Robert D. Loring, a specialist on eyes; Major Edward A. Supple, surgery; Major Donald V. Beker, surgery; Major George W. Morse, surgery; Major Peter Owen Shea, surgery;

Captain E. Fred Murphy, medical; Captain Thomas F. Harrington, medical; Dr. Nathaniel Morse. medical; Captain Dewitt Wilcox, medical; Captain John W. Dewis, medical.

Mrs. William H. Lothrop, director of civilian relief for New England, called the Red Cross workers together by telephone for this trip. She received her authority from W. Frank Perona of Washington, D.C., director-general of civilian relief of the American Red Cross.[4]

Boston Relief Rushing To City

More Doctors, Nurses And Heavy Supplies Are Taken Aboard The Massachusetts Special

By Roy Atkinson, Post Staff Representative

On Board Massachusetts Relief Train Via Amherst, N.S., Dec. 7 — As this train of mercy rushes forward at full speed to the assistance of thousands upon thousands of injured at Halifax, the horror that has come upon that city grows. At the pause of the train at Moncton, the members of the relief party were told that fully 2000 men, women and children had lost their lives, and that the number of injured will total 5000 persons.

Refugees at St. John and at Moncton told the men and women from Massachusetts who are on this mercy train harrowing stories of death and destruction they had witnessed when Halifax was nearly wiped out of existence by an explosion so terrific that buildings were destroyed for miles around and thousands of lives snuffed out in a moment.

Tonight, as the relief train rushes forward through Canada, a blinding snowstorm is whirling over the bleak hills and through the sombre pines. It is a desolate scene and brings to the

minds of the workers what must be the suffering of those rendered homeless in Halifax.

Since 11 o'clock last night, Canadian time, this train has been breaking all former speed records in carrying the doctors, nurses and Red Cross workers on their errand of mercy. Never before in the history of the Maine Central, Boston & Maine and Canadian Pacific has such a run been made and never before has the need been so urgent.

At St John, N. B., a pause was made while medical and surgical supplies were purchased and taken on board. Gallons of alcohol, yards of gauze, surgical instruments, antiseptic supplies and other necessary supplies were rushed to the train.

Two hours after this train left St. John another relief train, laden with supplies, was made up and started on its way to Halifax [from Saint John].

At Moncton A.C. Ratshesky, at the request of General Manager Hayes of the Halifax office of the Canadian Government Railways, telegraphed the Boston Red Cross to make up and send at once a train load of supplies to Halifax. It is said that this train would be starting from Boston at once.

General Manager Hayes also wired that the loss of life was estimated at from 1000 to 2000 people and the list of wounded and missing will run high in the thousands. He added that the coming of the relief train from Massachusetts was one of the bright spots in the otherwise dark sky.

All along the line, through Portland, Bangor, Lincoln, Vanceboro, St John, N. B., and other points, the mercy train and its occupants have attracted wide attention. Crowds of sober-faced people have thronged the depots as the workers paused for a moment in their journey.

At St. John, N.B., the crowd was especially large, for 50 bandaged refugees had arrived from stricken Halifax earlier in the day and the interest was intense. At this station it was learned that eight girls from the Mt. St. Vincent Seminary at Rockingham had arrived on a train at 6:15 o'clock this morning. They had escaped with minor injuries.[5]

Bay State's Work Wins High Praise
Premier Borden Visits Hospital; Weeps at Scenes
Boston Nurses Busy All Day And Night
Doctors Help Victims and Bring Great Relief to City

By Roy Atkinson, Staff Correspondent of the Post

Halifax, Dec. 9 — With the arrival of a special train of Red Cross workers from Massachusetts and Maine late this afternoon the Bay State is really taking the lead on the work in this city of sorrow.

Headed by A. C. Ratshesky, Governor McCall's special representative, the relief party got the large hospital in readiness for occupancy yesterday and commenced the treatment of 100 wounded victims of the disaster early this morning.

Among the nurses from Boston are several young women who volunteered their services who are prominent in the social circles of that city. They have been and are working night and day, unflinchingly, amidst harrowing scenes.

Men and women who have read of the great distress that has come to this city are pouring in here by the hundreds freely offering their services. At the rate this work is going forward a large proportion of the task in sight will be accomplished in a few days more.

When Premier Borden visited the Bellevue Hospital, which is being used by the first Massachusetts unit to arrive, he wept when he observed how tenderly the victims are being cared for. "It is magnificent," he ejaculated finally, "I have never seen anything in all my experience like it. These men came here yesterday, and today they have a perfect and smooth running hospital. It is indeed magnificent."

Premier Borden went from cot to cot, speaking to the wounded men, women and children, many of whom he knew personally. He assured them that he would do everything in his power to assist them.

Massachusetts sailors from the hospital ship Old Colony, who have done so much to help in the past few days, continued their activities today. Half a hundred of them volunteered for service at the hospital, placing themselves at the disposal of Major Howard G. Giddings.

Miss Elizabeth Choate, daughter of

Charles H. Choate, the Boston lawyer, worked hard the most of last night and today caring for the wounded in houses and those brought to the hospital. She did not once flinch at the cries of agony all about her. Other nurses, who come from some of the leading families of Boston, had similar experiences.

Hundreds of injuries to the eyes are being brought to the attention of the Massachusetts doctors. Fortunately many of them have had wide experience in such work.

When the first Red Cross base hospital train from Massachusetts and Maine arrived this afternoon it was found that it had on board, in charge of Dr. William E. Ladd, 65 nurses, 25 doctors, 500 cots ready to set up and a complete hospital equipment. Several hospital orderlies also accompanied the train.

The Maine contingent included 13 doctors and four nurses together with several orderlies. They brought with them 100 blankets and 750 cots.

Representatives of Governor Milliken accompanied the Maine delegation. The entire train was composed of nine baggage cars and three Pullmans.

Thus far only one person from the entire United States has been injured in this great catastrophe. This man is vice-counsel of this port, Theodore Fisher, who was slightly wounded.

The Post correspondent made a tour of the devastated district today, where in the snow and slush, the scene was more desolate than it at first appeared.

Many people who were homeless were forced to spend the night out of doors, some of them making up beds in wagons and other vehicles.

It was a matter of surprise to Premier Borden that the children in the various hospitals are as brave as they are. When he went through the Massachusetts hospital he picked one youngster, with a terribly burned face, up in his arms, inquiring how he was. "I am all right, Sir Robert," the little boy answered.

A gig from the flagship of the British fleet now in this vicinity was sent to the aid of the Belgian relief ship, the Imo, after it rammed the Mont Blanc.[6] It was hoped to turn the ship toward the Dartmouth shore. When the explosion came, according to Admiral Chambers, the tiny boat was blown to fragments and all but one of the men lost. This sailor has been in such a dazed condition since that time that he has been unable to describe this happening. The flagship was not injured.[7]

Ratshesky To Leave For Boston
Coming Home Tomorrow With First Unit
By Roy Atkinson, Post Staff Correspondent

Halifax, Dec. 12 — After a banquet in their honor at one of the leading hotels in the city, A. C. Ratshesky, Collector of the Port Edmund Billings, doctors and nurses, who came on the first relief special sent from Boston to Halifax, will leave for their homes Friday morning [14 December].

At the dinner that is to be given as a token of esteem and thanks by the leading citizens of this city, Mr. Ratshesky and other members of the party, including Major Harold G. Giddings, will be praised and thanked for the work they have accomplished in relieving suffering in this community.

Today the Bellevue Hospital, where the first detachment of Massachusetts doctors established their headquarters was formally turned over to the Red Cross doctors and nurses from Rhode Island.

The Rhode Island unit is made up as follows: major in charge, Dr. Garry Dehough, New Bedford, John G. Hathaway, New Bedford, A.H. Mandell, New Bedford, Dr. Baker, superintendent of Rhode Island State Hospital; J. B. Ferguson, surgeon in chief; F. Hussey and Matt Gifford, surgeons; E. S. Porter, E. S. Brackett, chief of out-patient department; N. D. Hardy, oculist; Dr. Messenger, assistant; F.N. Bigelow, ear specialist; Harry Kimball, skin specialist; William H. McGill, skin specialist; Harold DeWolf, chief medical officer, and Dr. Halsey. There are also several internes (*sic*).

The collector of the port of Boston has been busily engaged in superintending the unloading of the steamer Calvin Austin ever since early morning. He managed to get about three hours sleep after his arrival in this city last night [Tuesday 11 December].

There is a general cargo of goods on the Calvin Austin. It is believed that everything will be unloaded by tomorrow morning. Collector Billings said that the trip to Yarmouth, where he disembarked, was the roughest he has ever experienced.

It became known today that Christian Lantz of Salem, who has had much to do with the reconstruction of that city, has been telegraphed to come here to help in the work of rebuilding Halifax.

Today, A.C. Ratshesky established a bureau of information, which is wide and far reaching. He has a large corps of workers, who have made a canvas of the city. The hundreds of telegrams from all parts of the world are turned over to the workers, and when the information desired is obtained it is wired to the questioner and a record is made of the event. The work is so well systematized that quick and accurate results are obtained.

St. Mary's College hospital was opened this morning by Red Cross doctors and nurses of the New England division of the New England Red Cross. Included in their numbers are some of the most eminent physicians and surgeons in New England. Men who charge fees for operations and professional services running into the thousands of dollars pulled off their coats and helped clean up the large school building. It was littered with broken glass and other articles, so that much work was necessary to get in into shape for occupancy.[8]

Richard Sears, *Boston American*

Richard "Dick" Sears was born in Boston, Massachusetts, on 11 October 1881. The son of a sea captain, he started as a newsboy in 1898 and in 1902 became staff photographer for the *Boston Traveler*. In a fifty-year career as a newspaper reporter, photographer and cameraman, he worked for the *Traveler*, *Boston Journal* and *Boston American*, Pathé News, International News Service press service and International News Photo.[1]

Sears photographed Presidents Theodore Roosevelt, Woodrow Wilson, Calvin Coolidge, Herbert Hoover and Franklin Roosevelt and covered

major news assignments, including the
Harry K. Thaw trial in 1907, the return
of Admiral Peary from the North Pole
in1909 and the *Squalus* submarine
disaster in 1939. During World War I
Sears was a lieutenant and served as a
photographer in the Signal Corps with
the 80th Division. In World War II he
served as a lieutenant-colonel with the
Army Signal Corps.[2]

In 1911 Sears became the first
photographer to take pictures in New
England from an airplane and made the
first shot from a balloon when he took a
ride over the Massachusetts Institute of
Technology for International Newsreel.
He was also credited with being the
first news photographer to take baseball
action shots from the edge of the playing field.[3] His most famous photograph
was an exclusive taken of Christian
Science founder Mary Eddy Baker at
her Mount Pleasant estate in Concord,
New Hampshire. In July 1934 he took a
newsreel picture of American boxer Max
Baer soon after he won the Heavyweight
Champion of the World title. During the

Richard Sears in 1918 serving as a photographer in the US Army Signal Corps. Courtesy Vermont Senator Dick Sears

1950s Sears worked on special assignment for Universal Film Exchanges.
He died in Brookline, Massachusetts on 11 November 1955.

Sears's Photographs

There is no evidence Sears wrote despatches for the *Boston American*,
but between 8 and 10 December he took a series of Explosion-related
photographs. Ten of these shots were published in a photo gallery in the
Boston American on 11 December.[4] Each photo contained a caption and
was copyrighted International Film Service. Collectively they captured the
magnitude of the disaster's aftermath.

*Where The Sudden Shock Of The Explosion And Hurricane Of Flame Wrecked The Proud
Spires Of Halifax.*[5] (Damaged Grove Street Presbyterian and St. Joseph's Catholic
Churches.)

Digging In Halifax Tenement House Ruins For Bodies.[6] (Soldiers digging for seven bodies in a Barrington Street house.)

Ruins, Desolation And Wounded Humanity Left By Halifax Explosion Holocaust, As Revealed By The Camera[7] (Seven photographs: a snow-covered panorama of the area near Pier 6, wounded survivors Arthur Compton and John Sullivan, three families in Gottingen Street on a sled loaded with furniture, Prime Minister Borden and A.C. Ratshesky following his arrival on the first Massachusetts relief train, a view of the dockyard and *Imo* beached on the Dartmouth shore and St. Joseph's School on Kaye Street.[8] At the bottom of the page is the caption "These pictures will be shown in the leading theatres in a current issue of the Hearst-Pathe News.")[9]

James Hare, *Leslie's Weekly*

James "Jimmy" Hare was born in England on 3 October 1856 and immigrated to the United States in 1889. He was a photojournalist for *Collier's Weekly* (1898–1914) and *Leslie's Weekly* (1914–1922) and was the leading photographer during the Spanish-American War (1898), Russo-Japanese War (1904 and 1905), Mexican Revolution (1911 and 1914), First Balkan War (1911 and 1914) and World War I. With *Collier's* he photographed the aftermath of the 1906 San Francisco earthquake and the Wright brothers' early test flights. In April 1912 Hare was rushed by *Collier's* to Halifax to photograph the erroneously reported arrival of *Carpathia* with *Titanic's* survivors. When Hare joined *Leslie's* to cover World War I, the magazine also offered him a chance to write news stories. As a correspondent he was known for his "terse, picturesque, human interest dispatches."[1] With *Leslie's* he photographed two events in Canada: the Halifax Explosion and the 1919 Winnipeg general strike.[2] Hare died in New York on 24 June 1946.

Described as "five foot two, with aggressive, pointed beard, firm-set mouth and determined eyes,"[3] at sixty-one Hare was the oldest journalist covering the Explosion story. He arrived in Halifax from Long Island, New York, on 9 December and presented his press credentials to local military authorities.[4] After obtaining permission from commanding officer of Military District No. 6 Major-General T. Benson's immediate subordinate, Colonel W. "Ernie" Thompson, Hare took a series of photographs of the blast's aftermath on 11 December.[5]

On 29 December 1917 *Leslie's* published three articles by Hare. "In Stricken Halifax" and "The Destruction of a City" together provided seven captioned images bylined "Photographs by James H. Hare, Staff War Photographer." These photographs show *Imo* on the Dartmouth shore (Number 1), relief workers salvaging flour from a wrecked storehouse (Number 2), a view down the Richmond slope across the Narrows to

Jimmy Hare (left) with USA Geological Survey photographer/explorer W.H. Jackson, c. 1940. Courtesy Elizabeth Morrison

the Dartmouth shore (Number 3), a second view of the Richmond slope (Number 4), a tree cut off at its base by the blast (Number 5), a severely damaged house (Number 6), and a load of bedding and furniture being salvaged for the wounded (Number 7). Photograph Number 4 is the only image to quote a survivor, almost certainly a soldier: "'I have lain among the dying in Flanders, I have gone over the top, crossed No-Man's Land, treading underfoot my own comrades still trembling with their death wounds and I have witnessed the agony of the aftermath of a bootless counterattack,' said one witness of the Halifax disaster, 'but I have seen nothing worse than this.'"[6]

"The Ruins of Halifax," bylined "As Seen by James H. Hare, Staff War Photographer," is a 600-word story featuring seven photographs.

The Ruins of Halifax
As seen by James H. Hare, Staff War Photographer

Out of a clear blue sky on a bright morning on December 6th one of the greatest disasters of years occurred at Halifax N.S. It is impossible at the present moment to ascertain the exact number of killed and injured, but conservative estimates suggest about 1400 to 1500 killed outright.[7] The regrettable part of the whole occurrence is the fact that it was accidental — caused by culpable negligence.

The *Mont Blanc*, a heavily loaded French munition ship passing the *Imo*, a Norwegian ship, carrying relief to the Belgians, in the narrow channel misunderstood each other's signals — somebody lost his head — after the ships had almost cleared each other safely.[8] The *Imo* crashed into the floating arsenal which carried tons of T.N.T., picric acid, and benzol, and the inevitable happened.

When I arrived on the scene I could almost believe I was back on the firing line in France.[9] Small piles of brick, mortar, wood and iron were all that remained of a thickly populated district. Trees were splintered and down from the force of explosions, fires were still

burning in coal heaps, and hundreds of people were working in the debris, frantically digging to find the bodies of their loved ones. Scores of these rescue workers were bandaged and looked for all the world like men wounded in battle.

As usual in accidents of this kind, there is a diversity of opinion as to how many explosions actually took place. Evidently there was a smaller one at first which caused people to rush to the windows to see what was happening.[10] Then came the main blast which blew in the glass windows and that I think accounts for so many people losing their eyes, and being cut about the head and face.

A mile from the explosion I saw great slivers of plate glass sticking horizontally in the walls of the office of the chief of police, like arrows that had been propelled by a bow. So one can partly realize what an inferno must have raged for a few moments.

Great bars of iron from the doomed ship wrought into fantastic shapes and hurled through the air were picked up at widely separated points.

The tragedy seemed to me even

December 29, 1917   889

The Ruins of Halifax

As seen by JAMES H. HARE, Staff War Photographer

This house shows the force of the explosion. Note how the side nearest the explosion has been blown in by the concussion.

Canadian soldiers are searching the ruins for injured and dead. The work of the men in uniform of all branches of the service did much to relieve suffering.

OUT of a blue sky on a bright morning on December 6th one of the greatest disasters of years occurred at Halifax, N. S. It is impossible at the present moment to ascertain the exact number of killed and injured, but conservative estimates suggest about 1400 to 1500 killed outright. The regrettable part of the whole occurrence is the fact that it was accidental—caused by culpable negligence.

The *Mont Blanc*, a heavily loaded French munition ship passing the *Imo*, a Norwegian ship, carrying relief to the Belgians, in the narrow channel misunderstood each other's signals—somebody lost his head—after the ships had almost cleared each other safely. The *Imo* crashed into the floating arsenal which carried tons of T. N. T., picric acid, and benzol, and the inevitable happened.

When I arrived on the scene I could almost believe I was back on the firing line in France. Small piles of brick, mortar, wood and iron were all that remained of a thickly populated district. Trees were splintered and down from the force of explosions, fires were still burning in coal heaps, and hundreds of people were working in the debris, frantically digging to find the bodies of their loved ones. Scores of these rescue workers were bandaged and looked for all the world like men wounded in battle.

As is usual in accidents of this kind, there is a diversity of opinion as to how many explosions actually took place. Evidently there was a smaller one at first which caused people to rush to the windows to see what was happening. Then came the main blast which blew in the glass windows and that I think accounts for so many people losing their eyes, and being cut about the head and face.

A mile from the explosion I saw great slivers of plate glass sticking horizontally in the walls of the office of the chief of police, like arrows that had been propelled by a bow. So one can

Above, at the left, relief workers are loading the injured on trains for transportation to hospitals in neighboring cities and towns. At the right is a team of horses and a wagon which caught the full force of the explosion.

partly realize what an inferno must have raged for a few moments.

Great bars of iron from the doomed ship wrought into fantastic shapes and hurled through the air were picked up at widely separated points.

The tragedy seemed to me even greater than at "the front" as it came so suddenly, absolutely without the slightest warning, whereas the damage on the battlefield is accomplished by degrees and people are expecting the terrible destruction.

The houses that were not entirely destroyed, but badly wrecked, had all the earmarks of buildings wrecked in Zeppelin raids on London and Paris. Sides of houses were smashed in, glass scattered in all directions, roofs lifted bodily and turned around, or dumped off entirely, interiors demolished and furniture wrecked.

Some families were wiped out entirely, but even more heartrending were the many cases of families broken up. Some lost fathers or mothers. In others the little ones were killed or maimed and one or both parents, who no doubt would willingly have given their lives to protect their babes, were either killed by the explosion or burned to death by the fire that followed.

To add to the horrors, the weather changed suddenly and a blizzard raged just as people were trying to extricate their injured. This also hampered the arrival of the small army of doctors and nurses that rushed to volunteer their services. No sooner was one snow-storm over than another commenced—three bad storms in two days whose icy cold blasts piercingly cut into the even well-appareled person.

One bright ray of sunshine that stood out prominently in this great havoc and gloom was the splendid offers of assistance in money, clothes, food and medical service that was received by cable at the earliest possible moment from the neighboring towns of Canada and of the United States.

This house collapsed when the explosion came, burying its inmates. When the relief workers began their task, the dead lay about in the streets, huddled against walls where they had been hurled, pinioned under burning buildings, and unconscious beneath the fallen walls.

Little Katherine Arnold, whose mother and two sisters were killed, left her father in Halifax at the side of her dying brother. She is on her way to Providence, R. I., with her uncle.

This Protestant school collapsed on hundreds of pupils and the death list is shocking. In another school not a child was killed, though the building was badly damaged.

"The Ruins of Halifax," photo story by James Hare, Leslie's Weekly *29 December 1917, 889*

greater than at the "the front" as it came so suddenly, absolutely without the slightest warning, whereas the damage on the battlefield is accomplished by degrees and people are expecting the terrible destruction.

The houses that were not entirely destroyed, but badly wrecked, had all the earmarks of buildings wrecked in Zeppelin raids on London and Paris. Sides of houses were smashed in, glass scattered in all directions, roofs lifted bodily and turned around, or dumped off entirely, interiors demolished and furniture wrecked.

Some families were wiped out entirely, but even more heartrending were the many cases of families broken up. Some lost fathers or mothers. In others the little ones were killed or maimed and one or both parents, who no doubt would willingly have given their lives to protect their babies, were either killed by the explosion or burned to death by the fire that followed.

To add to the horrors, the weather changed suddenly and a blizzard raged just as people were trying to extricate their injured. This also hampered the arrival of the small army of doctors and nurses that rushed to volunteer their services. No sooner was one snow-storm over than another commenced — three bad storms in two days whose icy cold blasts piercingly cut into even the well-appareled (*sic*) person.

One bright ray of sunshine that stood out prominently in the great havoc and gloom was the splendid offers of assistance in money, clothes, food and medical service that was received by cable at the earliest possible moment from the neighboring towns of Canada and the United States.[11]

Hare's Photographs

James Hare's seven captioned photographs in "The Ruins of Halifax" include three images of ruined buildings (Numbers 1, 5 and 7), soldiers searching in the ruins for the injured and dead (Number 2), relief workers loading the injured onto a hospital train (Number 3), a team of dead horses and a destroyed wagon (Number 4) and a little girl with her uncle (Number 6).

With the exception of Numbers 6 and 7, the captions are accurate.[12] Number 6 shows a little girl accompanied by an older man. The caption reads "Little Katherine Arnold, whose mother and two sisters were killed, left her father in Halifax at the side of her dying brother. She is on her way to Providence, R.I. with her uncle." In fact, the little girl was seven-year-old Catherine Arnold, and one sister [Harriet] and one brother [Tristam] were burned to death in their Veith Street home. The unidentified man was Catherine's uncle Charles T. Richmond of Providence, Rhode Island. The dying brother Wilfred survived though he lost the sight of one eye. In June his father took him to Providence.[13]

Number 7 shows a collapsed building with a large bare tree trunk in the foreground. The caption reads "This Protestant school collapsed on hundreds of pupils and the death list is shocking. In another school not a child was killed, though the building was badly damaged." The Protestant school at Richmond and Roome Streets did not collapse on hundreds of children. Rather, two children perished in the building and eighty-seven died on their way to school or at home. The building Hare described as "this Protestant school" might have been the Protestant Orphanage at 1274 Barrington Street, which had a hospital and one-room school. Three adults and twenty-five children were killed here.[14]

Aside from the inaccuracy of two captions, there is some possibility that Hare used photographs for his story from wire services or from one or more taken by W.G. MacLaughlan, the official military photographer for the city of Halifax and the photographer authorized by Major-General Benson to photograph the Explosion's aftermath.[15] Supporting this possibility is the absence of negatives of Hare's Explosion photographs in the 2,400 negatives, prints and lantern slides of the James H. "Jimmy" Hare Papers and Photography Collection in the Humanities Research Center at the University of Texas, Austin. However, it is also true that during a long and noteworthy career Hare may have taken tens of thousands of photographs, and it is most likely that the photographs in the "Ruins of Halifax" photo-story have not survived the passage of time.[16]

What is certain is that Hare did obtain permission from Halifax military authorities to take photographs on condition he was accompanied by an escort to ensure they did not disclose military secrets or compromise war-related operations. If the officer who accompanied Hare brought him to the same locations photographed by MacLaughlan, the background scenes for both photographers would have been similar, especially if the photographs were taken on the same day. Finally, Hare's Number 6 is not among the many taken by MacLaughlan and it has a strong American connection as the "uncle" in the photograph is from Providence, Rhode Island, and is taking Catherine Arnold back to the United States.

Staff Correspondent, *Providence Journal/Bulletin*

During the morning of 8 December a relief train left Providence, Rhode Island, and forty hours later arrived in Halifax.[1] On board was a staff correspondent from the *Providence Journal/Bulletin* with two assignments: to report the story and open the Providence Journal Information Bureau.[2] On 8 December the paper announced the establishment in Halifax of the bureau under the direction of a "Staff Correspondent" and invited "any person desiring information about relatives or friends to communicate with the City Editor at the office of the Providence Journal."[3] According to the paper's correspondent, more than 150 Rhode Islanders provided the paper with names and addresses of relatives in Halifax.[4] In addition, many of the doctors and nurses on the relief train were natives of the Halifax district and had relatives there.[5] Given this number of people connected to the disaster, the paper treated it as a local story.

On 9 December the *Providence Journal/Bulletin* published its correspondent's despatch en route to Halifax.[6] The next day the paper ran the reporter's first of four despatches from Halifax between 10 and 13 December.[7] The following are the stories of 10 December in the *Journal* and 12 December in the *Bulletin*.

Rhode Island's Red Cross Relief Train Reaches Devastated Halifax

Unit, Worn By 40-Hour Journey, Will Take Over Care Of 500 Injured Immediately, Party Sent From This State Largest To Arrive In Stricken City 2,000 Hurt Without Even First Aid Treatment More Than Three Days After Disaster — Journal's Correspondent Opens Information Bureau

From a Staff Correspondent of The Providence Journal

Halifax N.S — Dec. 10 (On Board the Rhode Island Red Cross Relief Train) Rhode Island's Red Cross Relief unit worn by the 40-hour run from Providence, pulled into devastated Halifax at 12:50 o'clock this morning and will take over the care of 500 of the injured at 6 o'clock.

The unit will be on a 12-hour shift until further notice.

Last night, three days and a half after the explosion that wrecked the city, 2000 of the 500 injured had not received even first aid treatment. Although doctors and nurses from all over Nova Scotia have been on the scene three days, during which time they have worked almost continuously they have been unable to come anywhere near meeting the needs of the situation.

The Rhode Island unit is welcome especially as it is the largest that has reached Halifax from any point.[8] It is as large as the three units from Boston and New York combined. Relief trains from Montreal and Ottawa are on the way, but have not arrived.

Fires Still Smoulder

Fires were still smouldering in the ruins

of the stricken city when the Rhode Island train came in. Relief work, Red Cross officials said, was becoming more organized, but the greater part of it is yet to be done. Scores of injured have died because of the impossibility of giving them even temporary treatment. Many others have frozen or died in the ruins before they could be gotten out. But information here at 1 o'clock this morning was that the final death list will near 3000 names.

All of the Rhode Island unit stood the long trip here well, except Dr. Frank M. Adams of Providence who is confined to his berth with a slight attack of indigestion.

Hardly had the Rhode Island relief train pulled up on the siding assigned to it when the staff correspondent of the Journal was handed a long telegram giving the names and addresses of more than 150 families for whom inquiries had been made by anxious relatives in Rhode Island.

Information Bureau

Enlisting the services of several Halifax workers, he at once proceeded the work of investigation necessary. The bureau was confronted with discouraging conditions for speedy results. In the first place the wire service here is in bad shape. Then, in sections of the city where no lives were lost and only slight injuries were suffered by individuals, houses were untenanable (*sic*) by the shattering of windows as a result of the explosion, and the occupants were forced to seek shelter elsewhere. This of course will cause some delay in finding parties sought even in cases where addresses were given.

There is a good supply of food in the city

There has been but one telegraph wire out of Halifax working. Additional lines will be in operation to-day. A telegraphic clearing house has been opened at Truro with extra operators brought from Boston to help clear away the flood of messages that overwhelmed the usual force. Truro, 62 miles from Halifax, is filled with injured from the devastated district.

The Rhode Island party got its first glimpse of damage at Sackville [Nova Scotia], when the relief train passed a string of more than 20 passenger cars with every inch of glass smashed out and the interior of half of them burned out. They were on a side track at Halifax, two miles from the water front when the explosion occurred.

After a night of delays the relief train reached Moncton, N.B. at 11:30 yesterday morning Atlantic time. Indications then were that the train would arrive in Halifax about 6 o'clock last night, but delays made this impossible.[9]

Halifax Relief Unit In Charge Of Hospital Now
Rhode Island Nurses And Doctors Busy Helping Injured — Do House To House Work In Blizzard — Several Members Return Home

From a Staff Correspondent of The Evening Bulletin

Halifax, Dec. 12 — The Rhode Island Red Cross relief unit has assumed charge of Bellevue Emergency Hospital, and every member is working hard in relieving the suffering of those brought in. For two days the members of the unit went from house to house in a raging blizzard and searched for the wounded.

For this great work they have been personally complimented by Col. Bell, commanding medical officer, who visited headquarters last night. There is a great deal of medical work before the doctors, and cases of terrible injury are demanding attention. There are thousands of people to be treated.

Several members of the unit left last night for home. These members found it absolutely necessary, for various reasons, to get back and could be spared. Carl B. Marshall, who is business manager of the unit, to-day received a telegram from Rathbone Gardner congratulating the unit on its work, and announcing that many other physicians and nurses in Rhode Island are ready to go to Halifax if needed.[10]

The money from the Rotary Club has been received. Because of the great disorganization of everything here, it is very hard to find relatives and friends of Providence people.

Notwithstanding that the first reports from Halifax indicate that some of the people for whom inquiries are being made are missing or even included in the list of possibly killed, relatives here have not given up hope, realizing that the missing persons may have taken shelter in some other parts of the city.

Mrs. John McEachern, daughter of Muriel, and son Jesse, are missing. Their home at 7 Richmond street, Halifax, is entirely gone and it is believed they were burned to death while pinned in the cellar. The Bulletin correspondent reports that he found the wreckage of the house still smouldering. Mrs. McEachern and her children were aunt and cousins of Miss Olive McEachern, who makes her home at the Providence Y.W.C.A. Miss McEachern's parents also lived in Halifax and she has not received any information concerning them as yet.

Blair W. Mosher and family, consisting of himself, wife and four children, 38 North street are missing and classified as dead as the house was levelled. Information concerning this family was sought by Mrs. W.H. Wilson of East Providence and also by Jesse A. Medberry.

Martin G. Marks of 67 Brunswick street is missing. Mrs. F. Cowan of 30 Felix street, sought information concerning Mr. Marks.

Richard J. Burgess of 30 Pearl street, this city, who inquired concerning Robert Burgess and family, has been notified that Mrs. Burgess and two of the four children in the family are dead. Mr. Burgess and the two remaining children are safe, one of the children being in a hospital.[11]

Epilogue

To become a newspaperman you need the hide of a dinosaur, the stamina of a Chinese coolie, the wakefulness and persistence of a mosquito, the analytical powers of a detective and the digging capacity of a steam shovel.

— Roy Greenaway, *The News Game*

The accounts by reporters, editors, correspondents, photojournalists and record keepers contained in *Bearing Witness* played a major role in the story of the Explosion in Halifax harbour. As Canon Charles Vernon of Halifax observed, "[press reports] written in graphic style, and full of human interest was probably the greatest factor in starting the magnificent wave of sympathy and of practical assistance which swept over the American continent, and indeed, over the world." The day after the disaster, 400 copies of the one-sided *Halifax Herald* featuring Peter Lawson's "Halifax Wrecked" story were circulated to Nova Scotia communities, and George Yates's graphic "pen picture" story for Canadian Press appeared in daily newspapers across the nation on 10 December. With a circulation of 50,000, *Canadian Courier* magazine published an eye-witness description by the event's official historian, Archibald MacMechan, on 22 December 1917, and a week later another story featuring eight sketches by artist Arthur Lismer. Also on 29 December, *Leslie's Weekly* magazine, circulation 379,000, published three articles and fourteen photographs of the aftermath by internationally famous photojournalist and war correspondent James Hare.

A hundred years after the Explosion rocked Halifax and Dartmouth the body of work represented by the news despatches, magazine articles and sketches of local and visiting chroniclers still forms an essential and compelling historical record. However, beyond the five W's and How of these accounts are the remarkable personal experiences of the men and women who struggled under difficult circumstances to obtain and convey the story to the public.

Eye-Witness Journalists and Record Keepers

John Ronayne raced to Pier 6 to investigate the burning *Mont-Blanc* and died in the line of duty; within 30 minutes of the Explosion James Hickey found a working telegraph and sent the first bulletin to the outside world; Peter Lawson made his way on foot through the devastated North End to Rockingham to telegraph news to Truro and beyond; Leo Hinch rushed home to the North End to face the death of his mother, two brothers and three sisters; May O'Regan identified colleague John Ronayne in one of the city's morgues; within hours of the blast the editor of the *Nieuw Amsterdam Courant* newspaper on board *Nieuw Amsterdam* in Bedford Basin published an account for passengers and crew; Hervey Jones boarded *Imo* late in the day and helped to find the body of Pilot William Hayes; James L. Gowen ventured into a blizzard on the night of the blast to obtain information on victims and surviviors; and Arthur Lismer began drawing sketches within forty-eight hours of the event.

Visiting Journalists and Record Keepers

On the day of the Explosion Alfred Coffin drove three hours in a taxi to Halifax from Truro to gather information and returned the same day with a carload of injured men, women and children; Stanley Smith made a windowless room liveable and shared it with a soldier; Tommy Gorman barged onto a Halifax-bound American relief train in Saint John to cover the story, found accommodation in Halifax in a dead man's hotel room and purloined a typewriter from a smashed shop storefront; Grattan O'Leary discovered his despatches were being delayed by a local censor; James Hare persuaded military officials to allow him take a series of photographs of the disaster's aftermath; George Yates provided Canadians across the country with a visceral account of the devastated North End; Thomas O'Leary slept overnight in a damaged house with practically every window blown out; and Jerome Keating obtained a pre-enquiry statement from *Mont-Blanc* captain Le Médec explaining events leading up to and immediately after the blast.

The Explosion in Halifax harbour was the biggest story of its kind in Canadian history, newsworthy because it involved elements of danger, courage, sacrifice, tragedy, heroism, blame and sheer history. What the local, regional, national and international public wanted and received was up-to-date and reliable information. In journalism the difference between news and truth is that news signals an event and truth reveals the facts and causes underlying the event. It is evident from the unrelenting and evocative accounts presented in *Bearing Witness* that the journalists and record keepers who gathered information and wrote about the disaster provided both news *and* truth.

Appendix A

Timeline of Activities for Journalists and Record Keepers

The following timeline indicates the activities of journalists and record keepers between 6 and 16 December 1917.

6 December 1917, 9:04:35 a.m. Atlantic Standard Time

Halifax Canadian Press (CP) Bureau Superintendent James Hickey and telegraph operator Maxwell Backer are in an office of the Chronicle Building at 85–93 Granville Street. Hickey is working at his desk and Backer is receiving news of a munitions plant explosion in Pittsburgh, Pennsylvania.

Sixteen-year-old CP messenger boy Leo Hinch is exiting the Chronicle Building.

Former *Montreal Gazette* telegraph editor William Barton is eating breakfast in the Halifax Hotel at 97–103 Hollis Street.

Official historian of the Explosion and Dalhousie University professor Archibald MacMechan is home at 72 Victoria Road reading a newspaper in his dining room.

Patriot editor Joseph Sheldon is in a meeting at the paper's waterfront office at 48 Commercial Street, one block east of the Dartmouth ferry terminal.

Herald news editor Peter Lawson is asleep in a rooming house on Buckingham Street.

Victoria School of Art and Design principal Arthur Lismer is home at 8 Cliff Street in Bedford about to eat breakfast with his wife and daughter.

Echo reporter John "Jack" Ronayne is investigating the burning *Mont-Blanc* near Pier 6.

Echo editor Hervey Jones is home at 88 Cedar Street.

Herald reporter Arthur Pettipas is in Dartmouth.

The editor of the *Nieuw Amsterdam Courant* paper is on the Holland-America passenger and freighter *Nieuw Amsterdam,* anchored in Bedford Basin.

Canada's Chief Press Censor (CPC) Lieutenant-Colonel Ernest Chambers is in Ottawa.

Unidentified *Herald* reporter (possibly Henry B. Jefferson) is in Truro.

Colchester Sun and *Truro Citizen* manager/editor William Foster is in Halifax.

News publisher/editor Alfred Coffin is in Truro.

Echo newspaper boy Thomas Raddall (future writer of history and historical fiction) is in a Grade 9 class at Chebucto Road School.

6 December, Post-Explosion

James Hickey was thrown through a shattered glass office door and suffered cuts on his left arm and hand. Shaking off shock and injury he gathered news and at approximately 9:35 a.m. wired the first bulletin on the Explosion to Associated Press in New York via Havana from the Halifax and Bermuda Cable Company in the Dennis Building at 108 Granville Street. He then went home to 175 Morris Street and found two of his children injured and his house partially damaged. Later he gathered details for a despatch wired in the afternoon from the Canadian Pacific Railway (CPR) Telegraph Company in the Dennis Building.

Maxwell Backer had just received the word "explosion" over the wire about the Pittsburgh munitions story when *Mont-Blanc's* concussion shook the office and broke his line. Before 10 a.m. he arrived at 116 Edward Street to find his wife seriously injured, his two young children unharmed and his house badly damaged. Backer did not return to the CP office that day.

Leo Hinch survived the Explosion and went home to 18 Richmond Street in the North End.

William Barton survived the blast and left the Halifax Hotel. After assisting the injured, he was joined by two friends. They first went to the Citadel and then the Armouries.

When the concussion hit, MacMechan thought the boiler had burst in the kitchen. The glass in the passage by the front door was smashed but his wife Edith and other occupants of the house were unhurt.

Joseph Sheldon backed away from the office's window and into a stock room from which he emerged unharmed. He left the building and encountered wounded men, women and children.

Lawson was awakened by the blast and discovered the door and windows smashed. A messenger from *Herald* publisher Senator William Dennis soon arrived with a note directing him to begin covering the story. Lawson crossed Sackville Street, ran across the citadel in the shadow of the

Old Town Clock and viewed the blast cloud over Richmond. He made his way to Richmond then north along the damaged railroad line to the nearest working telegraph at Rockingham where he wired news of the Explosion to Truro. He then returned to Halifax to gather news for his 7 December "Halifax Wrecked" story.

Fatally injured John Ronayne was found lying in the road [Barrington Street] near the railway foot bridge by his friend Roger Amirault.

Lismer, his wife and daughter were seated at the kitchen table when the blast occurred. The painted glass of the front door blew in and narrowly missed hitting them. During the morning he tried to reach Halifax but was turned back by a military cordon at Fairview [Lawn Cemetery] bridge.

During the morning *Ottawa Citizen* reporter Tommy Gorman left Ottawa for Halifax.

Alfred Coffin drove three hours and 100 kilometres in a taxi from Truro to Halifax to obtain news of the disaster for CP. He was the first visiting journalist to arrive in the city and witness the Explosion's aftermath. During the afternoon he visited Halifax newspaper and printing offices to place his paper's plant at their disposal.

Prior to 11:40 a.m. the *Nieuw Amsterdam Courant* publication on board *Nieuw Amsterdam* went to press. During the afternoon the paper featuring the article "Catastrophe in Halifax" was circulated among the passengers.

In Ottawa at 11:50 a.m. Eastern Standard Time (EST) CPC Ernest Chambers approved news of the Explosion by the *Sydney Record*.

In the afternoon Lismer arrived in Halifax and found the premises of his Victoria School of Art and Design at 24 George Street severely damaged.

At 3:45 p.m. (EST) Chambers telegraphed George Perry, General Manager of the Great North West Telegraph Company and J.J. McMillan, Manager of Canadian Pacific Railway Telegraph Company requesting co-operation to facilitate transmission of news of the disaster from Halifax. One hour later Chambers contacted CP General Manager Charles Knowles to offer assistance with news transmission by Halifax CP Bureau staff.

Hervey Jones accompanied *Mont-Blanc's* Captain Le Médec by car to the French Consulate. In the evening Jones joined a boarding party from Pickford and Black shipping agency to inspect *Imo*. The search party located Pilot William Hayes' body and Captain From's dog Ralph which they shot.

About 7:00 p.m. *Echo* reporter James L. Gowen left his Morris Street residence to gather news in a snowstorm that after midnight became a blizzard.

By 9:00 p.m. two *Toronto Star* staff reporters left Toronto by train for Halifax.

At 10:00 p.m. the first relief train for Halifax left Boston. Among the passengers were journalists Anthony Philpott *Boston Globe*, Roy Atkinson *Boston Post*, Richard. Sears *Boston American*, Jerome Keating *Boston Herald-Journal* and Richard Simpson Associated Press.

At 11:00 p.m. Coffin left Halifax with a carload of injured people for Truro.

Prior to midnight, Philpott wired his first despatch to the *Boston Globe* from Portsmouth, New Hampshire and Atkinson his first despatch to the *Boston Post*.

Also before midnight, Chambers telephoned a synopsis of press service reports to the Halifax Naval Department.

7 December

After 1:30 a.m. *St. John Daily Telegraph* city editor Stanley Smith left Saint John on a relief train for Halifax. At Stewiacke, Nova Scotia he attempted to wire his first despatch.

At 3:00 a.m. Gowen returned home in deep snow from news gathering. Later in the day he was sent by the *Echo* to all known shelters and hospitals to compile lists of casualties.

At 4:00 a.m. Lawson watched the single page "Halifax Wrecked" story he had reported, written and helped hand set come off the *Herald's* handpress.

At 7:00 a.m. the Boston relief train arrived in Saint John, New Brunswick. Philpott wired another story. Tommy Gorman, who had arrived earlier during the day in Saint John via Montreal, secretly boarded the train for Halifax.

In Ottawa, Chambers continued to facilitate transmission of news. He telegraphed George Creel, the Commissioner of Public Information for the United States government, offering to help American editors transmit news of the Explosion.

A special representative of the *News* began coverage in Halifax.

Lismer began a series of sketches depicting the early hours of the blast, the 7 December snowstorm that followed and survivors' shock. The sketches were requested by Augustus Bridle, editor of *Canadian Courier* magazine in Toronto.

An unknown *Echo* reporter interviewed *Mont-Blanc's* Captain Le Médec but he was unwilling to talk.

At 3:00 p.m. the Boston relief train arrived in Moncton, New Brunswick.

John Ronayne's body was identified at one of the city's morgues, first by his mother and then by a *Chronicle* female reporter, most likely Mary 'May' O'Regan.

At 5:00 p.m. George Yates, Sir Robert Borden's personal secretary, arrived in Halifax with the Prime Minister in a private rail car from Charlotte-town, Prince Edward Island.

At 6:00 p.m. Smith arrived in Halifax. He found accommodation above a café near the Queen Hotel and after midnight wired a 1,500-word despatch from the CPR Telegraph Company.

Prior to midnight, Atkinson wired his second despatch from Amherst, Nova Scotia.

8 December

At 1 a.m. Smith retired for the night. His room had the window blown out and he had to do his own repairs.

At 3:00 a.m. the Boston relief train arrived at Rockingham after a trip of twenty-nine hours. At 6:00 a.m. the train left Rockingham and arrived one hour later at Halifax's south end yet-to-be built terminus. Gorman disembarked and walked into the city. Later in the day he joined a group of Canadian and American newspapermen (almost certainly the Boston reporters) in a tour of the devastated North End district.

At 8:30 a.m. a staff correspondent of the *Providence Journal/Bulletin* left Providence on the Rhode Island relief train for Halifax.

Before 9:00 a.m. the *News*' special representative phoned in an update of the situation in Halifax.

In Ottawa, Chambers continued to facilitate transmission of news.

Prime Minister Borden arranged accommodation for the five Boston journalists in the Halifax Club on Hollis Street.

Gorman found accommodation in a waterfront hotel. By noon, his first story was wired to the *Ottawa Citizen*.

Between 9:30 a.m. and 6:00 p.m. Smith visited morgues, hospitals, ruins and inquiry stations. He also met with Halifax publisher Gerald Weir who provided an eye-witness account of the Explosion and its immediate aftermath.

From noon until 3:00 p.m. Yates toured the North End with one of the Boston journalists (most likely *Boston American* photographer/reporter Richard Sears) who took photographs.

During the day Associated Press correspondent Richard Simpson visited the North End.

At 4:00 p.m. *Montreal Standard* staff correspondent William Stuart and *Ottawa Journal* staff representative Grattan O'Leary arrived in Halifax.

Montreal Star reporter Eldred Archibald and *St. John Daily Globe* reporter
   Thomas O'Leary arrived in Halifax.

At 7:00 p.m. the Rhode Island relief train arrived in Bangor, Maine and the
   Providence Journal's correspondent sent his first despatch.

During the evening Yates wrote a story about his 8 December tour of the
   ruined Richmond district.

By midnight Gorman had filed 5,000 words on the disaster.

9 December

In the morning Yates delivered his story to the CPR telegraph office with
   instructions to wire it to CP.

At 11:00 a.m. Smith returned to Saint John.

At 11:30 a.m. the Rhode Island relief train arrived in Moncton.

A *Toronto Daily Star* male reporter interviewed Explosion survivors and
   citizens in Truro.

Arthur Pettipas began supervising Dartmouth's #2 relief food depot near
   Victoria Road and assisting with Dartmouth's Fuel Relief Committee.

Leslie's Weekly photo-journalist James Hare arrived in Halifax from Long
   Island, New York and obtained permission from army headquarters to
   take photographs of the disaster's aftermath.

MacMechan began the first part of an article for the *Canadian Courier*. Later
   in the day he finished the second part, sent both parts by train at 7:30
   pm to Toronto and telegraphed Augustus Bridle. "Halifax in Ruins", appeared in the magazine's 22 December 1917 issue.

Stuart visited Chebucto School morgue, the Armouries, Common, relief stations and the Richmond district.

Thomas O'Leary visited several hospitals and City Hall. During the day he
   wrote two despatches for the *St. John Daily Globe*.

Grattan O'Leary visited the ruined Richmond district as well as morgues
   and hospitals.

Eldred Archibald and *Boston Post* reporter Roy Atkinson toured the North
   End.

10 December

A *Toronto Star* woman reporter joined her male colleague in Halifax. During the day he toured the downtown and North End and in the evening
   interviewed survivors in the Queen Hotel.

At 12.50 p.m. the *Providence Journal* staff correspondent arrived on the
   Rhode Island relief train in Halifax. Thirty minutes later he was handed
   a telegram with the names and addresses of more than 150 families in
   Halifax with Rhode Island relatives.

The *Chronicle* published a story bylined by Associated Press reporter Richard

Simpson under the headline "Richmond District Worse Than Battle Fields Of France."

Yates left Halifax with Prime Minister Borden.

During the afternoon Jerome Keating and Roy Atkinson obtained a statement from Captain Le Médec.

11 December

Accompanied by a military escort, Hare visited the North End and took a series of photographs which appeared in the 29 December 1917 issue of *Leslie's Weekly*.

The *Providence Journal's* correspondent visited the Richmond district.

Gorman attended and reported funeral services for military victims at the Admiralty building.

12 December

Chambers left Ottawa for Halifax.

Atkinson and Grattan O'Leary filed their last despatches from Halifax.

December 13

Prior to an early morning departure from Halifax to Boston, Abraham Ratshesky, head of the Boston Relief Committee in Halifax from 8-12 December, congratulated local newspapers and the press as well as the five Boston journalists for their supportive role in the aftermath.

Halifax Herald cub reporter Harold Jefferson and *Echo* reporter James L. Gowen began covering the Wreck Commissioner's Inquiry held in courtroom #1 at the County Court House on Spring Garden Road. Gowen's son, James E., acted as a runner for his father and the paper.

Keating, Gorman and the *Providence Journal* reporter filed their last despatches from Halifax.

On or about this date Lismer sent sketches of the Explosion's aftermath to the *Canadian Courier*. Eight drawings were featured in an article titled "The War Comes to Halifax …As Seen by the Artist." in the magazine's 29 December 1917 issue.

14 December

Chambers arrived in Halifax to discuss security and censorship problems caused by the Explosion with Major-General Thomas Benson, the commanding officer of Military District No. 6 which included Halifax.

15 December

Chambers convened a meeting at the Halifax Hotel of local press representatives from the *Herald, Mail, Chronicle, Echo* and *Recorder* to discuss guidance of the press in the treatment of Explosion related matter.

Hickey represented the Halifax CP Bureau. There were no visiting Canadian or American journalists present.

Inaugural Chair of the Rehabilitation Committee Dugald MacGillvray met MacMechan at 11 a.m. on Hollis Street and requested him to write an official history of the disaster. Later in the day, MacMechan visited the Chronicle Building to meet *Daily Echo* editor Hervey Jones about renting office space for the Halifax Disaster Record Office.

16 December

Philpott filed his last despatch from Halifax to the *Boston Globe*.

MacMechan obtained Room 24 in the Chronicle Building for the Halifax Disaster Record Office.

Appendix B

Acadian Recorder 7 December 1917 Front-Page Public Information Notice

1. That all parents or guardians seeking lost children and all persons who are housing lost children are requested to call at the City Clerk's office and register.
2. All persons who are homeless or who need shelter are also requested to register with the City Clerk when they will be assigned quarters as soon as possible.
3. All persons who are willing to provide accommodation for survivors are requested to file their names, together with accommodations available with the City Clerk.
4. As there will likely be a shortage of the available supply of glass all persons removing glass are earnestly requested to do so with as little breakage as possible. A large quantity of the glass required will be sizes as small as 8 X 10 and 10 X 18 inches. If persons assisting in this way will telephone the City Clerk's office such glass will be sent for.
5. All persons removing sashes to have same made with small lights in order that small sizes of glass may be used.
6. All outside towns contributing relief furnish as far as possible the following articles: Glass, Beaver Board, Tarred Paper, Lumber, Putty, Bedding and Blankets.

Carpenters, glaziers, masons and plasterers are urgently needed and as quickly as possible.

Notes

Introduction

1. Although the word "munitions," meaning military weapons, ammunition and equipment, is usually spelled in the plural, it was frequently spelled "munition" in contemporary newspaper accounts of the Explosion.

2. In a CBC radio interview originally broadcast in 1958 and re-broadcast on 3 October 1967, *Mont-Blanc* Pilot Francis Mackey characterized the munitions on the ship as a "damned bad cargo." Francis Mackey, 1958, CBC's Bob Cadman interviews Captain Mackey. According to the original New York City manifest and shipper's export declaration, when *Mont-Blanc* left New York at 11:00 p.m. on 1 December there were 2,366.475 tons wet and dry picric acid [a chemical used in the manufacture of explosives], 250 tons TNT, 62.062 tons gun cotton [nitrocellulose, a highly flammable nitrate compound] and 246.022 tons benzol for a total of 2,924.559 [short] tons of explosive material on *Mont-Blanc*. Alan Ruffman and Colin D. Howell, co-editors, *Ground Zero: A Reassessment of the 1917 Explosion in Halifax Harbour*, 296. Henry Jefferson, a twenty-four-year-old cub reporter who covered the inquiry into the disaster for the *Halifax Herald*, indicated that the benzol was contained in 494 barrels on *Mont-Blanc's* decks. Henry B. Jefferson "Day of Disaster," *Atlantic Advocate* (1958): 17. In addition to the picric acid, TNT, gun cotton and treated benzol, there were between 350 and 400 rounds of 90 mm and 95 mm shells on board for the fore and aft cannons. Joel Zemel, *Scapegoat: The Extraordinary Legal Proceedings Following the 1917 Halifax Explosion*, 22.

3. *Imo's* destination was New York to collect emergency relief supplies for civilians in war-torn Belgium. The ship had been originally scheduled to leave Halifax during the afternoon of 5 December, but a delay in coaling postponed its departure.

4. In the January 1918 *Canadian Railway and Marine World* issue an unattributed article provides the following non-metric description of both ships. "The s.s. Mont Blanc was a single screw steamship of 3,121 tons gross, 320 ft., 44 ft., beam and 15 ft. deep ... The s.s. Imo was ... length 430 ft., beam 45 ft., depth 30 ft. 2 ins., tonnage 5,043 gross."

5. The *Ottawa Journal's* Grattan O'Leary reported that the words "Belgian Relief" were "blazoned on both her sides in letters three feet deep," 10 December 1917, 16.

6. Eye-witness Lieutenant-Colonel Frederick McKelvey Bell wrote that the morning "dawned both fine and fair...air was clear and crisp but the bright sunshine tempered the slight touch of frost," Frederick McKelvey Bell, *A Romance of the Halifax Disaster*, np.

7. Archibald MacMechan, official historian of the Explosion, indicated that "the collision occurred about seventeen minutes to nine," Graham Metson, *The Halifax Explosion Dec. 6, 1917*, 13.

8. Joan Payzant and Lewis Payzant, *Like a Weaver's Shuttle: A History of the Halifax-Dartmouth Ferries*, 145.

9. During the inquiry into the Explosion, Crown prosecutor Andrew Cluney KC, who represented the Office of the Attorney General of Nova Scotia, referred to *Mont-Blanc* as a "floating arsenal." John Armstrong, *The Halifax Explosion and the Royal Canadian Navy: Inquiry and Intrigue*, 182.

10. Owen McCarron, *A Tribute to the Halifax Fire Department on the 85th Anniversary of the Halifax Explosion. An Historical Docu-Comic*, 2. The "Patricia" carried a six-man crew; Fire Chief Edward Condon and Deputy Chief William Brunt followed in an automobile. The fire call box number was confirmed in an *Acadian Recorder* story published on 7 December.

11. The railway footbridge spanned from the bottom of Duffus Street to the head of Pier 7. *Chronicle Herald*, 4 December 2000 A3.

12. Excluding *Mont-Blanc's* captain Le Médec and his forty-man crew, only one person in Halifax knew the full extent of the munitions on board *Mont-Blanc*: Mate Terrance Freeman was informed of the entire cargo via the ship's manifest when he boarded *Mont-Blanc* on 5 December. However, it is unlikely that he was aware of the true nature of each of the dangerous substances. The author thanks Joel Zemel for this information.

13. According to *Dartmouth Patriot* editor Joseph Sheldon, *Mont-Blanc's* gun landed in Albro Lake "where it now lies, exposed to view." "Death Calls Too Soon – Scenes at Chebucto Morgue" in Syd Gosley, *The Harbour Catastrophe*, n. p. On 23 May 1918 *Mont-Blanc's* anchor shank was "hoisted out of a four foot deep hole in the ground on Gabriel Edmond's property 'Hiddenhurst.'" Public Archives of Nova Scotia (hereafter PANS) MG 1 Volume 2124, #108.

14. Owned by the Norwegian South Pacific Trading Company, *Imo* was repaired and re-launched in 1920 as the whale-oil tanker *Guvernøren* (*Governor*).

15. Helmsman John Johansen was the sole crew member on *Imo's* bridge to survive.

16. Ronayne was the only Halifax-Dartmouth reporter to die as a result of the Explosion. See Chapter 2.

17. Sydney is 434 kilometres northeast of Halifax and Yarmouth 273 kilometres south. Visiting *St. John Daily Telegraph* city editor Stanley Smith stated that "two distinct sounds of the explosion" were also heard in Louisburg, 398 kilometres from Halifax. Stanley Smith, *Heart Throbs of the Halifax Horror*, 95.

18. McAlpine's 1917 Halifax City Directory lists the population at 65,000. Separate figures for Dartmouth vary. Harry Chapman indicates that by 1917 Dartmouth was incorporated as a town with a population of 6,000. Harry Chapman, *Dartmouth's Day of Anguish*. Armstrong indicates that the number of soldiers in the area in December 1917, including medical troops, totalled approximately 5,000. Armstrong *op. cit.* 11.

19. In a special fifty-six-page Reconstruction issue of the *Halifax Evening Mail* on 22 March 1918, the Herald building was described as "250 feet long by 75 feet deep, with its aggregate floor space of 73,000 feet."

20. Nova Scotia newspaper historian Gertrude Tratt suggests that the circulation of the *Acadian Recorder* in 1917 was 2,500. Gertrude Tratt, *Preliminary Survey and Listing of Nova Scotia Newspapers 1752-1954*, 42. The 1917 Canadian Newspaper Directory indicates the circulation of the *Morning Chronicle* as 12,001, *Daily Echo* 7,251, *Herald* 10,741, and *Evening Mail* 14,181. The *Halifax Herald, Halifax Evening Mail, Morning Chronicle, Daily Echo, Acadian Recorder, Dartmouth Patriot* and *Truro*

Daily News hereafter known as the *Herald, Mail, Chronicle, Echo, Recorder, Patriot* and *News*.

21. Both morning papers, the *Chronicle* and *Herald*, were home-delivered prior to the Explosion. See the *Boston Globe*, 12 December 1917, 9, and Hugh MacLennan, *Barometer Rising*, 167, 171 and 172. The 6 December *Chronicle* was headlined "British Have Situation in Control at Cambrai" and the *Herald* "Germans Start New Offensive to Take Venice."

22. On 7 December the *News* was also available in Halifax. A notice in the 8 December morning edition reminded readers the paper was "compiled and printed after 6:30 o'clock in the morning and was on the streets at 9 o'clock." *News*, 8 December 1917, 1.

23. The *Patriot's* next issue appeared on 15 December and was described by the paper's editor Joseph Sheldon as "a small edition." *Patriot*, 15 December 1917, 1. According to Tratt, the *Patriot's* all-time high circulation was 2,260, in 1915. Tratt *op. cit.* 42. The weekly *Nova Scotian* was published by the Chronicle Publishing Company. Unfortunately, no hard or microfilm copies of the paper exist.

24. In 1917, newspapers and magazines were the major mass media used by the public to obtain news. Commercial radio was not available at the time and not in Halifax until 1926. *Mail Star*, 6 December 1975, 7. The election was set for 17 December. Prime Minister Sir Robert Borden held a Halifax seat.

25. Mark Nichols, *(CP) The Story of Canadian Press*, 134-135. As will be seen in Chapter 2, Hickey had previously wired news of the Explosion to Associated Press (AP) in New York half an hour after the disaster occurred.

26. With the exception of bulletins on the commission of inquiry into the disaster, by 13 December the Explosion story was no longer front-page news in most Canadian newspapers, and Saint John, Toronto, Ottawa and Montreal newspapers recalled their reporters from Halifax. American papers waited a few more days to recall their correspondents. For example, *Boston Herald-Journal's* Jerome Keating's final despatch ran on 14 December and *Boston Globe* reporter Anthony Philpott's last despatch from Halifax appeared on 16 December.

27. The official title was the Wreck Commissioner's Inquiry.

28. Mackey recovered his pilot's licence on 14 February 1922 and continued piloting vessels until 1937. For an excellent narrative of his efforts at reinstatement as a Halifax pilot see Janet Maybee *Aftershock The Halifax Explosion and the Persecution of Pilot Francis Mackey*. Captain Le Médec continued serving as captain in the Compagnie Generale Transatlantique until 1922 and in 1931 received the Chevalier de la Legion d'Honneur (Legion of Honour) for thirty-five years of service in the French merchant marine. After Wyatt's discharge from the Royal Canadian Navy, he and his wife moved to the United States. He worked for twenty years in the merchant marine and after retirement lived for sixteen years in Sarasota, Florida, where he died at age eighty-nine. The author thanks author and Explosion historian Joel Zemel for information on Le Médec and Wyatt.

29. The earliest publications were Archibald MacMechan's "Halifax in Ruins" (*Canadian Courier* 22 December 1917), "When the War Came to Halifax…As Seen by the Artist" (*Canadian Courier* 29 December 1917) edited by Augustus Bridle and sketches by Arthur Lismer, Harold T. Roe's *Views of the Halifax Catastrophe*

Showing Effects of Explosion December Sixth 1917 (1917), Stanley Smith's *Heart Throbs of the Halifax Horror* (1918), Joseph Sheldon's *A Bolt from the Blue* (1918), Lt. Col. F. McKelvey Bell's novel *A Romance of the Halifax Disaster* (1918), Canon Charles Vernon's "Some Impressions of the Great Disaster Which Befell Halifax and Dartmouth December 6th, *1917*" (*Church Work* 14 February 1918) and Samuel Prince's *Catastrophe and Social Change* (1920). These were followed several years later by Hugh MacLennan's novel *Barometer Rising* (1941), Thomas Raddall's *Halifax, Warden of the North* (1948), Michael Bird's mix of fact and fiction *The Town That Died: The True Story of the Greatest Man-Made Explosion Before Hiroshima* (1962), Thomas Raddall's *In My Time: A Memoir* (1976), Graham Metson's *The Halifax Explosion, Dec. 6, 1917* (1978) and Jim Lotz's novel *The Sixth of December* (1981). Later publications included Janet Kitz's *Shattered City: The Halifax Explosion and the Road to Recovery* (1989) and *Survivors: Children of the Halifax Explosion* (1992), Harry Chapman's *Dartmouth's Day of Anguish* (1992), Alan Ruffman and Colin Howell's co-edited *Ground Zero: A Reassessment of the 1917 Explosion in Halifax Harbour* (1994), James and Rowena Mahar's *Too Many to Mourn: One Family's Tragedy* (1998) and Robert MacNeil's novel *Burden of Desire*. More recent works are those by John Armstrong's *The Halifax Explosion and the Royal Canadian Navy: Inquiry and Intrigue* (2002), David Flemming's *Explosion in Halifax Harbour: The Illustrated Account of a Disaster That Shook the World* (2004), Laura MacDonald's *Curse of the Narrows: The Halifax Explosion, 1917* (2005), Janet Kitz and Joan Payzant's *December 1917 Re-Visiting the Halifax Explosion* (2006), Jon Tattrie's novel *Black Snow* (2009), Jennie Marsland's novel *Shattered* (2011), Joel Zemel's *Scapegoat: The Extraordinary Legal Proceeding Following the 1917 Explosion* (2012), Steven Lafolley's novel *The Blue Tattoo* (2014) and Janet Maybee's *Aftershock The Halifax Explosion and the Persecution of Pilot Francis Mackey* (2015).

30. Sources used to identify the journalists and record keepers include government documents, archival records, correspondents' memoirs, diaries, manuscripts and letters, descendants' recollections and photographs, morgue (newspaper library) files, magazine articles, news-wire copy and newspaper bylines, headlines, despatches, interviews and editorials. In 1917 the majority of Canadian daily newspapers maintained reporter anonymity, and most published material was unsigned or identified by such generic appellations as "staff reporter" or "staff correspondent." However, bylines were sometimes given to recognize a reporter's original contribution and hard work on a story. The only Halifax-Dartmouth journalist given a byline was *Dartmouth Patriot* editor Joseph Sheldon. Visiting journalists given bylines include Grattan O'Leary (*Ottawa Journal*), William Stuart (*Montreal Standard*), Anthony Philpott (*Boston Daily Globe*), Jerome Keating (*Boston Herald-Journal*), Roy Atkinson (*Boston Post*) and James Hare (*Leslie's Weekly*). Also, on 10 December the *Chronicle* published a story headlined "Richmond District Worse Than Battle Fields of France" signed by visiting AP correspondent Richard Simpson. *Chronicle*, 10 December 1917, 4. The identities of the *Daily News* reporter, *Nieuw Amsterdam Courant* editor, *Truro News* special representative, both *Toronto Daily Star* reporters and the *Providence Journal/Bulletin* staff correspondent remain unknown. The author of the article "When War Came to Halifax…As Seen by the Artist" may have been the magazine's editor Augustus Bridle; the sketches were drawn by Arthur Lismer.

Chapter 1 The Role of Canada's Chief Press Censor, Lieutenant-Colonel Ernest J. Chambers

1. For a thorough examination of Chambers' role as CPC see Jeffrey Keshen's *Propaganda and Censorship During Canada's Great War*.
2. Mark Bourrie, *The Fog of War*, 24.
3. W.A. Craick, *A History of Canadian Journalism 11*, 109.
4. Between June 1915 and April 1919 Chambers banned 253 publications, including 164 in a language other than English or French, and 70 after war ended on 11 November 1918.
5. Library and Archives Canada (hereafter LAC), Secretary of State – Chief Press Censor (CPC) File RG 6E Volume 621, File 350 Microfilm T-102, *Sydney Record* to Chambers, 6 December 1917.
6. CPC File RG 6E Volume 621, File 350, Chambers to *Sydney Record*, 6 December 1917. The telegram arrived from the *Record* in Ottawa at 11.38 a.m. Eastern Standard Time (EST) and Chambers replied at 11:50 a.m. (EST). Given the one hour difference between EST and Atlantic Standard Time (AST), it appears the *Record's* representative sent the telegram approximately three hours and thirty minutes after the Explosion.
7. CPC File RG 6E Volume 621, File 350, Chambers to George Perry, General Manager, Great North West Telegraph Company, Montreal and J.J. McMillan, Manager Canadian Pacific Railway Telegraph Company, Montreal, 6 December 1917.
8. In October 1915 Chambers appointed Knowles one of two Toronto-based press censors. With headquarters in Montreal, CP began operations on 2 September 1917 serving 117 member newspapers. Knowles supervised fifteen staff in Toronto; there were fourteen telegraph operators and forty-three editorial and administrative employees spread over eight bureaus. Gene Allen, *Making National News: A History of Canadian Press*, 49.
9. CPC File RG 6E Volume 621, File 350, Chambers to Knowles, Canadian Press, Toronto, 6 December 1917. Unknown to Chambers, on the day of the Explosion every CPR Company Telegraph operator in the Halifax office but one was "more or less seriously injured." *News*, 6 December 1917, 1.
10. CPC File RG 6E Volume 621, File 350, McMillan to Chambers, 6 December 1917. McMillan's reply was sent from Montreal at 4:43 pm (EST). Given the communications delay for CPR Telegraph Company officials in Halifax to assure McMillan in Montreal that a wire was now available for outside communication, a Halifax CP despatch could have been filed for distribution after 4:00 p.m. (EST). In the special Reconstruction edition of the *Evening Mail* under the headline "Triumph Wrought by C.P.R. Telegraphers," Halifax CPR Telegraph Company officials provide a detailed description of the service following the Explosion. Through "the organizing genius" of Eastern superintendent A.C. Fraser, the company recovered one line within thirty minutes of the Explosion and was obtaining details of the disaster when directed by military authorities to leave office headquarters in the Dennis Building. By evening the office had six direct multiplex wires to Montreal, three to Saint John and one each to Boston and New York. *Mail*, 22 March 1918.
11. CPC File RG 6E Volume 621, File 350, Perry to Chambers, 6 December 1917.
12. CPC File RG 6E Volume 621, File 350, Memorandum for Office File, 6 December 1917. Chambers kept the CPC Ottawa office open from 9 a.m. to midnight Monday

through Saturday and 8 p.m. to midnight on Sunday. Keshen *op.cit.* 72.

13. *Mail*, 22 March 1918. The city of St. John was officially renamed Saint John in 1925. Hereafter Saint John will be used in reference to the city and St. John for 1917 newspapers.

14. *Mail*, 22 March 1918.

15. To spike a story is to withhold it from publication. Discarded copy was originally impaled on a spike.

16. CPC File RG 6E Volume 621, File 350, Chambers to C.O. Knowles, 7 December 1917. As CP did not send any agency reporters to Halifax, Chambers' reference to "special correspondents despatched to Halifax" referred to visiting correspondents.

17. The local papers were the *Ottawa Citizen* and *Ottawa Journal* as both sent reporters to Halifax.

18. From Chambers' memorandum it is known he tried unsuccessfully to reach Curren by phone "about ten o'clock." CPC Memorandum for Office File, 7 December 1917. CPC File RG 6E Volume 621, File 350, Chambers to Colonel A.E. Curren, 7 December 1917.

19. CPC File RG 6E Volume 621, File 350, Chambers to Creel, Washington, 7 December 1917. George Creel, former journalist and politician, was Chambers' counterpart in the United States.

20. CPC File RG 6E Volume 621, File 350, Chambers to McMillan, 8 December 1917.

21. See Chapter 3 for O'Leary's *Ottawa Journal* coverage.

22. CPC File RG 6E Volume 621, File 350, Chambers to Perry, 9 December 1917.

23. Armstrong *op. cit.* 116 117, 124. The request by Gwatkin came via Major-General Thomas Benson in Halifax.

24. CPC File RG 6E Volume 621, File 350, Chambers to Hickey, 18 December 1917. From CPC records no representative from the weekly *Dartmouth Patriot* nor visiting Canadian or American journalists were present at the "little conference."

25. LAC, RG 24 Vol. 4547 File 86-1-3 Part 7, Chambers to Gwatkin, 18 December 1917.

26. Ratshesky *op. cit.* 27.

27. Smith *op. cit.* 44.

Chapter 2 Journalists and Record Keepers Who Experienced the Explosion Firsthand

1. The author thanks Ryerson University Professor Gene Allen for information on EAP and CP. Pearson became chairman of the Halifax Relief Commission's construction committee and also provided an office in the Chronicle building for the Halifax Disaster Record Office directed by Archibald MacMechan.

2. McAlpine's Halifax Directories for 1917–18 and the 1918–19 Halifax Phone Directories list "Canadian Press Ltd." in December 1917 at 92 Granville Street. As well, the 1918 City Directory and the 7 December 1917 *Recorder* masthead show 90–94 Granville Street as the location of the *Recorder* and Blackadar Bros. Printers, both owned by the Blackadar family [brothers Charles, Hugh and Henry]. As the 1919–20 Halifax City Directory indicates the Halifax CP office as Rm. 6, Chronicle Building, 85-93 Granville Street, it is likely that the wire service bureau moved to the Chronicle Building [home to the *Chronicle* and *Echo*] sometime in 1918 or 1919.

3. Carlton McNaught, *Canada Gets the News*, 65–66. According to information in the

March 1981 interview with Janet Kitz and Jim Gowen (hereafter PANS Kitz/Gowen interview), in 1917 *Echo* reporter James L. Gowen provided copies of his stories to James Hickey, a routine practice under CP guidelines.

4. Despatches were wired from CP Montreal to bureaus in Ottawa, Toronto, New York, Winnipeg, Calgary, Edmonton and Vancouver. With the exception of Ottawa, each bureau acted as a relay point. CP historian Nichols states a review of American papers of 6 December reveals the Canadian wire service supplied *"more than ninety per cent"* (my italics) of the Halifax story used by AP newspapers. Nichols *op. cit.* 66, 134.

James Hickey and Maxwell Backer, Halifax Canadian Press Bureau

1. According to CP personnel records, when the Halifax CP bureau was established on 1 September 1917, the first superintendent was American-born, thirty-three-year-old Andrew D. Merkel (CP records his official title as editor). For several years before joining CP, Merkel had been editor of the *Daily Echo*, but prior to the Explosion Merkel was transferred to Montreal as Maritime news editor. The author thanks Esther Bye, CP Human Resources Advisor, for providing Merkel's employment details.

2. McAlpine's Halifax Directory for 1917 (effective July 1917) lists Backer as "night operator Chronicle." When the Halifax CP bureau was established in September 1917 he likely transferred to the new press service and became the agency's day operator.

3. When the Explosion occurred, Hinch had just exited the Chronicle Building. Following the blast he went home to 18 Richmond Street in the North End. Although his father survived the Explosion, Hinch lost his mother, two brothers and three sisters.

4. In the 1954 Halifax-Dartmouth City Directory, Hickey is listed as "writer Halifax Herald."

5. The author thanks Hickey's granddaughter Pat Brennan for the information.

6. Hickey's obituary appeared in the *Chronicle Herald* on 29 November 1954. The author thanks Spring Garden Road Reference Department staff for a copy.

7. Journalism historian W.H. Kesterton verifies that Hickey was involved in the coverage of the *Titanic* story. W.H. Kesterton, *A History of Journalism in Canada*, 109.

8. *Chronicle*, 20 June 1949, 26. Hickey retired in 1951 after serving as a Halifax news reporter for sixty-six years.

9. *New York Times*, 10 December 1917. There are no existing CP personnel records for Hickey and Maxwell Backer.

10. CPC, Chambers to Hickey, 18 December 1917.

11. PANS Accession 2007-066 Volume 002 AC 3647-3648 31, PANS Kitz/Gowen interview. In 1917 it was common practice for reporters and editors to supplement their incomes by providing news to outside newspapers and press services. These freelance correspondents were known as stringers.

12. *Chronicle Herald*, 29 November 1954.

13. The author thanks Nancy Ring and Joe McSweeney for information on Backer.

14. The author thanks Carolyn Simpson for information on Leo Hinch.

15. The Chronicle Building was on the southeast corner of Granville and Prince Streets. Built in 1907 it was three stories and constructed of ironstone clay brick. The printing

presses and composing room were on the main floor and offices on the upper floors. The building had natural light for all sides through plate glass windows and plate glass was particularly used in the Granville Street front. The author thanks Spring Garden Library Reference Department staff for information on the Chronicle Building. At the time of the Explosion the Halifax Publishing Company (home to the *Herald* and *Mail*) was located a few blocks west of the Chronicle Building, at the intersection of Argyle, Prince and Sackville Streets.

16. McAlpine's Halifax Directory for 1917 lists forty-two-year-old John Hagen as the senior operator of Halifax and Bermuda Cable Company Ltd and the company office on the first floor of the Dennis Building at 108 Granville Street. Hagen's 6 December 1917 message transmitted to Hamilton, Bermuda, was picked up by the company's station in Havana and relayed to Associated Press in New York.

17. Given the circumstances, Hickey would have had no time to make notes and as reported "dictated" the despatch to Hagen. While Hickey's news bulletin was the first to be wired from the stricken city on 6 December, it was not the only one. Later in the day his longer despatch was wired to the outside world by an operator in the CPR Telegraphs office in Halifax. *Royal Gazette* (Hamilton, Bermuda), 14 March 1918, 1. The author thanks Joe Zemel for a copy of the *Royal Gazette* story.

18. If Hickey's recollection of wiring the first despatch "half an hour" after the Explosion is correct, his bulletin was the *first* news that AP circulated throughout the United States.

19. *Chronicle*, 20 June 1949, 26. The wording in Hickey's 6 December telegram to AP is similar to the only one originating from Halifax in a series of telegrams sent from points outside Halifax on the morning of the Explosion. It reads: "12:26 p.m. P.M. Halifax NS (via Havana) – Hundreds of persons were killed and a thousand others injured and half the city of Halifax is in ruins as the result of the explosion on a munitions ship in the harbour today. It is estimated the property loss will run into the millions. The north end of the city is in flames." Telegrams: D. Johnstone, "The Tragedy of Halifax 1917," PANS, MFM 3824.

20. A follow up is a story written to report extra details, later developments, reaction and new issues related to a previously published story.

21. According to Kesterton, Hickey "starred" in the coverage of the Explosion. Kesterton *op. cit.* 109. A legman is a reporter whose job is to gather information at the scene of an event or by visiting various news sources. A spreader is a headline that extends across two or more columns of print.

22. Africville was Halifax's African Nova Scotian community located on the southern shores of Bedford Basin.

23. *Mont-Blanc* was obliterated by the blast.

24. *Imo* struck *Mont-Blanc* at Hold No. 1 on the starboard side in the ship's forward section. *Imo* did not shove *Mont-Blanc*. After *Imo* struck *Mont-Blanc* the Belgian relief vessel separated from *Mont-Blanc* and attempted to steer to Bedford Basin. *Mont-Blanc's* crew abandoned ship.

25. The force of the Explosion produced a tsunami which caused the *Imo* to be beached on the Dartmouth shore north of the town's ferry terminal.

26. *Montreal Gazette,* 7 December 1917, 1.

27. According to McAlpine's Halifax Directory for 1917, Backer and Hickey resided in

the south end of the city: Backer at 116 Edward Street and Hickey at 175 Morris Street.

28. *Manitoba Free Press,* 8 December 1917, 19.

29. It is likely that Muriel Backer was in the cradle as she was thirteen months (born 25 November 1916) and her brother Lawrence over two years (born 27 September 1915).

30. *New York Times,* 10 December 1917, 3. The reference in the *Times* story to a "three-storey structure" supports the author's belief that Hickey and Backer were in an office in the Chronicle Building.

31. *New York Times,* 7 December 1917, 2. From this report day operator Backer left the Chronicle Building after the disaster to determine the fate of his family and did not return to the bureau that day; an unidentified substitute, who replaced Backer, in turn left his key at 10:00 p.m.

32. *Montreal Gazette,* 7 December 1917, 1.

33. *St. John Daily Telegraph,* 7 December 1917, 3. The hospital was located in the Rockhead Prison in the city's North End near the intersection of Leeds and Gottingen Streets.

CP Historians Mark Nichols and Peter Buckley

1. Neither author mentions Ernest Chambers' 6 December 1917 telegraph to CP general manager Charles Knowles; both authors fail to acknowledge the day one accomplishments of Hickey and Backer. In addition, neither historian mentions the role played in facilitating transmission of the Explosion's news coverage by CP reporter George MacDonald and Maritime News Editor Andrew Merkel in Montreal. MacDonald was CP's resident correspondent stationed in Montreal. He reported news for CP in Quebec, the rest of eastern Canada and at times the eastern United States. According to information provided by his grandson Hugh Doherty (see hughdoherty.tripod.com/george.htm). "George MacDonald: Half a century of news"), MacDonald "covered" the Halifax Explosion for CP. There is no evidence his grandfather was present in Halifax at the time of the Explosion and its aftermath, and it is more likely that MacDonald's news coverage involved receiving James Hickey's despatches from Halifax and relaying them from Montreal to CP headquarters in Toronto. According to a story written prior to Merkel's retirement, his "intimate knowledge of the entire Halifax area made it possible for the Canadian Press to give its papers accurate coverage" of the Explosion. J.M. Redditt "A.D. Merkel to Leave CP Post in Halifax," *Editor & Publisher* (20 April 1956, 44).

2. The author believes this bulletin was based on the despatch previously sent to AP in New York by Hickey.

3. As previously indicated, at 4:43 p.m. CPR Telegraph Manager J.J. McMillan assured Chambers that a wire was now available for Halifax CP. Therefore, Nichols' assertion that "a [CP] dispatch was filed for distribution at 4 p.m." appears accurate.

4. On 6 December the *News* reported forty-two-year-old Alfred Coffin's trip to Halifax. "Mr. A. R. Coffin of the News has rusht (*sic*) thru to Halifax by automobile to assist the Canadian Press Association in all possible ways to get the story of the Halifax disaster for the Canadian Association." *News,* 6 December 1917, 4. In the same issue, the paper stated: "The News reporter visited the newspaper and printing offices in Halifax and placed its plant at their disposal if needed." *News,* 6 December 1917, 1. However, none of Halifax's five dailies accepted the offer to use *News* plant facilities.

5. Nichols *op. cit.* 134–135.

6. The telegraph operator was Vincent Coleman, who died moments later when the *Mont-Blanc* detonated.

7. From the *Manitoba Free Press* 8 December and *New York Times* 10 December press reports at the time of the blast *both* Backer *and* Hickey were in the CP bureau.

8. Peter Buckley, *The National (CP) Link. 1917: Halifax Explosion First Test*, n. p. The author thanks Ryerson University Professor Gene Allen for a copy of Buckley's two-page description.

William Barton, Former *Montreal Gazette* Telegraph Editor

1. Although a *former* journalist, Barton's description of the Explosion's aftermath has been included as it was reported in several North American newspapers and is one of the few accounts by a visitor with professional news experience.

2. The four-storey Halifax Hotel was located on the east side of Hollis Street, approximately 3.5 kilometres south of the immediate blast area. All of its plate-glass windows were shattered but the building did not suffer major structural damage.

3. The interview with Barton was likely conducted by CP's Hickey on either 6 or 7 December. AP obtained the interview via its news sharing agreement with CP.

4. A.H. Chipman, another guest having breakfast in the Halifax Hotel at the time of the Explosion, provided the number. A.H. Chipman to My Dear Brother, 13 December 1917. Chipman's letter was published in the *Berwick Register* on 9 January 1918.

5. Chipman also confirmed Barton's description of the damage to the hotel's hallway and lobby. "Glass was crashing in all directions. The hallway and lobby were two inches deep in small pieces of thick plate for the pressure came equally upon each square foot of glass. Through the swivel doors we stepped with a stoop to sidewalk and street." A.H. Chipman to My Dear Brother, 13 December 1917.

6. The Armouries was located at the southeast corner of North Park and Cunard Streets.

7. After 12 December entry into the devastated area required an official pass. According to a *Toronto Daily Star* (hereafter *Toronto Star*) reporter, it was necessary to obtain this permit from Halifax's Chief of Police Frank Hanrahan as "a safe-conduct through all military lines except in fortified areas." "A city of stopped clocks keeps strange, sad Sunday" *Toronto Star*, 11 December 1917, 18.

8. *New York Times*, 8 December 1917, 2.

Joseph Sheldon, *Dartmouth N.S Patriot*, Arthur Pettipas, *Halifax Herald*, and Mary "May" O'Regan, *Morning Chronicle*

1. McAlpine's Halifax Directory for 1917 lists Sheldon at an unnumbered Victoria Road residence. Nova Scotia Vital Statistics records indicate he married Violet Umler on 10 March 1915.

2. Although McAlpine's Halifax Directories between 1916 and 1918 list the address of the *Patriot* as Water without a street number, prior to 1912 Water Street was called Commercial Drive. According to Dartmouth historian J.P. Martin, in 1912 the *Patriot's* street address was 48 Commercial Street. Martin, *The Story of Dartmouth*, page 509. This address placed the newspaper between Portland and Queen Streets, behind the ferry terminal and outside the immediate blast area of Tuft's Cove and

Dartmouth's north end. The author thanks Spring Garden Road Library Reference Department staff and Dartmouth Heritage Museum curator Crystal Martin for information leading to the location of the *Patriot*.

3. *Patriot*, 15 December 1917, 1.

4. "Death Calls Too Soon: Scenes at Chebucto" can be found in a four-page pamphlet *The Harbour Catastrophe* by Syd Gosley, n.d. The author thanks Crystal Martin for a copy of Gosley's pamphlet.

5. Biographical details on Pettipas are based on information in H. Millard Wright's *One Region Many Leaders*, 42-43. Pettipas was mayor of Dartmouth between 1948 and 1950.

6. *Halifax Mail Star*, 28 July 1975. The author thanks *Chronicle* librarian Louise Le Pierres for a copy of Pettipas's obituary.

7. *Patriot*, 16 December 1917, 1.

8. May was the youngest of four children. Her father died accidentally in 1901 leaving his wife Johannah to raise four children under eleven on earnings as a seamstress. The author thanks May's nephew Jim O'Regan for this information.

9. Berton Robinson "The Chronicle building comes down," *Chronicle Herald* (December 1972). The author thanks Jim O'Regan for a copy of the *Chronicle* article.

10. Marjorie Lang, *Women Who Made the News*, 117. See also Doris McCubbin, "The Women of Halifax," *Chatelaine* (June 1954), 16. The author thanks Jim O'Regan for a copy of the *Chatelaine* article and Louise Le Pierres for a copy of May O'Regan's obituary.

11. Janet Kitz, *Shattered City: The Halifax Explosion and the Road to Recovery*, 31.

12. Information provided to the author by Jim O'Regan.

13. See note 35 in Chapter 2 on Hervey Jones, James L. Gowen and John Ronayne.

14. *Chronicle*, 21 December 1917, 11. The author thanks Jim O'Regan for a copy of the column.

15. *Chronicle*, 27 December 1917, 6. The author thanks Jim O'Regan for a copy of the story.

16. See "Sensational Local Events Recorded in Half-Century" *Halifax Mail-Star* 10 April 1951, 6. The author thanks Jim O'Regan for a copy of the story.

17. A deck is one or more shorter headlines inserted between the main headline and the story.

18. The brief information about Sheldon (the writer) is known in journalism as a "blurb."

19. According to Alan Ruffman and David Simpson there were several "pre-cursor" explosions caused by exploding barrels of benzol on *Mont-Blanc's* deck prior to the main blast. Ruffman and Simpson *op. cit.* 314. Aside from these preliminary explosions, they emphasize there was only one main explosion, which caused a seismic ground wave, an air wave or shock wave, with the sound wave travelling through the ground faster than the air wave, and a sea water wave — the tsunami. At a distance of one kilometre from ground zero the sound of both waves would have been only one second apart but at five kilometres the sounds would have been about ten seconds apart, accounting for the reporting of a first and then second explosion close to ground zero. Ruffman and Simpson *op. cit.* 317–318.

20. Oland's brewery at Turtle Grove was within 125 metres of the grounded *Imo*. According to Sheldon, when the blast levelled the building, the owner, Cornelius

[Conrad] Oland, and every employee, except one, were killed. Sheldon, *A Bolt from the Blue*, n. p.

21. Harry Chapman lists the names of fifty-two Dartmouth residents reported killed and missing as a result of the Explosion. Chapman *op. cit.* 43.

22. In the *Patriot's* 15 December issue Sheldon detailed the damage to the paper on the day of the Explosion and reported it was impossible to publish on 8 December. *Patriot*, 15 December 1917, 1.

23. In fact the *Patriot* did republish on 15 December.

24. *Toronto Star*, 10 December 1917, 19.

Peter Lawson, *Halifax Herald*

1. Biographical information on Lawson is based on obituaries in the *Beaumont Enterprise* 10 September 1949 and *Berwick Register* 15 September 1949 as well as details in Albert J. Perry, *The History of Knox County, Illinois*, 1069–70 (transcribed by Danni Hopkins). The author thanks Dr. Scott Pigford for a copy of the *Berwick Register* obituary and Joel Zemel for a copy of the information on Lawson in *The History of Knox County, Illinois*.

2. Lawson never received his BA after returning in 1897. The author thanks Creighton Barrett, digital archivist, Dalhousie University, for information on Lawson's academic record.

3. Maude Tryon's husband Frank and Peter Lawson went sailing in 1908 and Frank drowned. Subsequently Peter married Maude and became step-father to her two-year-old son Lyman. In 1910 a daughter, Agnes, was born to Maude and Peter.

4. *Tremorvah* sailed from Halifax on 29 October 1914 and reached Rotterdam on 15 November.

5. *Beaumont Enterprise*, 16 October 1936, 3.

6. Jefferson *op. cit.* 21. The first working telegraph was at Rockingham Station, approximately six kilometres from the North Street Station. Jefferson does not indicate whether Lawson travelled to Rockingham by car or on foot. If on foot it would have taken him several hours to make the trip from Halifax to Rockingham and then back to Halifax.

7. Jefferson *op. cit.* 23.

8. Lawson's recollection was contained in a letter to the *Berwick Register* on 27 January 1943.

9. According to the 1918 Halifax-Dartmouth Directory, in 1917 Lawson was living in Dartmouth, and his Canada Registration Board confirmation letter indicates residence in Dartmouth on 22 June 1918. The author thanks Dr. Scott Pigford for the Canada Registration Board information. It is likely Lawson used Mrs. Connor's boarding house at 30 Buckingham Street as temporary living quarters.

10. Reporters who worked for a morning paper normally arrived at 1:00 p.m. the previous day. The usual deadline for a morning paper was midnight or earlier and for an afternoon [evening] paper noon of the previous day. "Put to bed" means when the newsroom signed off on all pages and the paper sent to the presses for printing.

11. Linotype machines were located in the paper's composing room and contained thousands of zinc pieces, known as slugs, from which newspaper pages were created. Gas-fed fires melted the metal ingots and the scalding-hot liquid (up to 300°C) would be set and hardened into lines of type, one line at a time. According to Bird,

the gas supply operating the linotype machines was interrupted for three days. Michael Bird, *The Town That Died*, 148–49. For additional details of damage to the *Herald* and *Mail* see the 22 March 1918 Reconstruction issue of the *Mail*, the front page of the 7 December 1917 issue, the 12 December 1917 front-page *Herald* article headlined "The task of getting out a paper in disaster," the 6 December 1967 Halifax *Mail-Star* story headlined "Publishing the news – Difficult task," the article headlined "Amid debris, printers struggled" *Mail Star* 6 December 1975.

12. There is more than one narrative of the circumstances surrounding the printing of the *Herald's* improvised issue of 7 December. The most detailed account is provided in the *Mail's* 22 March 1918, Reconstruction edition. According to this version, staff with knowledge of hand setting worked during the night of 6 December and into the early hours of 7 December to produce 400 copies (out of a regular run of 14,000) of a one-sided news sheet reduced to "one-sixteenth of the size of the original." Due to the continued absence of gas to operate the linotype machines, hand setting was required for the *Herald* until 13 December. *Mail*, 22 March 1918. A second version, likely based on the *Mail's* 22 March 1918 issue, is provided by author William March. He states that 400 copies of the one-page issue of the 7 December 1917 morning *Herald* were printed, "the equivalent of one for every 27 subscribers to the morning paper," and during the first four days following the Explosion, as many as sixteen pages of hand-set type may have been produced for the *Herald* alone. March, *Red Line: The Chronicle-Herald and the Mail-Star 1875–1954*, 135.

13. Letter from P.F. Lawson to the *Berwick Register* 27 January 1943.

14. *Mail*, 22 March 1918.

15. The author thanks Louise Le Pierres for a copy of the *Halifax Mail-Star* 6 December 1967 special edition.

16. *Mont-Blanc* drifted to Pier 6 not 8.

17. According to Kitz and Payzant, Campbell Road was renamed Barrington Street and also renumbered in July 1917. Janet Kitz and Joan Payzant, *December 1917: Revisiting the Halifax Explosion*, 26.

18. According to the *Mail*, when the Explosion occurred "work had been in progress for the production of the issue of that day [the afternoon *Mail*] for an hour or more" and the paper's editor [name unknown] was at his desk a "few inches from the direction taken by the flying fragments when the glass broke or otherwise his life would have most certainly have been lost." *Mail*, 22 March 1918. The next edition of the *Mail* was 7 December under the banner headline "Scenes at Morgues and Hospitals that Baffle Description." *Mail*, 7 December 1917.

19. *Mail-Star*, 6 December 1967, 1.

20. *Mail*, 22 March 1918.

21. *Mail-Star*, 6 December 1967, 1. On the back page of the fiftieth anniversary issue was reprinted the front page of the *Mail* for 8 December 1917 with the banner headline "Yet More Appalling." It is likely that this 8 December story was also written in part or whole by Lawson.

22. *Mail-Star*, 6 December 1967, 8.

Hervey Jones, James L. Gowen and John Ronayne, *Daily Echo*

1. Jones's first name on his birth and marriage certificates is Hervey although Harvey also appears in some sources. The author thanks Garry Shutlak for the birth and marriage information on Jones. Jones became the *Echo's* editor on 1 September 1917.
2. From information in McAlpine's Halifax Directory 1917.
3. PANS MG 27, MGI Volume 2124 #161 Harvey Jones. On 17 December 1917 Jones provided a detailed description of the 6 December events he experienced to Archibald MacMechan, the disaster's official historian. MacMechan documented Jones's information in a three-page Personal Narrative. PANS MG 27, MGI Volume 2124 #161, #161a and #161b Harvey Jones.
4. *Chronicle* 1 August 1917, 4. Jones married Gertrude Murphy in Halifax on 31 July 1917.
5. PANS MG 27, MG 1 Volume 2124 #161a Harvey Jones.
6. The Common was a large area of grass fields behind the Citadel located between Camp Hill and Cunard Street.
7. PANS MG 27, MGI Volume 2124 #161 Harvey Jones. Pickford and Black acted as agents for many of the damaged ships, including *Imo*.
8. PANS MG 27, MG1 Volume 2124 #161 Harvey Jones. See also Zemel *op. cit.* 65. According to the *Herald*, Hayes' body was removed from *Imo* on 9 December, transferred to Snow's morgue and interred at Herring Cove Cemetery on 12 December. The author thanks Joel Zemel for a copy of the 11 December 1917 *Herald* article headlined "Pilot Hayes Died at His Post of Duty."
9. The *Echo* was the evening or afternoon edition of the *Chronicle*. Prior to the Explosion, the *Echo's* issue for 6 December was "ready" for circulation with a headline of "Enemy Massing Guns And Men on the Asiago Front for a Renewal of Heavy Offensive." *Echo*, 6 December 1917. The paper republished on 7 December under the banner "Death Toll In Great Disaster Growing." The next day the *Chronicle* reported the disaster accompanied by an account of the Explosion and subsequent events reprinted from a 7 December story in the *Recorder* headlined "Halifax Suffers." Throughout its history the *Recorder* was four pages and hand-set on a flatbed press. March *op. cit.* 55. Hand-setting the paper contributed significantly to its publication on 7 December.
10. Above the banner and *Echo's* masthead on 7 December ran a larger banner announcing "A Stricken City."
11. The identity of the reporter who interviewed *Mont-Blanc's* captain is unknown.
12. *Echo*, 7 December 1917, 1.
13. Information in an undated 1918 newspaper clipping provided to the author by Gowen's granddaughter Margaret Brooker.
14. *Sydney Post-Record*, 14 April 1936 obituary. The author thanks Margaret Brooker for a copy of the obituary.
15. *Sydney Post*, 14 April 1936. The author thanks Margaret Brooker for a copy of the *Post's* newspaper clipping.
16. *Chronicle*, 14 April 1936. The author thanks Louise Le Pierres for a copy of Gowen's obituary.
17. PANS Kitz/Gowen interview. In support of Gowen's statement about the timing of the snowstorm, eye-witness Thomas Raddall mentions that snow began to fall "by

dark" on 6 December and during the night became "a howling blizzard." Thomas Raddall, *In My Time: A Memoir*, 37.

18. Janet Kitz, *Shattered City*, 76-77.

19. PANS Kitz/Gowen interview.

20. Gowen was referring to the fire department's new chemical pumper "Patricia." Crewed by six fire fighters "Patricia" raced from Station 2 to Pier 6 after a phone call from grocer Constant Upham. Following closely behind "Patricia" in his 1911 McLaughlin roadster was Fire Chief Edward Condon and his deputy, William Brunt.

21. "Patricia's" driver Billy Wells was injured but survived.

22. *Echo*, 7 December 1917, 1

23. Laura MacDonald, *Curse of the Narrows*, 277.

24. PANS MG 1 Volume 2124 #360 p.6.

25. The 1916 Halifax phone directory lists a line to Mrs. Elizabeth Ronayne with the number Lorne 912-W. Lorne refers to the central telephone location. John Ronayne's great niece Rhonda Leblanc suggested to the author that the newspaper may have phoned him. Roger Amirault married Martha Ronayne in 1921. Emails, Rhonda Leblanc to author 20 and 21 March 2013.

26. In December 1917 a tram line ran along Barrington Street/Campbell Road to Duffus Street. Don Artz and Don Cunningham, *The Halifax Street Railway*, 30. Taking a cab was also a possibility as Howard Quinn, who lived a few blocks from Ronayne at 188 North Street, operated a taxi company. MacDonald *op. cit.* 119–21.

27. Smith *op. cit.* 58. The overhead bridge was Canadian Government Railway property and acted as a pedestrian walkway over the tracks from the bottom of Duffus Street to the head of Pier 7. It may have been built in 1912. There are several unproven details related to the bridge in Mahar and Mahar *op. cit.* 14, 24, 34, 39 and 53.

28. *Mail-Star*, 4 December 2000 A3. Bystanders on the bridge were approximately 300 metres from Pier 6.

29. PANS MG 27, MG 1 Volume 2124 #161b Harvey Jones.

30. Smith *op. cit.* 18. According to later information, as a result of the Explosion the bridge was wrenched from its concrete abutment and ejected onto its side near the railroad tracks and Pier 7. Sessional Papers of the Dominion of Canada, 1919, Vol. 7, Appendix 2, 42.

31. PANS MG 27, MG 1 Volume 2124 #161b Harvey Jones. The "road" was most likely Barrington Street/Campbell Road. At the time of the Explosion many people still referred to Barrington Street as Campbell Road.

32. *Chronicle*, 8 December 1917, 3. The Halifax Explosion Book of Remembrance (novascotia.ca/archives/virtual/remembrance) lists the cause of Ronayne's death as "shock, due to injuries."

33. Email, Rhonda Leblanc to author 20 March 2013.

34. Mount Olivet Cemetery records indicate John Ronayne buried in Section 2 Plot T Grave 51. However according to Rhonda Leblanc a marker only exists for John's father Ambrose, with whom John shares a plot. Email, Rhonda Leblanc to author 18 June 2013 and on 3 December 2013 the author was taken to the Ronayne grave site by Rhonda Leblanc.

35. According to an 8 December 1917 story in an American newspaper, after the

Explosion a *Chronicle* "girl reporter" and Ronayne's "desk neighbour" found him "among the dead" when she was sent to obtain a list of the injured at the "infirmary." *Oswego Daily Times*, 8 December 1917, 10. The author believes the "girl reporter" was the *Chronicle's* twenty-six-year-old columnist Mary "May" O'Regan. It is not certain whether O'Regan or Mrs. Ronanyne first identified John Ronayne's body on 6 December.

36. *Chronicle*, 8 December 1917. There is more than one version of Ronayne's last minutes. See *Recorder*, 8 December 1917, 1 and Smith *op. cit.* 20 and 23.

Editor, *Nieuw Amsterdam Courant*

1. Alan Bartlett "A Dutchman duly taxed," Magazine of the American Society for Netherlands Philately, (2007): 111. Bartlett's numbers are suspect. According to a 29 December 1917 article in the *Nieuw Rotterdamsche Courant*, there were 350 passengers and 304 crew on *Nieuw Amsterdam*. The author thanks Joel Zemel for a copy of the *Nieuw Rotterdamsche Courant*.

2. *The Sun* (New York), 7 December 1917, 2. Most likely the grain was in the form of wheat. A follow up story in the *New York Times* reported that the ship's 10,000 tons of provisions were for the Belgian Relief Fund. *New York Times*, 16 December 1917.

3. *Daily Kennebec Journal*, 29 December 1917, 4. The *Journal* was the daily paper of Augusta, Maine. The author thanks Joel Zemel for a copy of the newspaper.

4. According to Armstrong, on 6 December there were between thirty and forty merchant vessels in Bedford Basin. Armstrong *op. cit.* 25.

5. The editor may have been the ship's fifty-six-year-old administrator/purser, Johs Arnoldus Van Wyk, or the vessel's forty-six-year old printer, Jans Gerardus. In 1918 Gerardus was listed on the *Nieuw Amsterdam's* manifest as printer and on another voyage in July 1917 as Dutchman Jans Jacs. Gerardus, 46 (passenger #8, Position in Ship's Company: Printer). The author thanks Joel Zemel for information on Van Wyk and Gerardus.

6. In 1918 Johnstone moved to Dartmouth and wrote the 159 page account of the disaster and its aftermath. The complete text of "Catastrophe in Halifax" can be found at PANS in MFM 3824 Dwight Johnstone, "The Tragedy of Halifax: The Greatest American Disaster of the War," Halifax: Unpublished manuscript, c. 1919. Chapter VIII "Twice Told Tales" pp. 95–96.

7. The location of the *Nieuw Amsterdam* in Bedford Basin prevented passengers and crew from seeing the burning *Mont-Blanc* and explains the editor's assumption of an ammunition dump's explosion.

8. The steamer was most likely the heavily damaged cargo ship SS *Curaca* of New York, which was blown across the harbour from Pier 8 to Tuft's Cove and thus visible to passengers and crew on the *Nieuw Amsterdam*.

9. The "decided wave" was the northward moving portion of the tsunami created when *Mont-Blanc* detonated. This is the only reported observation of the tsunami travelling out into the Bedford Basin. The author thanks Alan Ruffman for this information.

10. It appears there was not enough time to verify the source of the blast with the boat's occupants before the paper went to press.

11. *Nieuw Amsterdam Courant*, 6 December 1917.

12. *Nieuw Rotterdamsche Courant*, 29 December 1917, 4, in Dutch language. On 29

December *Nieuw Rotterdamsche Courant* published the article "De binnenkomst van de Nieuw Amsterdam" (The Arrival of the *Nieuw Amsterdam*). In this account several details of the disaster were provided by the executive officers of the ship including the number of people killed (1,500–2,000), the number made homeless (20,000), the distance of the ship from the blast (2 miles) and the time between the collision of *Imo* and *Mont-Blanc* and the Explosion (20 minutes). The author thanks Paulus Vrijmoed for a translation of pertinent passages in *De binnenkomst van de "Nieuw Amsterdam."*

Archibald MacMechan, Official Historian of the Disaster

1. Details on MacMechan's life and career are based primarily on his biographical history in the Dalhousie University Archives.
2. Archibald MacMechan fonds MS-2-82 Box 1-4 Diaries and Private Memos. Hereafter MacMechan Diary. The Rehabilitation Committee was established on 12 December. At the time of the Explosion MacGillivray was also President of the Halifax Board of Trade, President of the Halifax Club and Halifax branch manager of the Bank of Commerce. The author thanks Barry Cahill for this information.
3. MacMechan Diary. According to MacMechan, on 16 December he "engaged Room 24 for the Halifax Disaster Record Office at $12 per month."
4. In an undated notice titled Circular No. 1, MacMechan listed six categories of urgently desired information including impressions and testimony of eye-witnesses. Archibald MacMechan Diary.
5. On 9 December MacMechan began writing the first part of an article for the *Canadian Courier*. Later that day he finished the second part while in the Chronicle Building, sent both parts by train at 7:30 p.m. to Toronto and wired Augustus Bridle to that effect. The article ran on 22 December on pages 6, 23 and 25 and was preceded by a full-page drawing on page 5 captioned "Now doth the city sit solitary, that was full of people! how (*sic*) is she become as a widow! she (*sic*) that was great among the nations and princess among the provinces."
6. Not all children in North End schools were assembled in class when the Explosion occurred. At St. Joseph's Catholic School, where nearly 400 attended from grades 1 to 9, classes for girls started at 9:30 a.m. and in the afternoon for boys.
7. According to the ship's original manifest, *Mont-Blanc* carried 250 tons of TNT.
8. As previously indicated, only Mate Terrance Freeman knew the full extent of the munitions on board *Mont-Blanc*.
9. MacMechan was incorrect as *Imo* struck *Mont-Blanc* at Hold No. 1 on the starboard side in the forward section of the ship.
10. *Mont-Blanc* did not drift to Pier 8 but to Pier 6, where it set the south side of the pier on fire.
11. MacMechan was almost certainly referring to HMCS *Niobe*, a former British warship which acted as the harbour's guard-ship, and to its commander, who sent men in a steam pinnace. HMS *Highflyer* also sent men in a whaler to investigate the fire on board *Mont-Blanc*. Both boats were destroyed in the Explosion with heavy loss of life.
12. MacMechan's figure of 20,000 is likely inaccurate as Halifax's population in 1917, excluding 5,000 military personnel, was 55,000.
13. At Richmond School 421 students attended grades 1 to 9 in seven classrooms;

eighty-eight were killed, two at the school and eighty-six at home or on their way to school.

14. At St. Joseph's School twenty-three girls and fifty-five boys who attended the school died. Four girls were killed at school and four died later due to injuries, fifteen of the girls who were absent died and the fifty-five boys died outside of school.

15. Three adults and twenty-five children were killed at this orphanage.

16. Harry Chapman lists the names of fifty-two Dartmouth residents reported killed and missing as a result of the Explosion. Chapman *op. cit.* 43. It is not clear whether this total includes fatalities from the Mi'kmaq settlement at Tuft's Cove.

17. See note 5.

18. Archibald MacMechan "Halifax In Ruins" *Canadian Courier* (1917): 6.

Arthur Lismer, Principal, Victoria School of Art and Design

1. Marjorie Lismer Bridges, *Red Rock,* 11.

2. Lismer arrived in Halifax on the Cunard Line ship *Corsican* on 28 January 1911. The author thanks Caroline Michaud of the Canadian Museum of Immigration at Pier 21 and Alan Ruffman for this information.

3. The other members of the Group of Seven were Frederick Varley, A.Y. Jackson, Lawren Harris, Frank Johnston, J.E.H. MacDonald and Franklin Carmichael.

4. Lismer's house at 8 Cliff Street overlooked the Sackville River. See Shelagh Mackenzie (ed), *Halifax Street Names: An Illustrated Guide,* 13.

5. Bridle was well acquainted with Lismer from their association in Toronto between 1911 and 1916. It was logical that Bridle would contact Lismer for images of the disaster as he was living in Halifax at the time of the Explosion. The author thanks Alan Rufman for providing the timeframe when Lismer sent the sketches.

6. In early 1918 the *Canadian Courier's* circulation passed 50,000. The author thanks Alan Ruffman for this information.

7. The article appeared on 29 December on pages 10 and 11, and the issue's cover was an image (not a Lismer sketch) of a damaged area in the city's North End.

Chapter 3 Visiting Canadian Journalists and the Aftermath

Alfred Coffin, *Truro Daily News*

1. Coffin also served on Truro Town Council, including two terms as mayor.

2. Buckley *op. cit.* n.p. and Nichols *op. cit.* 134–35.

3. The distance between Truro and Halifax is 100 kilometres, but winter road conditions made travel time for the trip longer than usual on the day of the Explosion.

4. In 1917 many newspapers used a street level bulletin board to exhibit news items.

5. The two stories in the *News* on 7 December were based on eye-witness observations by Coffin during his 6 December visit to Halifax as well as information provided to the *News* by its "special representative" on 7 December via telegraph and telephone from Halifax. It is possible that the "special representative" in Halifax was *Colchester Sun* and *Truro Citizen* manager/editor William Foster. According to to information provided to the author by Foster's granddaughter Patricia Poll, he was in Halifax when the Explosion occurred and remained in the city for a few days. His wife Edith was very upset that he did not contact her during this time.

6. On 7 December the *Herald* published "Halifax Wrecked," and the *Recorder* published

an edition, albeit also reduced in length. As well, on the afternoon of 6 December the liner *Nieuw Amsterdam* published and circulated the onboard paper *Nieuw Amsterdam Courant* with a story about the Explosion.

7. By "magazine" Coffin may have been referring to *Mont-Blanc's* cargo of TNT, or the ship's total cargo of TNT, dry and wet picric acid, gun cotton and benzol.

8. *News*, 7 December 1917, 1.

9. *Imo* struck *Mont-Blanc* on the starboard side.

10. *Imo* did not strike *Mont-Blanc* in the engine room, nor did the flames originate from the ship's boilers.

11. In fact *Imo* attempted to steer back to Bedford Basin and was driven onto the Dartmouth shore by the force of the Explosion and ensuing tsunami.

12. *Mont-Blanc's* destination in France was Bordeaux.

13. Of the fifty-three employees at the foundry, forty-five died, including owner Frank Hillis.

14. The Richmond Railway Station did not disappear because of the blast and the Acadia Sugar Refinery and Cotton Mills [Dominion Textile] buildings were not completely obliterated.

15. Reporting a figure of 1,000 dead indicates the story was written during the early hours of 7 December.

16. Fires in the North End continued to burn during the evening of 6 December and into the next day.

17. One crew member of the *Mont-Blanc* and seven on board *Imo* died as a result of the blast.

18. *News*, 7 December 1917, 2.

George Yates, former *Montreal Gazette* telegraph editor

1. *Ottawa Citizen*, 1 December 1942. A review of Borden's Halifax Explosion related files reveals Yates's frequent involvement as the prime minister's private secretary. See Borden Papers MG 26H Volume 90 Microfilm Reel 4325 Documents 46,728 and 46,727.

2. Douglas Eaton Eagles and Elizabeth Joan Eagles (Yates). *Hopper-Caldwell-Yates and Allied Families in the Ottawa Valley*, 120. Quote used by permission of Carol Eagles, Yates's great granddaughter. The author thanks Miss Eagles for a copy of the self-published family history of George Yates.

3. Eagles and Yates, *op. cit.* 118.

4. MacDonald *op. cit.* 179.

5. Smith, *op. cit.* 101. The *Montreal Gazette* reported Borden in King's County, Nova Scotia, on 12 December and the next day in Ottawa.

6. They were C.C. Carstens, Red Cross, Secretary, Civilian Relief Committee and General Secretary of the Massachusetts' Society for the Prevention of Cruelty, J. Prentice Murphy, Secretary, Boston Children's Aid Society, and William H. Pear, American Red Cross representative of the Boston Provident Association. Metson *op. cit.* 137. The Boston "camera man" was almost certainly Richard Sears of the *Boston American*. See note 13.

7. Eagles and Yates *op. cit.* 119–120. Quote used by permission of Carol Eagles. Also, according to Smith, Yates wrote the story "at the request of the Canadian Press." Smith *op. cit.* 78.

8. Both the *Herald* and *St. John Daily Telegraph* published portions of Yates's story on 11 December.

9. Yates began his tour in a car with Carstens, Pear and Murphy. MacDonald *op. cit.* 184.

10. As *Mont-Blanc* was obliterated in the Explosion, Yates was mistaken about the presence of the French ship's remains. The prow likely belonged to the wooden tug *Stella Maris,* which was approximately 200 metres away from *Mont-Blanc* when it exploded. The author thanks Joel Zemel for this information.

11. A reference to *Echo* reporter John Ronayne.

12. While in Halifax, Borden issued two official press statements: an undated [but certainly 7 December] "Message to the press" and a 9 December "Statement for the Halifax local papers and the Canadian Associated Press." LAC Borden Papers MG 26H Volume 89 Microfilm Reel 4325 Documents 46,363 and 46,410. A third statement reported in the *Echo* on 8 December was attributed to Borden.

13. Given his experience as a newspaper photographer and newsreel camera operator, it is likely that the "camera man for a Boston paper, who was making a series of photographs" was Richard Sears of the *Boston American.* See Chapter 4 for Sears's Explosion related material. There is a note in the CPC file dated 10 December 1917 titled "Extract From Canadian Press Service" in which the following statement from Yates's story is quoted and underlined "turned to look at a camera man for a Boston paper who was making a series of several photographs in the vicinity." Documentation of this passage is a reminder of Chambers' ongoing security concern over photographs taken after the Explosion by Canadian and American correspondents in Halifax and vicinity. The CPC Halifax Explosion file contains several communications concerning this issue.

14. *Toronto Evening Telegram*, 10 December 1917.

Stanley Smith, *St. John Daily Telegraph*

1. The author thanks Amber McAlpine-Mills of the New Brunswick Museum for details of Smith's journalism career.

2. *Boston Globe*, 9 December 1917.

3. Smith's book went through three editions in 1918 although the text in each is identical. Compiled after he visited Halifax and reported the disaster's aftermath, the book underwent a cover change and then a title and format change and finally photos replaced with eleven drawings by Halifax artist Arthur Lismer. Details of each edition can be found in a 1917 Explosion Bibliography <www.halifaxexplosion.org/biblio/bilio17html>. The author thanks Alan Ruffman for the above information.

4. The term Great Disaster was chosen by a *Toronto Star* headline editor and was also used in the introduction to Joseph Sheldon's 14 December Explosion story in the *Star.*

5. Stewiacke is approximately 30 kilometres south of Truro, Nova Scotia. Though datelined "Stewiacke N.S. December 7," Smith's despatch did not appear in the *Daily Telegraph* until 10 December under the headline "Telegraph Reporter Sees Gruesome Scenes."

6. The Queen Hotel was a five-storey building at 107–115 Hollis Street. Like the nearby four-storey Halifax Hotel, the Queen did not suffer major structural damage from the Explosion.

7. This did not apply to the five American reporters who had arrived in Halifax on the first Boston relief train. Prime Minister Borden found accommodation for them in the Halifax Club on Hollis Street.

8. A transom is a horizontal pane of glass across the top of a door.

9. For additional details on the damage caused by the blast see *Chronicle Was Hard Hit* on page 2 of the paper's 8 December issue, 14 December *Chronicle* editorial *Our Own Part*, *Mail Star* article 6 December 1917, 7, a description in *Heart Throbs*, Smith *op. cit.* 74 and details in PANS Accession 2007-066 Volume 002 AC 3647-3648.

10. In *Heart Throbs* Smith described the reporter as "One lone *outside* (my italics) newspaper man." Smith *op. cit.* 74. By referring to the correspondent as outside, the author believes Smith meant *visiting*. This reporter could have been from the *News*.

11. In 1913 the *Herald* and *Mail* moved to Argyle Street and its previous location, the Clayton and Sons Building at 108 Granville Street, was rebuilt and two storeys added. The refurbished structure was renamed the Dennis Building. March *op. cit.* 82.

12. Visiting reporters normally recorded observations and interviews on notepads using longhand, personal, Pitman or Gregg shorthand. These notes were then typed into a story and the copy given or dictated to a telegraph operator. It appears Smith submitted hand written work to the telegraph operator.

13. Smith claimed he was able to put through his first special despatch to the *St. John Daily Telegraph* "before 3 o'clock Saturday morning." Smith *op. cit.* 34. On 12 December the *Telegraph* confirmed Smith "was able to get through the first special despatch sent to any paper from Halifax." *St. John Daily Telegraph*, 12 December 1917, 3.

14. The *Daily Telegraph* published this story under the headline "Grim Finds Of Telegraph Correspondent In Ruins." *St. John Daily Telegraph*, 10 December 1917, 2.

15. As the dead reporter was John Ronayne, the "competitor on the rival paper" would have been from either the *Herald* or *Mail*. The *Herald's* Peter Lawson was news gathering soon after the Explosion and it is possible he was the reporter.

16. Blind baggage refers to a railway baggage, express or postal car that has no door opening at one end.

17. *Toronto Star*, 15 December 1917, 6.

Thomas O'Leary, *St. John Globe*

1. (Saint John) *Evening Times Globe*, 24 July 1943. The author thanks Thomas O'Leary for biographical information on his father and a copy of his 24 July 1943 obituary.

2. *Evening Times Globe*, 24 July 1943.

3. The *St. John Globe* reporter was not given a byline but the author believes he was Thomas O'Leary. The 1917 St. John City Directory lists three *Globe* reporters: O'Leary, Howard Codner and Joseph Mooney. However, Mooney was sixty years old and Codner was a cub reporter. It is therefore most likely that thirty-three-year-old O'Leary, who had been a reporter with the paper since 1913, was given the assignment. The author thanks Amber McAlpine-Mills for identifying the *Globe's* reporters in 1917.

4. *St. John Globe*, 10 December 1917.

5. On 20 June 1877 Saint John was devastated by a great fire.

6. *St. John Globe*, 11 December 1917.

Grattan O'Leary, *Ottawa Journal*

1. Frederick Griffin, *Variety Show*, 29. In 1917 Griffin was a reporter with the *Toronto Star's* Ottawa bureau but was at the paper's Toronto headquarters when the Explosion occurred.
2. Grattan O'Leary, *Recollections of People, Press, and Politics*, 195.
3. Published in 1977, O'Leary's memoirs contain many details of his *Ottawa Journal* coverage in New York of the *Titanic* story. Unfortunately, the work does not mention his Explosion reporting.
4. *Ottawa Journal*, 19 April 1912, 1.
5. Tom Van Deusen fonds, R11596 Volume 21.
6. Ottawa Journal, 6 December 1917, front page. In 2012 the author spoke with Grattan O'Leary's grandson, Barry O'Leary. He recalled his grandfather acknowledging coverage of the Explosion but downplaying his journalistic accomplishments with the assignment.
7. Box is a newspaper term referring to type that has a solid frame around it for prominence. Next to O'Leary's photograph ran George Yates's 8 December 1917 CP story from Halifax headlined "Death Overtook Even The Man Who Turned In Alarm."
8. During the morning of 8 December Crate contacted CPC Chambers complaining about the delayed transmission of press despatches the day before. After wiring CPR Telegraphs manager J.J. McMillan, Chambers resolved the situation and by the next day O'Leary was able to wire two despatches via the Halifax office of the CPR Telegraph Company.
9. The closest O'Leary came to "working on Halifax city newspapers" was in 1911 when he was a *St. John Standard* reporter.
10. Lieutenant-Colonel Frederick Mackenzie McKelvey Bell was assistant director of medical services (ADMS) for the Canadian military and Military District No. 6's senior medical officer. He played a key role in the medical response to the Explosion. Armstrong *op. cit.* 96–97, 104, and Metson *op. cit.* 142–144, 146.
11. *Ottawa Journal*, 10 December 1917, 1.
12. This particular scenario involving Hayes and Mackey was not only unlikely prior to the Explosion but also never discussed at the official inquiry, and is an example of O'Leary injecting an element of sensationalism into his despatch.
13. *Ottawa Journal*, 10 December 1917, 14.
14. On 14 November 1917 Borden and Union candidate A.K. Maclean were speakers at a public pre-election gathering in Halifax's Market Building. According to O'Leary he was present at the gathering.
15. The Intercolonial Railway (ICR) operated from 1872–1918 but after 1915 was officially the Canadian Government Railway (CGR). Despite the name change, for many years the railway continued to be referred to locally as the ICR or Intercolonial.
16. The railway station was damaged but not obliterated.
17. *Ottawa Journal*, 12 December 1917, 1.

Tommy Gorman, *Ottawa Citizen*

1. *Ottawa Citizen*, 1 February 1947.
2. Michael Dupuis, "The Titanic Disaster," *History Magazine* (April/May 2012): 21. Halifax journalists James Hickey and James Gowen were also involved in *Titanic's*

April 1912 news coverage.

3. The National Hockey League's first games occurred two weeks before the Halifax Explosion.

4. Information from the unpublished journal of Tommy Gorman (hereafter Gorman journal). The author thanks Tommy Gorman's grandson David Gorman for details in the journal via e-mails on 25 and 26 November 2013.

5. Unlike Stanley Smith it appears Gorman typed his story before submission to the telegraph operator.

6. This story by Finn on Gorman was No. 9 in a series titled *Behind The Headlines.*

7. There is no evidence to confirm the presence of 20–25 reporters waiting in Saint John for a train to Halifax.

8. On 10 December the *Citizen* published Gorman's first Halifax despatch datelined 9 December. Headlined "Amazing Scenes To Those Arriving In Capital N. Scotia," the story appeared on the front page and spilled over to page 12. Other Explosion news appeared on pages 2, 3 and 5, and on page 11 there was a list of casualties. The next day the *Citizen* ran a follow up story by Gorman datelined 10 December and headlined "Four Ottawans In The Dead Roll In Halifax Disaster." In this despatch Gorman provided details on the deaths of the wife and three children of Ottawa resident Robert Donnelly, an able seaman on the HMCS *Niobe* who was out at sea when the blast occurred.

9. *Ottawa Citizen*, 1 February 1947, 2.

10. The *Citizen* did not permit Gorman a byline.

11. The *Ocean Limited* travelled from Montreal to Halifax.

12. The party of newspaper reporters included the five American reporters on the first Boston relief train.

13. A reference to the Boston reporters. Among the Canadian reporters were Gorman and possibly Stanley Smith.

14. This scenario was highly speculative and never discussed at the official inquiry.

15. *Ottawa Citizen*, 10 December 1917, 1.

16. The Boston doctor was incorrect in his statement. For example, *Echo* reporter John Ronayne, who was near ground zero when the *Mont-Blanc* exploded, did not die instantly.

17. Many survivors in the North End did in fact burn to death after being trapped in the ruins of their houses.

18. Only Pier 6 was on fire.

19. The photographer was almost certainly *Boston American* journalist Richard Sears. See Chapter 4 for Sears's material.

20. *Ottawa Citizen*, 11 December 1917, 2.

21. Although 150 *Titanic* victims were buried in three Halifax cemeteries in April 1912, their bodies were recovered at sea and not, as Gorman stated "washed ashore nearby." Gorman is also mistaken about unclaimed bodies being buried at St. John's Anglican Cemetery. They were buried at Fairview Lawn Cemetery.

22. *Ottawa Citizen*, 13 December 1917, 2. According to Armstrong, the military funeral covered by Gorman went unreported by the local newspapers. Armstrong *op. cit.* 109.

William Stuart, *Montreal Standard*

1. According to Lovell's City Directory, in 1917 Stuart lived at 2336 Park Street in Montreal.
2. The *Maritime Express* travelled from Montreal to Halifax.
3. Two days after Stuart's story appeared in the *Standard* referring to the publication of Explosion-related photographs [the series of ten pictures including one of *Imo* beached on the Dartmouth shore was published on 22 December], Chambers wrote to the Nova Scotia-born Yorston questioning the use of certain "panoramic pictures." CPC, Chambers to Yorston, 19 December 1917. Yorston replied to Chambers on 21 December 1917 attaching a report by Stuart.
4. The reference is to fourteenth-century Italian poet Dante Alighieri who wrote the epic poem *Divine Comedy*. The first part of the poem is about a journey through Inferno (Italian for Hell).
5. The figure of 30,000 inhabitants for the Richmond district is likely too high.
6. If Stuart was referring to Richmond School at 88 Roome Street, his figures are incorrect. Eighty-eight students were killed, two at the school and eighty-six at home or on their way to school.
7. James Hickey, Joseph Sheldon, Peter Lawson, James L. Gowen and Hervey Jones are the Halifax-Dartmouth journalists known to have reported the immediate aftermath of the Explosion.
8. Stuart was referring to the Norwegian general cargo vessel *Hovland*, which at the time of the Explosion was in the Halifax Graving Dock. As a result of the blast five crew members were killed and the ship's upper works were seriously damaged.
9. Captain James W. Harrison of Furness Withy Company knew the SS *Picton* had a cargo of explosives. On the day of the Explosion he managed to board the vessel and anchor it in the middle of the Narrows.
10. *Montreal Standard*, 17 December 1917, 32.

Toronto Daily Star Reporters

1. Griffin *op. cit.* 182. In December 1917 Griffin was the *Star's* telegraph editor and assigned the task of handling all Explosion related telegraph copy, correlating, heading and getting it into the paper. Griffin *op. cit.* 38.
2. In his memoirs Griffin recalls that within twelve hours of the disaster "staff reporters were started by train for the scene." Griffin *op. cit.* 38.
3. In a 10 December despatch headlined "Bandaged People In Streets Of Halifax" the *Star's* male reporter wrote "I took my first walk through the stricken city this morning." The author assumes that both reporters were not female. It is quite possible the woman reporter sent to Halifax was Claire Irene Prime. In December 1917 Prime was twenty-five, single, a member of the Toronto Women's Press Club and a staff writer for the *Star's* women's page.
4. Eldred Archibald, the *Montreal Star's* reporter in Halifax, was almost certainly referring to the *Toronto Star's* female correspondent, who had arrived in Halifax on 10 December, when he wrote "You may see a Toronto 'sob sister' in a hotel lobby, weeping over her own touching notes." *Montreal Star*, 11 December 1917, 5. Though MacDonald mentions the presence of a "newspaperwoman" at the 17 December afternoon funeral for unidentified bodies, neither the woman reporter nor her paper are named. MacDonald *op. cit.* 247. It is possible the newspaperwoman was May O'Regan.

5. Griffin *op. cit.* 38.
6. A dateline provides the name of the city/town and the date at the start of a story that is not of local origin.
7. The exact time between the collision of *Imo* and *Mont-Blanc* [and the start of the fire] and the Explosion at Pier 6 is not known though it is now estimated at between seventeen and eighteen minutes. Ruffman and Simpson, *op. cit.* 307.
8. Truro converted the court house, academy and fire hall into hospitals. For further details on Truro as a relief centre, see Metson *op. cit.* 72–73 and *News*, 6–8 December 1917.
9. *Toronto Star*, 10 December 1917, 5.
10. It is likely both *Star* reporters stayed at the Queen's Hotel.
11. *Toronto Star*, 10 December 1917, 8.
12. *Toronto Star*, 11 December 1917, 18.
13. *Toronto Star*, 12 December 1917, 9. The *Star* reporter's 11 December conversation with Colonel Low was confirmed in a front-page story in the *Chronicle*. *Chronicle*, 12 December 1917, 1.
14. *Toronto Star*, 13 December 1917, 24. According to Stanley Smith, due to the Explosion the polling day for the 17 December 1917 election was postponed in Halifax until 28 January 1918. In addition, just before nomination day Dr. Edward P. Blackadder, Laurier Liberal, and Ralph Eisenor, labour candidate, announced their withdrawal, allowing Hon. A.K. MacLean and Mayor Martin to be elected unopposed. Smith *op. cit.* 104.
15. *Toronto Star*, 14 December 1917, 7.

Eldred Archibald, *Montreal Star*

1. Although the *Montreal Star* did not provide Archibald with a byline, it is almost certain he was the correspondent sent to Halifax. In 1917 he was on staff at the paper and residing in Montreal. In addition, a comparison between his *Toronto Star* reporting of the *Titanic* story in April 1912 from New York City and his Explosion despatches for the *Montreal Star* demonstrate a similar writing style. Finally, Archibald's experience in reporting the *Titanic* disaster would have made him the ideal reporter for the *Montreal Star* to send to Halifax.
2. In 1917 G. Fred Pearson was the *Chronicle's* owner/publisher, F.B. McCurdy [Pearson's brother-in-law] news editor and Alvin MacDonald editor-in-chief; Hervey Jones was the *Echo's* editor. Senator William Dennis was the *Herald's* proprietor/publisher, his nephew William Henry Dennis vice-president and general manager, W.R. McCurdy news editor and Hiram Weir senior editorial writer. The *Recorder's* proprietor/publisher was Charles Coleman Blackadar and the paper's editorial writer was Dr. Edward Blackadder.
3. *Montreal Star*, 8 December 1917, 1.
4. Only Pier 6 was "wiped out" above and below the waterline.
5. Eldred Archibald was mistaken about the identity of the vessel. The prow belonged to the tugboat *Stella Maris*, which was approximately 200 metres away when *Mont-Blanc* exploded. After the Explosion the remains of *Stella Maris* came to rest near Pier 6 and not Pier 8 as Archibald claimed. The author thanks Joel Zemel for this information.
6. *Montreal Star*, 10 December 1917, 5.
7. *Montreal Star*, 11 December 1917, 1.

Chapter 4 Visiting American Journalists and the Aftermath

1. The relief train left Boston at 10:00 p.m. on 6 December and arrived at 3:00 a.m. on 8 December at Rockingham outside of Halifax. Four hours later it arrived at the south end railway terminus.
2. For example, Philpott's last despatch was published in the *Boston Globe* (hereafter *Globe*) on 16 December and Keating's last despatch in the *Boston Herald-Journal* (hereafter *Herald*) on 14 December.
3. The author thanks Professor Jacob Remes at suny Empire State College for this information.
4. A. C. Ratshesky Collection, P-586, American Jewish Historical Society, Box 4, Item 3, Scrapbook. The author thanks Professor Remes for information in the Ratshesky Collection. It is unknown why there was not a credential letter for *Boston American* journalist Richard Sears.
5. *Providence Journal*, 9 December 1917. Providence is 66 kilometres south of Boston.
6. A review of several New England daily newspapers, including the *Kennebec Journal*, *Bangor Daily News*, *Eastern Argus*, *Manchester Union-Leader*, *Hartford Courant*, *Burlington Daily Free Press* and *Burlington Daily News*, between 6 and 24 December 1917 indicates they provided news coverage of the disaster but did not send reporters to Halifax.
7. For example, the *New York Times* published Simpson's account on the front page of its 9 December issue under the headline "Richmond An Appalling Waste After Explosion And Fires" and on the same day the *Providence Journal* ran an edited version of his despatch under the headline "20,000 in Devastated District Are In Desperate Need Of Help."

Anthony Philpott, *Boston Globe*

1. *Boston Globe*, 1 March 1952, 12.
2. Philpott's Halifax-based despatches appeared in the *Globe* on 10, 11, 12, 13 and 16 December.
3. *Boston Globe*, 6 December 1917, 1. Philpott's despatch from Amherst, Nova Scotia, also ran 7 December on the *New York Times's* front page.
4. The number of injured was approximately 9,000.
5. Steam railways were streetcars or trams and a steam road was a road independent of tracks used by vehicles powered by a steam engine. To the author's knowledge there were no steam roads in existence in Halifax at the time of the Explosion; Halifax's trams ran on electrical engines in1917.
6. The linotype machines in the Chronicle and Herald buildings were temporarily put out of service when the Explosion destroyed the gas storage tanks supplying heat for the metal pots. See *Mail Star*, 6 December 1975, 7.
7. *Boston Globe*, 7 December 1917, 3. A cross-check of the surgeons and doctors, Red Cross representatives, nurses, railroad officials and representatives of the press listed by Ratshesky in his official report to Massachusetts governor Samuel McCall confirms that with the exception of misspelling a few names, Philpott accurately reported individuals on the first relief train from Boston in his 7 December 1917 story. Metson *op. cit.* 137–38.
8. Philpott was mistaken as there was only one major explosion which occurred at 9:04 35s.

9. Borden's presence in Halifax was also reported by Yates, Smith and Grattan O'Leary.

10. An inaccurate number.

11. A pinnace is a light boat propelled by oars and used as a tender; a whaler is a boat that is narrow and pointed at both ends to facilitate backwards and forwards movement. Depot ship HMCS *Niobe* sent men in a steam pinnace, and light cruiser HMS *Highflyer* sent men in a whaler to investigate the fire on board *Mont-Blanc*. Both were destroyed in the Explosion with heavy loss of life.

12. Neither the steam pinnace nor whaler towed *Imo*.

13. *Boston Globe*, 9 December 1917, 1.

14. As previously indicated, there was only one main explosion; the "second" explosion was the arrival of the slower air wave which did most of the damage to buildings and exposed personnel.

15. Philpott was referring to W.A. Henry K.C., a highly respected and long-serving Halifax lawyer appointed by the Minister of Marine and Fisheries to represent the federal government in the inquiry. Zemel *op. cit.* 81-83. Whether Henry was a "legal maritime expert" is uncertain.

16. There was no evidence presented at the inquiry to indicate either Pilot Mackey or Pilot Hayes experienced "nervousness."

17. *Imo* never signalled that it was going to starboard; it signalled with two blasts indicating it intended to keep to port.

18. There is no evidence to suggest that Pilot Hayes was "confused."

19. The time frame of 10 minutes is incorrect; allowing for the time to row their lifeboats to the Dartmouth shore, it was about fifteen minutes until *Mont-Blanc* detonated.

20. The current was not a factor in preventing *Imo* from reaching the Dartmouth shore; in fact the ship was attempting to return to Bedford Basin.

21. HMCS *Niobe* was a *former* British warship.

22. *Mont-Blanc* drifted to Pier 6 not Pier 8.

23. Once again Philpott incorrectly reported two explosions.

24. Soon after the Explosion a cloud of steam rose from the ventilators at the Garrison ammunition magazine at Wellington barracks. Although a fire associated with the cloud was soon extinguished, the situation quickly led to rumours of a second explosion and an exodus of people to the Commons, Citadel Hill and Point Pleasant Park.

25. *Boston Globe*, 16 December 1917, 14.

Richard Simpson, Associated Press

1. The author thanks Katie Devine, Boston Public Library Reference Librarian, for information on Simpson, including a copy of his 31 May 1953 obituary in the *New York Times*.

2. As with CP, it was not AP practice to permit correspondents' bylines on despatches. However, in this case the *Chronicle* allowed Simpson to sign his name at the end of the story.

3. Neither Pilot Mackey nor Pilot Hayes was a "Government" pilot. They belonged to the Pilotage Commission, which was a separate and independent organization. As a result of the inquiry into the disaster the federal government invoked the War Measures Act and took over the Pilotage Commission in March 1918. The author thanks Joel Zemel for this information. *Imo* struck *Mont-Blanc* at Hold No. 1 on

the starboard side in the forward section of the ship. *Imo* was in ballast and had no cargo.

4. *Mont-Blanc's* engine room was not near the point of contact. The benzol that spilled over the side from the ruptured barrels contacted the fire which ignited when the vessels disengaged. The author thanks Joel Zemel for this information.

5. Simpson may have been referring either to Richmond School at the corner of Roome and North Albert Streets or St. Joseph's Catholic School on Kaye Street. At Richmond School 421 students attended grades 1 to 9 in seven classrooms. As a result of the Explosion 88 students were killed, 2 at the school and 86 at home or on their way to school. At St. Joseph's School nearly 400 students attended grades 1 to 8. Classes started at 9:30 a.m. for girls and in the afternoon for boys: 23 girls and 55 boys who attended the school died. Four girls were killed at school and four died later due to injuries, fifteen of the girls who were absent died and the fifty-five boys died outside of school.

6. Simpson is mistaken as *Mont-Blanc* was blown to pieces by the Explosion. The vessel he refers to was most likely the heavily damaged cargo ship ss *Curaca* of New York, blown across the harbour to the entrance of Bedford Basin.

7. The figure of 1,400 railway cars destroyed is too high.

8. Most likely Simpson was referring to St. Joseph's Roman Catholic Church at the corner of Gottingen Street and Russell Streets. Following the Explosion the building had only three walls standing. All four churches in Richmond were either badly damaged or destroyed.

9. An inaccurate number.

10. The tents were erected on the Commons near the citadel.

11. Simpson was referring to Chebucto School.

12. The figure of 4,000 killed is too high.

13. A pung is a low box-like sleigh designed to be pulled by one horse.

14. According to the unpublished journal of Dwight Johnstone, during the Explosion's aftermath there were incidents of opportunistic criminal behaviour, including looting. Ruffman and Howell *op. cit.* 102. Also, Smith reported the theft of cigarettes from a tobacco store on December 6. Smith *op. cit.* 24.

15. *Chronicle*, 10 December 1917, 4. Simpson's story first appeared on the *New York Times's* front page on 9 December under the headline "Richmond an Appalling Waste After Explosion and Fires."

Jerome Keating, *Boston Herald*

1. The author thanks Katie Devine at the Boston Public Library for information on Keating, including a copy of his 8 March 1974 obituary in the *New York Times*.

2. His despatches were published in the *Herald* on 11, 12, 13 and 14 December.

3. The Note of Protest was notarized on 8 December by W.A. Henry, the federal government's legal representative at the Wreck Commissioner's Inquiry. Zemel *op. cit.* 309-310.

4. The dailies included the *Washington Observer* on 11 December and the *Lewiston Morning Tribune* on 12 December; Canadian dailies included the *Regina Morning Leader* on 12 December.

5. The statement reportedly issued by Le Médec may have been dictated by him but likely read by someone else, possibly French Consul Emile Garboury. Although Le

Médec could understand English, he did not speak the language fluently and during the inquiry was provided with interpreter Louis D'Ornano from Ottawa. Zemel *op. cit.* 96.

6. According to the vessel's original manifest there were 494 barrels of benzol on *Mont-Blanc.* Ruffman and Simpson op. cit. 298.
7. *Mont-Blanc* drifted to Pier 6 not Pier 8.
8. *Boston Herald*, 11 December 1917, 4.

Roy Atkinson, *Boston Post*

1. *Lewiston Daily Sun*, 24 December 1938.
2. Atkinson's despatches appeared in the *Post* on 10, 11, 12 and 13 December. The paper published two more despatches on December 11 — one of which was headlined "Mont Blanc Captain's Own Story." *Boston Post*, 11 December 1917, 10. From this account it appears that Atkinson was present along with *Boston Herald* reporter Jerome Keating when Captain Le Médec provided his 10 December statement of the "complete story" of the collision between *Mont-Blanc* and *Imo.*
3. Atkinson was referring to the Great Fires of Chelsea, Massachusetts, on 12 April 1908 (2,835 buildings destroyed and 16,000 homeless) and Salem, Massachusetts, on 25 June 1914 (1,792 buildings burned and 16,000 homeless).
4. *Boston Post*, 7 December 1917, 15.
5. *Boston Post*, 7 December 1917, 7.
6. The "gig" was the whaler sent from HMS *Highflyer* to investigate the burning *Mont-Blanc.*
7. *Boston Post*, 10 December 1917. 1, 8. There was damage to the *Highflyer,* three members of the crew were killed and fifty injured.
8. *Boston Post*, 13 December, 1917, 8.

Richard Sears, *Boston American*

1. Publisher William Randolph Hearst added the *Boston American* to his newspaper chain on 21 March 1904. Five years later he established International News Service (INS) to compete with Associated Press and United Press Association wire services and in 1914 added picture service International News Photo (INP). Between 1904 and 1918 Sears worked for all three organizations.
2. *Daily Boston Globe*, 12 November 1955. Sears's service record indicates he enlisted in the 80th Division on 27 June 1918 [six months after covering the Explosion] and was discharged on 15 September 1919. His World War II record indicates he enlisted in the Army Signal Corps on 23 December 1940 and was discharged on 23 December 1943.
3. *Washington Post and Times Herald*, 12 November 1955.
4. Several of Sears's snapshots in the *Boston American's* 11 December photo galley were published in other American newspapers: 12 December in the *Evening Public Ledger* [Philadelphia, Pennsylvania], 20 December, *Ward County Independent* [North Dakota] and 21 December, *North Platte* semi-weekly *Tribune* [North Platte, Nebraska]. In addition, one of Sears's photographs appeared on 5 January 1918 in the *Illustrated London News* [London, England]. The author thanks Joel Zemel for the above information.
5. *Boston American*, 11 December 1917, 1, two photos.

6. *Boston American*, 11 December 1917, 2, one photo.
7. *Boston American*, 11 December 1917, 3, seven photos.
8. The caption for the photograph incorrectly states "where forty children lost their lives." Twenty-three girls and fifty-five boys who attended the school died. Four girls were killed at school and four died later due to injuries, fifteen of the girls who were absent died and the fifty-five boys died outside of school.
9. *Boston American*, 11 December 1917, 3.

James Hare, *Leslie's Weekly*
1. Lewis Gould and Richard Greffe, *Photojournalist: The Career of Jimmy Hare*, 116.
2. For Hare's work on the Winnipeg general strike see Michael Dupuis, *Winnipeg's General Strike: Reports from the Front Lines*, 68, 71–72.
3. Carnes *op. cit.* 2.
4. Hare's presence in Halifax was reported by *Montreal Star* correspondent Eldred Archibald on 11 December. *Montreal Star,* 11 December 1917, 5 and mentioned in Carnes *op. cit.* 264 and Lewis Gould and Richard Greffe *op. cit.* 141.
5. According to Chambers, Colonel Thompson was in charge of the "photographic Dept." LAC, RG 24 Vol. 4547 File 86-1-3 Part 7 Chambers to Ernest Ouimet [Director Specialty Film Import], 14 December 1917. On 12 December Benson wrote his superior in Ottawa, Major-General Gwatkin, indicating any photographer permitted to take pictures of the ruins was accompanied by an officer to "see that the regulations were not violated and to censor their pictures.' LAC, RG 24 Vol. 4548 File 86-1-4 Major-General T. Benson to Major-General Gwatkin, 12 December 1917.
6. James H. Hare, "The Destruction of a City," *Leslie's Weekly*, 29 December 1917, 888.
7. The official death toll in the virtual Halifax Explosion Remembrance Book is currently 1,946 and has been so since December 2012. The author thanks Lois Yorke, Nova Scotia Archives for the above information. See novascotia.ca/archives/virtual/remembrance/. However, as not all bodies were recovered after the blast, it is purported that as many as 2,200 may have actually died.
8. There is no evidence to support Hare's assertion that "somebody lost his head."
9. Hare was *Leslie's* war correspondent during World War I.
10. In using the phrase "smaller blast" Hare may have been describing the last in a series of explosions caused by exploding barrels of benzol on *Mont-Blanc*'s forecastle deck. The "major blast" Hare referred to was the Explosion at 9:04 35s.
11. *Leslie's Weekly*, 29 December 1917, 889.
12. Both captions and material for the story as well as captions in "In Stricken Halifax" and "The Destruction of a City" articles would have been based on Hare's notes. According to one biographer, Hare never faked a picture and his name over a photograph guaranteed it was "just what the caption says it is, and was made just where it purports to come from." Lewis Gould and Richard Greffe *op. cit.* 139
13. The author thanks Garry Shutlak, Senior Reference Archivist, PANS, for clarifying information in the caption. See also *Providence Bulletin* 12 December 1917.
14. Janet Kitz and Joan Payzant *op. cit.* 44.
15. LAC, RG 24 Vol. 4548 File 86-1-4 Major-General T. Benson to Major-General Gwatkin, 12 December 1917. In this letter Benson stated he appointed "Mr. McLaughlin (*sic*)…to take photographs generally for official purposes, all to be

censored by me personally." The author thanks John Armstrong for a copy of the 12 December 1917 Benson to Gwatkin letter

16. The author thanks Roy Flukinger, Senior Research Curator at the Harry Ransom Center, University of Texas, Austin, for information on Hare's images in the James H. "Jimmy" Hare Papers and Photography Collection.

Staff Correspondent, *Providence Journal*

1. *Providence Journal*, 10 December 1917. According to a separate 10 December story in the *Journal*, the train went to Halifax by way of Worchester, Massachusetts, and Portland, Maine.
2. The *Bulletin* was the *Journal's* afternoon edition; the paper's staff correspondent acted as reporter for both papers.
3. *Providence Journal*, 8 December 1917. However, it wasn't until the paper's correspondent arrived on 9 December that the information bureau was formally opened.
4. *Providence Journal*, 10 December 1917.
5. *Providence Journal*, 8 December 1917.
6. The existing microfilm copy of the reporter's despatch is poor quality. What can be determined is the headline "R.I Relief Train Delayed By Storm," dateline "Bangor, ME (Aboard Rhode Island Red Cross Relief Train) – Dec. 8" and the reporter's byline "From A Staff Correspondent of The Providence Journal."
7. The despatches of 10, 11, 12 and 13 December appeared in both the *Journal* and *Bulletin*.
8. The train did bring the largest American relief contingent: 50 doctors, 50 nurses, 1 chauffeur, 1 druggist, 3 secretaries and 2 social workers.
9. *Providence Journal*, 10 December 1917.
10. Rathbone Gardner was a lawyer, Rhode Island State senator and chair of the Providence Chapter of the Red Cross.
11. *Providence Bulletin*, 12 December 1917. In the Halifax Explosion Remembrance Book, Mrs. McEachern, 55, and children Muriel, 23, and Jesse, 14, are listed as dead, no members of the Mosher family are listed, Martin Marks, 55, of 107 Maynard Street (Dartmouth) is listed as dead, and Mr. Burgess and the four children are not listed.

References

Primary

Government Documents — Canada

Library and Archives Canada (LAC)

Michael Grattan O'Leary Collection MG 32 C37

Military District 6 RG 24 Volume 4547 File 86-1-3 Pt. 7 and Volume 4548 File 86-1-4

Robert Borden Papers MG 26H Volumes 89, 90 Microfilm Reel 4325

Secretary of State, Chief Press Censor File (CPC), RG 6E Volume 621, File 350, Microfilm T-102

Sessional Papers of the Dominion of Canada, 1919, Volume 7, Appendix 2

Tom Van Deusen Fonds R11596 Volumes. 1, 20, 21

Other Archive Material

Dalhousie University Archives and Special Collections

MS-2-82, 1-63 Volume 39 Archibald MacMechan Fonds

MS-2-326 Andrew Merkel Papers

Government of Nova Scotia

Nova Scotia Vital Statistics records

Jewish Historical Society, Newton Massachusetts

A.C. Ratshesky Collection, P-586

Public Archives of Nova Scotia (PANS)

Accession 2007-066 Volume 002 AC 3647-3648 Janet Kitz Interview with Jim Gowen 31 March 1981

MFM 3824 Dwight Johnstone. *"The Tragedy of Halifax: The Greatest American Disaster of the War."* Halifax: Unpublished manuscript, c. 1919

MGI Volume 2124 Archibald MacMechan Personal Narratives

MG 1/498 H.B. Jefferson Papers

MG 20, Volume 529-532 Halifax Relief Commission

MG 27 Volume 1-2, Miscellaneous explosion related material

Microfilm: Biography: Power N.L. (Capt.): Log Book Microfilm No. 10967

Newspapers

Acadian Recorder, Bangor Daily News, Beaumont Enterprise, Berwick Register, Boston American, Boston Daily Globe, Boston Herald- Journal, Boston Post, Burlington Daily Free Press, Burlington Daily News, Daily Echo, Eastern Angus, Dartmouth N.S Patriot, Evening Public Ledger, Halifax Morning Chronicle, Halifax Chronicle-Herald, Halifax Evening Mail, Halifax Herald, Halifax Mail-Star, Hartford Courant, Kennebec Journal, Lewiston Daily Sun, Manchester Union-Leader, Manitoba Free Press, Montreal Gazette, Montreal Herald, Montreal Standard, Montreal Star, New York Times, Nieuw Amsterdam Courant, Nieuw Rotterdamsche Courant, North Platte Tribune, Nova Scotian, Oswego Daily News, Ottawa Citizen, Ottawa Journal, Royal Gazette, Providence Evening Bulletin, Providence

Journal, St. John Daily Globe, St. John Daily Telegraph, Saint John Evening Times Globe, Toronto Daily Star, Toronto Evening Telegram, Toronto Globe and Mail, Truro Daily News, Ward County Independent, Washington Post and *Times Herald, Winnipeg Telegram, Winnipeg Tribune*

Magazines
Canadian Courier, Leslie's Weekly

Miscellaneous Printed Material
Devastated Halifax Views of the Greatest Disaster in the history of the American Continent; caused by the explosion that followed the collision of the French Munition ship "Mont Blanc" and the Belgian Relief Ship "Imo" in Halifax Harbor, December 6, 1917. Halifax: Gerald E. Weir, 1917

Halifax Phone Directory 1916–1919

Johnston, H.C. *30 Views of the Dartmouth Disaster Showing Effects Of Explosion December 6th, 1917.* Dartmouth: A.W. Griswold, 1917

Lovell's Montreal City Directory 1917–1918

McAlpine's Halifax Directory 1917–1920

Might Directories Limited — City of Toronto 1917 and 1918

Pettipas, Arthur C. Illustrated Souvenir Booklet — Program in Honor of 169th Anniversary of the Settlement, and 46th Anniversary of the Incorporation of Dartmouth. Peace Celebration and Welcome To Our Brave Soldier Boys, Thursday, Aug. 7, 1919

Ratshesky, A.C. *Report of the Halifax Relief Expedition December 6 to 15, 1917.* Boston: Wright and Potter Printing Company, 1918

Roe, Harold T. *Views of the Halifax Catastrophe Showing Effects of Explosion December Sixth.* 1917. Halifax: Royal Print & Litho Ltd., 1917

____. *40 Views of the Halifax Disaster Showing Effects Of Explosion December 6th 1917 And Official List Of Identified Dead.* Halifax: Royal Print & Litho Ltd., 1917

Books
McKelvey Bell, F. *A Romance of The Halifax Disaster.* Halifax: Royal Print & Litho Ltd., 1918

Sheldon, Joseph. *A Bolt From The Blue.* Halifax: Cox Bros. Company, 1918

Smith, Stanley K. *Heart Throbs of the Halifax Horror.* Halifax: Gerald E. Weir, 1918

The Canadian Newspaper Directory. Montreal: A. McKim, 1917 and 1918

Articles
Bridle, Augustus (ed.) and Lismer, Arthur [artist]. "When War Came To Halifax… As Seen By The Artist." *Canadian Courier* Volume XX111 No. 5, 29 December 1917

Canadian Railway and Marine World January and February 1918

Hare, Jimmy. "In Stricken Halifax." *Leslie's Weekly* Volume CXXV No. 3251, 29 December 1917

___. The Destruction of a City." *Leslie's Weekly* Volume CXXV No. 3251, 29 December 1917

___. "The Ruins of Halifax." *Leslie's Weekly* Volume CXXV No. 3251, 29 December 1917

MacMechan, Archibald. "Halifax In Ruins." *Canadian Courier* Volume XX111 No. 4, 22 December 1917.

Nieuw Amsterdam Courant. "Catastrophe in Halifax." 6 December 1917.

Nieuw Rotterdamsche Courant. "De binnenkomst van de 'Nieuw Amsterdam.'" [The Arrival of the *Nieuw Amsterdam*] 29 December 1917.

O'Regan, May (pseudonym Cousin Peggy). "A Steady Stream Of Gifts—This Is What Cousin Peggy Asks." *Halifax Morning Chronicle*, 21 December 1917.

____. "How The 'Sunshine Rays' Sent Father Christmas 'To The Little Children.'" *Halifax Morning Chronicle*, 27 December 1917.

Tomkinson, Grace. "Little Stories From Halifax." *Canadian Courier* Volume XX111 No. 15, 13 March 1918.

Vernon, C.W. "Some Impressions of the Great Disaster which Befell Halifax and Dartmouth December 6th, 1917." *Church Work* 14 February 1918.

Secondary

Books

Allen, Gene. *Making National News: A History of Canadian Press.* Toronto: University of Toronto Press, 2013.

Amey, Gerry (ed.) *The Halifax Club 1862 to 1987.* Halifax: The Halifax Club, 1987.

Armstrong, John Griffith. *The Halifax Explosion and the Royal Canadian Navy: Inquiry and Intrigue.* Vancouver: UBC Press, 2002.

Artz, Don, and Cunningham, Don. *The Halifax Street Railway.* Halifax: by the authors, 2000.

Beed, Blair. *1917 Halifax Explosion and American Response.* Halifax: Nimbus Publishing, 1998.

Bird, Michael J. *The Town That Died: The True Story of the Greatest Man-Made Explosion Before Hiroshima.* Toronto: McGraw-Hill Ryerson, 1962.

Boileau, John. *Halifax & the Royal Canadian Navy.* Halifax: Nimbus Publishing, 2010.

Borrett, William C. *Tales Told Under The Old Town Clock.* Halifax: The Imperial Publishing Company Limited, 1942.

____. *More Tales Under The Old Town Clock.* Halifax: The Imperial Publishing Company Limited, 1943.

Bourrie, Mark. *The Fog of War: Censorship of Canada's Media in World War Two.* Vancouver: Douglas & McIntyre, 2011.

Bridges, Marjorie Lismer. *A Border of Beauty.* Toronto: Red Rock, 1977.

Buckley, Peter. *The National* (CP) *Link.* Toronto: The Canadian Press, 1997.

Carnes, Cecil. *Jimmy Hare, News Photographer Half a Century With a Camera.* New York: The MacMillan Company, 1940.

Chambers, Lenoir, and Shank, Joseph E. *Salt Water and Printer's Ink: Norfolk and Its Newspapers. 1865–1965.* Chapel Hill: University of North Carolina Press, 1967.

Chapman, Harry. *Dartmouth's Day of Anguish: The Halifax Harbour Explosion.* Dartmouth: Dartmouth Historical Society, 1992.

____. *The Dartmouthians.* Dartmouth: Dartmouth Historical Association, 2005.

Cornall, James. *Halifax South End.* Charleston, South Carolina: Arcadia Publishing, 1998.

Craick, W.A. *A History of Journalism in Canada ll.* Toronto: Ontario Publishing Company, 1959.

Dupuis, Michael. *Winnipeg's General Strike: Reports from the Front Lines.* Charleston: History Press, 2014.

Flemming, David B. *Explosion in Halifax Harbour: The Illustrated Account of a Disaster That Shook the World*. Halifax: Formac Publishing, 2004.

Gould, Lewis L., and Greffe, Richard. *Photojournalist: The Career of Jimmy Hare*. Austin: University of Texas Press, 1977.

Griffin, Frederick. *Variety Show*. Toronto: Macmillan, 1936.

Harkness, Ross. *J.E. Atkinson of the Star*. Toronto: University of Toronto Press, 1963.

Harper, J. Russell. *Historical Directory of New Brunswick Newspapers and Periodicals*. Fredericton: The University of New Brunswick, 1961.

Heyer, Paul. *Titanic Century: Media, Myth, and the Making of a Cultural Icon*. Santa Barbara: Praeger, 2012.

International Year Book and Statesmen's Who's Who 1978. London: Burke's Peerage, 1978.

Jobb, Dean. *Crime Wave: Con Men, Rogues and Scoundrels from Nova Scotia's Past*. Lawrencetown Beach: Pottersfield Press, 1991.

Keshen, Jeffrey. A. *Propaganda and Censorship During Canada's Great War*. Edmonton: University of Alberta Press, 1996.

Kesterton, W.H. *A History of Journalism in Canada*. Toronto: McClelland and Stewart, 1967.

Kitz, Janet. *Shattered City: The Halifax Explosion and the Road to Recovery*. Halifax: Nimbus Publishing, 1989.

____. *Survivors: Children of the Halifax Explosion*. Halifax: Nimbus Publishing, 1992.

Kitz, Janet, and Payzant, Joan. *December 1917: Re-Visiting the Halifax Explosion*. Halifax: Nimbus Publishing, 2006.

Lang, Marjory. *Women Who Made the News: Female Journalists in Canada, 1880–1945* Montreal: McGill-Queen's University Press, 1999.

MacDonald, Laura M. *Curse of the Narrows: The Halifax Explosion 1917*. Toronto: Harper Collins, 2005.

Maybee, Janet. *Aftershock: The Halifax Explosion and the Persecution of Pilot Francis Mackey*. Halifax: Nimbus, 2015.

Mackenzie, Shelagh (ed.), with Scott Robson. *Halifax Street Names, An Illustrated Guide*. Halifax: Formac Publishing, 2002.

MacLennan, Hugh. *Barometer Rising*. Toronto: Collins, 1941.

Mahar, James, and Mahar, Rowena. *Too Many to Mourn: One Family's Tragedy in the Halifax Explosion*. Halifax: Nimbus Publishing, 1998.

March, William. *Red Line: The Chronicle-Herald and the Mail-Star 1875–1954*. Halifax: Chebucto Agencies Limited, 1986.

Martin, J.P. *The Story of Dartmouth*. Dartmouth: Private Printing, 1957.

McNaught, Carlton. *Canada Gets the News*. Toronto: Ryerson Press, 1940.

Metson, Graham (ed.). *The Halifax Explosion Dec. 6, 1917*. Toronto: McGraw-Hill Ryerson, 1978.

Nichols, M.E. (*CP*) *The Story of the Canadian Press*. Toronto: The Ryerson Press, 1948.

O'Leary, Grattan. *Recollections of People, Press and Politics*. Toronto: MacMillan of Canada, 1977.

Payzant, Joan, and Payzant, Lewis. *Like A Weaver's Shuttle: A History of the Halifax-Dartmouth Ferries*. Halifax: Nimbus Publishing, 1979.

Perry, Albert J. *The History of Knox County, Illinois: Its Cities, Towns and People Volume 1*. Chicago: S.J. Clarke Publishing Company, 1912.

Prince, Samuel. *Catastrophe and Social Change.* New York: Columbia University Press, 1920.

Raddall, Thomas H. *Halifax: Warden of the North.* Toronto: McClelland and Stewart, 1948.

___. *In My Time: A Memoir.* Toronto: McClelland and Stewart, 1976.

Ruffman, Alan, and Howell, Colin D. (eds.). *Ground Zero: A Reassessment of the 1917 Explosion in Halifax Harbour.* Halifax: Nimbus Publishing and Gorsebrook Research Institute for Atlantic Studies at Saint Mary's University, 1994.

Smith, Marilyn Gurney. *The King's Yard An Illustrated History of the Halifax Dockyard.* Halifax: Nimbus Publishing Limited, 1985.

Stephens, David E. *Truro: A Railway Town.* Hantsport: Lancelot Press, 1981.

Tratt, Gertrude. *Preliminary Survey and Listing of Nova Scotia Newspapers 1752–1954.* Halifax: Dalhousie University, 1979.

Ware, William (ed.). *Printers' Journal.* Halifax: Halifax Typographical Union no. 130, 1952.

Wright, H. Millard. *One Region Many Leaders.* Halifax: Halifax Regional Municipality, 2002.

Zemel, Joel. *Scapegoat, the Extraordinary Legal Proceeding Following the 1917 Explosion.* Halifax: SVP Publications, 2012.

Articles

"After The Blast." *Time* (24 February 1975).

Allen, Graham. "Veteran Newsman Had Ringside Seat For City's History." *Halifax Chronicle-Herald — Bicentennial Edition- Mail-Star* (20 June 1949).

Bartlett, Alan. "A Dutchman duly taxed." *Magazine of the American Society for Netherlands Philately* (Vol. 31/5 May 2007).

Doane, Frank A. "Completes 50 Years in Business." *Truro Daily News* (12 October 1944).

Dupuis, Michael. "Piecing together the unwritten tale of Halifax explosion journalists." *Halifax Chronicle Herald* (28 January 2014).

___. "Fallout from 1917 Halifax Explosion reached all the way to the prairies." *Winnipeg Free Press* (1 December 2012).

___. "The Titanic Disaster." *History Magazine* (April/May 2012).

Ferguson, Charles. "The Halifax Explosion." *Journal of Education* (February 1968).

Finn, Joe. "Behind The Headlines. Meet 'Tommy' Gorman, Reporter. He Beat 'Em All In His Day." *Ottawa Citizen* (1 February 1947).

___. "Behind the Headlines. Tommy Gorman Finds a Man's Shirt and With It Identifies a Body." *Ottawa Citizen* (3 February 1947).

Fraser, R.L. "My Experience of the Halifax Explosion." *Atlantic Advocate* (Vol. 57, No. 5 January 1967).

Graham, Gayle, and MacDonald, Bertrum H. "The Halifax Explosion and the Spread of Rumour through Print Media, 1917 to the Present." *Journal of the Royal Nova Scotia Historical Society* (Vol. 17, 2014).

Jefferson, Henry B. "Day of Disaster." *Atlantic Advocate* (Vol. 48, No. 5, January 1958).

Jeffrey, Davene. "A tragic tale of a bridge too tempting." *Halifax Chronicle-Herald* (4 December 2000).

Keshen, Jeffrey. "All the News That Was Fit to Print: Ernest J. Chambers and Information Control in Canada, 1914–1919." *Canadian Historical Review* (LXX111, 3, 1992).

Kingsbury, Al. "Amid debris, printers struggled." *Halifax Mail Star* (6 December 1975).

Maybee, Janet. "The Persecution of Pilot Mackey." *The Northern Mariner* (XX, No. 2, April 2010).

McCubbin, Doris. "The Women of Halifax." *Chatelaine* (June 1954).

O'Regan, May. "Sensational Local Events Recorded In Half-Century." *Halifax Mail-Star* (18 April 1951).

J.M. Redditt, "A.D. Merkel to Leave CP Post in Halifax." *Editor & Publisher* (20 April 1956).

Reid, H. "Halifax Explosion How They Got the Message Out." *Atlantic Advocate* (Vol. 68, No. 5, January 1978).

Robinson, Berton "The Chronicle building comes down." *Halifax Chronicle Herald* (December 1972).

Ruffman, Alan. "Grim Visions: Arthur Lismer and the Halifax Explosion." Art Gallery, Mount Saint Vincent University, Halifax, 23 November — 16 December, 1990.

Scanlon, Joseph. "The Magnificent Railways Rail Response to the 1917 Halifax Explosion." *Canadian Rail* (No. 461, November-December 1997).

Smith, Douglas N.W. "The Railways and Canada's Greatest Disaster: The Halifax Explosion. December 6, 1917." *Canadian Rail* (No. 431, November–December 1992).

Pamphlets

Gosley, Syd. *The Harbour Catastrophe*. Dartmouth: Dartmouth Museum, 199?.

McCarron, Owen. *A Tribute to the Halifax Fire Department on the 85th Anniversary of the Halifax Explosion. An Historical Docu-Comic*. Halifax: By the author, 2002.

Other Documents

Eagles, Douglas Eaton, and Eagles (Yates), Elizabeth Joan. *Hopper-Caldwell-Yates and Allied Families in the Ottawa Valley*. Ottawa: By the authors, 1987.

Letter re the death of James L. Gowen by David MacDonald, Roving Editor *Readers Digest* (13 May 1983).

Mount Olivet Cemetery records.

Ruffman, Alan. Exhibition document *Grim Visions: Arthur Lismer and the Halifax Explosion*. Halifax: The Art Gallery, Mount Saint Vincent, 1990.

Tommy P. Gorman, unpublished manuscript, n.d.

Recordings

Francis Mackey, CBC Radio Interview, 3 October 1967. Bob Cadman interviews Captain Mackey. The 1967, 6:38 minute recording is a portion of the original 1958, 47 minute interview with Cadman. The full 1958 interview is held at PANS.

Websites

Halifax Explosion Remembrance Book <novascotia.ca/archives/virtual/remembrance/>.

<hughdoherty.tripod.com/George/htm> George MacDonald: half a century of news-by Hugh Doherty

Nova Scotia Historical Vital Statistics <novascotia.genealogy.com>.

<www.halifaxexplosion.org/biblio/biblio17html>.

Communications with Journalists' Descendants

Brennan, Pat. Telephone Conversation, E-Mails and correspondence 2014.

Brooker, Margaret. E-mails 2013.

Eagles, Carol. E-mails and correspondence 2013 and 2014.

Gorman, David. E-mails 2013 and 2014.

Gowen, David. E-mails 2013.

Leblanc, Rhonda. E-mails, telephone conversations and meeting in Halifax 2013.

Lynch, Susan. E-mails 2013 and 2014.

O'Leary, Barry. E-mails and telephone conversations 2012 and 2013 and meeting in Victoria 2016.

O'Leary, Thomas. E-mails 2014.

O'Regan, Jim. Telephone conversations and correspondence 2014.

Dr. Scott Pigford. Telephone conversations and e-mails 2015.

Rouse, Eileen. E-mails and correspondence 2014.

Sears, Richard. E-mails 2013.

Sheldon, Donna. E-mails 2013.

Zimber, Diana. E-mails 2013.

Index

About the Author

Michael Dupuis is a retired Canadian history teacher, writer and author. His writing focuses on the role played by journalists in historical events including *Titanic*, the Halifax Explosion, Winnipeg general strike, On-to-Ottawa trek and Regina Riot. In 2011 he was a consultant to CBC television for *Titanic: The Canadian Story*, and in 2012 contributed *Canadian Journalists in New York* in Paul Heyer's *TITANIC Century: Media Myth and the Making of a Cultural Icon*. In 2014 Michael published *Winnipeg's General Strike: Reports From The Front Lines*. He holds a BA (English) and MA (History) from University of Ottawa and a BEd from University of Toronto. Michael resides in Victoria, BC, with his wife Christine Moore and their two Golden retrievers. He can be reached at michaeldupuis@shaw.ca

FSC
www.fsc.org

MIX
Paper from
responsible sources
FSC® C013916